Eudora Welty, Whiteness, and Race

D1525023

Eudora Welty, Whiteness, and Race

EDITED BY HARRIET POLLACK

The University of Georgia Press   Athens and London

© 2013 by the University of Georgia Press
Athens, Georgia 30602
www.ugapress.org
All rights reserved
Set in Minion Pro by Graphic Composition, Inc., Bogart, Georgia
Manufactured by Thomson-Shore
The paper in this book meets the guidelines for permanence
and durability of the Committee on Production Guidelines
for Book Longevity of the Council on Library Resources.

Printed in the United States of America
17 16 15 14 13 P 5 4 3 2 1

Library of Congress Cataloging-in-Publication Data

Eudora Welty, whiteness, and race / edited by Harriet Pollack.
        p. cm.
    Includes bibliographical references and index.
    ISBN 978-0-8203-4432-4 (hardcover : alk. paper) —
    ISBN 0-8203-4432-X (pbk. : alk. paper) —
    ISBN 978-0-8203-4433-1 (hardcover : alk. paper) —
    ISBN 0-8203-4433-8 (pbk. : alk. paper)
1. Welty, Eudora, 1909–2001—Criticism and interpretation.
2. Whites in literature.
3. Race relations in literature. I. Pollack, Harriet.
    PS3545.E6Z675 2013
    813'.52—dc23   2012024176

British Library Cataloging-in-Publication Data available

Contents

Acknowledgments

This book originated from "Eudora Welty at One Hundred: The Eudora Welty Society Centennial Conference and Celebration," which met in Jackson, Mississippi, in 2009. Having the privilege and pleasure of organizing the conference and its program, I also had the opportunity to assign myself to a panel of my choice and so to promote and grow a particular topic of concern. I picked Welty and race without hesitation. Four of the papers here were first delivered at the conference, and many of the other papers started in conversations ignited by those four. So when I say that the book was a fruit of the Welty Centennial project, it is quite true.

In another sense, though, the volume is the product of a much longer trajectory of earlier academic adventures and the much-appreciated relationships that they produced. Each contributed to this volume's happening.

Work with Suzanne Marrs on our 2001 volume *Welty and Politics: Did the Writer Crusade?* illuminated the topic of Welty and race, and I want to thank Suzanne for having been—for decades now—a chief collaborator in my meandering self-education and persistent interest in Welty. Similarly, Rebecca Mark has in those same decades repeatedly caused me to see our unfolding interests in Welty and race freshly and from diverse angles. In 2004 she invited me to speak at "Unsettling Memories," a symposium on culture and trauma in the deep South that she and Alferteen Harrison hosted at Jackson State University. There I chaired a panel on Emmett Till in the literary imagination that included both Suzanne Jones, whose 2004 book *Race Mixing: Southern Fiction Since the Sixties* is a model for me, and Christopher Metress, who had edited *The Lynching of Emmett Till*, anthologizing responses to the 1955 racial murder in Mississippi that arguably became the first major media event of the civil rights movement. Before leaving the conference, Chris and I were working on *Emmett Till in Literary Memory and Imagination* (2008), and he became my cohort and guide in probing Mississippi's race history, a story that this volume continues to explore. Work on our Till book became for me a consciously chosen and deliberate preparation for reopening the topic of Welty, whiteness, and race.

Cornelius Eady and Sarah Micklem, lifelong friends, whose work to establish Cave Canem, the black poets workshop that has so much changed the landscape of literary concern and recognition, have also influenced my attention to the story of race in America, and I thank them for years and years of productive talk over good food.

I especially thank all the contributors to this volume for their collaboration on the project, and for the friendships that have grown—some from scratch and others from already important connections—in consequence of working together.

I'm also grateful to Peggy Prenshaw, who generously read the book and improved it with her suggestions. And I owe special recognition to Nancy Grayson, who shepherded this project for the University of Georgia Press and whose interest has always encouraged my work. Others at and associated with the press—Jon Davies, John Joerschke, John McLeod, Kathi Morgan, Daniel Simon, and Beth Snead—have also made essential contributions to the book's production.

The Bucknell Center for the Study of Race, Ethnicity, and Gender repeatedly supported me with funding for conference and research travel, and I am grateful to my colleagues there for their ongoing support and shared mission.

I want also to thank Jacob Agner, who came to me in 2010 as an assigned student assistant but had the spirit of a collaborator. By working helpfully on the editing stages of this book, he became its important first audience and markedly influenced the project, even as the project influenced his own evolving work.

Lastly and always, I want to lovingly thank the members of my family—Marc, Lauren, and David—who with great good nature continually accommodate and support a wife and mother whose nose is always in a pile of papers.

Eudora Welty, Whiteness, and Race

HARRIET POLLACK

Reading Welty on Whiteness and Race

Eudora Welty, Whiteness, and Race seeks to spotlight and clarify Eudora Welty's concern for and depiction of African Americans, the color line, segregation, and Jim Crow as well as her commentary on patterns of whiteness, including its patterns of blindness, insensitivities, and atrocities. The need for such a volume has grown clear following several decades during which critics, faced with Welty's preference for the oblique in literary performances that are anything but straightforward, have assumed either that Welty's work is not particularly concerned with these issues or that she was callously unaware of or ambivalent toward racism.

Diana Trilling's contemporary response to *Delta Wedding* in 1946 initially raised this important topic in an early reading that was only the first to severely underestimate the complexities of Welty's fiction and its treatment of race. Taking Welty and the South both to task and conflating the two, Trilling wrote, "It is difficult to determine how much of [my] distaste for Eudora Welty's new book . . . is resistance to the culture out of which it grows." Moreover, Trilling objected, "Doll's houses, birds, moonlight, snow, the minutiae of vulnerable young life and the sudden revelations of nature may have their distressingly persistent way of agitating the modern female literary psyche . . . but it seems to me that only on a Southern plantation could the chance remark of a gardener to the effect that he wished there 'wouldn't be a rose in the world' set the lady of the house to 'trembling . . . at some impudence.'"[1] Presupposing that Welty was "so fondly" describing Mississippi Delta culture, Trilling essentially oversimplified the novel and associated what she called the "tremulousness" of Welty's style with the temperament of a self-absorbed, unsympathetic, imperious, and imperceptive southern lady. This misreading is based on assumptions not only about Welty's relationship to her class and culture but about her relationship to

1

gender positions and the idea of the privileged and feminine white lady. Too simply interpreting the fiction as without "criticism of the Fairchild way of life" and believing that Welty cherished "the parochialism and snobbery of the Fairchild clan," Trilling felt she must "deeply oppose its values."

What followed Trilling's fundamental need to locate Welty's position in relation to social issues was not further exploration of the topic but a few decades of analytic response in which the topic of race was almost absent, a conspicuous omission that defined the limitations of the period's critical interests. Trilling's concern was not again directly addressed until the publication of Alfred Appel's "'They Endured': Eudora Welty's Negro Characters" (1965) and John E. Hardy's "Eudora Welty's Negroes" (1966). This developing shift in focus was a sign that Welty's readership was, in a period of cultural change, beginning to observe issues it had previously ignored in her fiction. Then, in Welty's 1980 introduction to *The Collected Stories*, as Julia Eichelberger points out in an essay here, the writer herself acknowledged her awareness of readers' uncertainty about her position: "I have been told, both in approval and in accusation, that I seem to love all my characters."[2] Welty registers this irony in her readers' finger-pointing charges, it should be noted, ten years after the publication of her 1930s photographs in *One Time, One Place* had documented her early attention to Mississippi life on both sides of the color line.

The meaning of those images, the record of what she was seeing as she looked at life around her in the 1930s, did not at first show the way to understanding her position on race. Discussions of individual works came close to the topic. But not until the mid-1980s were Trilling's concerns and contentions about *Delta Wedding* again addressed. Then, on the other side of the historical sensitivities brought by the civil rights era, Suzanne Marrs and Barbara Ladd each wrote essays that in a sense directly responded. In "The Metaphor of Race in Eudora Welty's Fiction" (1986), Marrs focused on the "almost unnoticed" black characters in *Delta Wedding* and *The Golden Apples* and Welty's attention to their "exclusion from white society," "despite intimate contact."[3] In "Coming Through: The Black Initiate in *Delta Wedding*" (1988), Ladd identified the Fairchild story as not at all about the status quo of the Mississippi Delta but precisely about their existence in the midst of social change. Ladd's forward-looking revelation was that no reading had "given any prolonged attention to [Welty's portrait of] signs of unrest among *Delta Wedding*'s black characters," signs now further probed in the recent treatments of the novel here.[4] Focusing on the marginalized but mystifying character Pinchy, Ladd—

unlike Trilling in 1946—noted the distance between the writer and her characters' points of view. "For Ellen Fairchild, Pinchy does not belong . . . For Eudora Welty, however, she does belong. We know that she belongs because, as absent as she is from Ellen's moral world, Pinchy remains conspicuous in Welty's scene, a clear, black absence standing right there."

Since the 1980s, much criticism has at least tangentially contributed to the sense that race is an important topic for Welty studies. In 2000, Patricia Yaeger's *Dirt and Desire: Reconstructing Southern Women's Writing, 1930–1990* shifted the paradigm in discussions of southern women writers generally toward attending "a crisis in whiteness" as well as the experience of African American lives.[5] Simultaneously, eleven Welty readers contributed to the volume *Eudora Welty and Politics: Did the Writer Crusade?*, a title in which the term "politics" purposely remained open-ended in order to embrace a number of historical and social issues, including race, the topic of Suzan Harrison's influential contribution, "'Racial Content Espied': Modernist Politics, Textuality, and Race in Eudora Welty's 'The Demonstrators.'" The collection brought into focus a shift in critical approaches to Welty. Then, in 2005, Marrs's *Eudora Welty: A Biography* assembled information about the patterns and details of the writer's life that would enrich and stimulate critical discussion. In the same time period, additional work by Suzan Harrison in "'It's Still a Free Country': Constructing Race, Identity, and History in Eudora Welty's 'Where Is the Voice Coming From?'" as well as new work by Brannon Costello in *Plantation Airs: Racial Paternalism and the Transformations of Class in Southern Fiction, 1945–1971* and by Minrose Gwin in her 2010 Lamar Lecture, *Remembering Medgar Evers: Writing the Long Civil Rights Movement*, have all extended the conversation about Welty and race.[6]

Still, the debate about Welty's position is in no way settled. If Trilling was the first to criticize Welty for not making it more evident in her fiction that she found Mississippi's racial hierarchy reprehensible, others followed. Rather than seeing her as a cultural critic, Claudia Roth Pierpont—in a 1998 *New Yorker* essay published while *Welty and Politics* was moving toward production—in contradiction to the critical readings, asserted that Welty's affectionate portraits of white Mississippians "turned her into Mississippi's favorite daughter—the besieged white public was only too happy to see itself in her adorable eccentrics."[7] And in his 2007 *Hudson Review* essay, "Welty and Racism," Dean Flower characterized Welty as "ambivalent," seemingly in the sense of "[liking] to keep hidden her deep resistance to the South and its relentless social pressures," at least until she wrote "Where Is the Voice Coming From?" in which—as he, I think incorrectly, argues—"Welty's fiction had at last found a way to voice things she had kept silent about before."[8] Believing Welty, like Faulkner, harbored a felt need to defend her home state despite her discomfort with its reprehensible race history, Flower is skeptical of the view, now prominent in Welty studies, that she crossed the color line in earlier fictions too. Incongruously, he contradictorily argues the established position in criticism, that "What she cared about most, and sought out in her fiction, was the deeper mystery of individuals" and that, as a result, her stories, including her earliest, were already "the best defense against" a charge of racism, citing "Keela," "Powerhouse," "A Worn Path," and "Livvie" as stories that, given their respect for their central black characters, do "not even need to be about racism." Nevertheless, responding to Suzanne Marrs's disclosure that "in the massive [Welty] correspondence available for research," the writer used the word "nigger" in four of her letters, Flower mockingly comments, "Why, Eudora is hardly guilty of racism at all."[9] His facetious indictment underappreciates how interesting it is both that, in what Marrs estimates to be more than 2,600 letters written by Welty, extant and available for research,[10] there seem to be only four instances of her use of the offensive word that was more than a daily commonplace in her society *and* that these particular four letters were all written to the same person, John Robinson, a topic Marrs takes up again in her essay here and discusses fully.

To some significant degree these recent readings, like Trilling's, are more about Welty's style than they at first seem to be; that is, they are responses to the writer's preference for the complex and indirect. What Flower reveals in his grumbling comment on an essay of hers—"her point, left so cryptic, gets lost . . ."—is a desire for directness that would not be typical of Welty, loved by many for her crafty and well-crafted complexity.[11] Sarah Ford's discussion of *Delta Wedding* in this volume interrogates the need to parse the varying distances between author, narrator, and characters, an examination which suggests that, as in the case of Charles Chesnutt's *The Conjure Woman Tales*, where the author's distance from the white narrating character's assumptions can be entirely overlooked depending on the reader, *Delta Wedding* can be read too simply. And Dean Flower, though brief on the novel, does seem to read *Delta Wedding* differently than do the essays here (by McWhirter, Ford, Griffith, and McMahand), which assert the novel's intricate implications over straightforward presentations.

By contrast then, in my view, "Where Is the Voice Coming From?" is a unique text in the Welty canon, not because it alone deals with whiteness, which would be an unsupportable statement, but because it is so straightforward that there can be no question about what Welty is saying about whiteness.

To this point, contrary to Flower's suggestion that Welty found her frank voice directly out of silence, it is unquestionably true that "Powerhouse" (1941), a story written at the very outset of her career, was already as much about whiteness as "Where Is the Voice Coming From?" (1965).[12] When we first meet Powerhouse, he is performing for a white group who, amused and scandalized, has come to marvel, to see not the artist behind the mask but the mask they expect. The narrator of the story's opening section has come to enjoy the black performer—"Nigger man?"—indulging a sense of the exotic (158).[13] To that initial white point of view, the black jazz musician looks "Asiatic, monkey, Jewish, Babylonian, Peruvian, fanatic, devil." Powerhouse, stomping and smooching on stage, improvises with these stereotypes that his white audience attributes to "people on a stage—and people of a darker race . . . them—Negroes—band leaders" (158, 160). In a Fats Waller or Louis Armstrong type of metaperformance, Powerhouse works a blackface imposed on him, turning it into a medium for expressing his private and individual self.

But the bulk of the audience on this particular rainy night in Alligator, Mississippi, is not ready to receive the man behind his mask. Instead of receiving his performance collaboratively, instead of sharing his effort and his eventual achievement, they even "feel ashamed for" the jazzman who seems to them to give everything (160), a spectacle before their eyes, holding nothing in reserve. The initial and clearly white narrator is curious, enthusiastic, but not in tune with artist. Powerhouse, attempting to give his music to these alienating spectators, seems to feel displaced, lost in a racial blues. While he wears the grimaces that reflect and fulfill his audience's expectations for a "vast and obscene" jazzman, he plays "Pagan Love Song," a sad song that confirms his estranged and racial mood. As an artist who makes use of his emotional self in his performance, and who momentarily but appreciably and tellingly veers toward racial depression, Powerhouse invents the suicide of Gypsy, a story that he at first tells with his "wandering fingers" (cs 133), that is, in a musical exchange perhaps accompanied by stage whispers. The story he improvises musically in his performance and then in narrative for the responsive black audience in Negrotown's World Café, expresses his blues: he invents a fictional telegram announcing "Your wife is dead," provocatively signed "Uranus Knockwood" (133–34). That name is both a smart-mouthed rebuff—hear it rudely enunciated one syllable at a time in his reply to his drummer's too literal, antagonistic questioning or musical drum counterbeat—and also a ward-off swagger mantra shooing (knock-on-wood) that body of the blues, that "no-good pussyfooted crooning creeper" who "takes our wives when we are gone" (138).

Knockwood is a creation personifying the source of sorrow; like whiteness itself, he brings misfortune, despair, and dejection, outraged loss of what is yours and what matters. Members of Powerhouse's band and of the all-black audience at World Café recognize the culprit during their collaborative call-and-response: "Middle size man . . . Wears a hat" (138). In this act of jazz swagger, Powerhouse changes a mood that loomed. His song has sad lyrics but an aggressive, transformative, increasingly joyous tone. Naming the bringer of the blues becomes a means of chasing them away. Mutating the black-and-blues that had their source in his alienation at the white dance and his frustration in performance there, he "comes out the other side." Members of his band agree: "you got him now," they say, and they feel the change. Back at the white dance, he approaches the piano as if "he saw it for the first time in his life." Then he "tested it for strength, hit it down in the bass, played an octave with his elbow, lifted the top, looked inside, and leaned against it with all his might . . . he produced something glimmering and fragile, and smiled" (140–41). His accomplishment and his challenge are measurable as he leaves his theme, "I got a telegram my wife is dead," to move to the number "Somebody Loves Me," and to sing out to his white audience aggressively and with wry, assertive defiance as well as collaborative deference: "Maybe it's you!"

As I pointed out many years ago in an essay that I wish had discussed these issues of race more explicitly, none of the story's complexity—which is to say its complexity on whiteness—is *necessarily* apparent to a reader.[14] What stands in the way of more immediate reception is Welty's technical intricacy. A reader may or may not tune in to Welty's two tricky complications. One of these is the relationship between Powerhouse's musical performance and his narrative one, seemingly two but actually one. But it is another stylistic hurdle that, jumped, clarifies the story's attitude toward whiteness. Welty risks opening with a point of view unmarked as a character's, one that may misleadingly appear to belong to an authorial narrator. The heart of the story, its revelation and strategy, is that the story leaves its initial white perspective to travel (toward intimacy and collaboration) with Powerhouse himself—moving us, possibly without even triggering notice that the story's point of view and our distance from the black jazz man has shifted. The change, only lightly marked by double-spacing between sections, moves readers into Powerhouse's receptive and collaborating audience when he, and we along with him, leave the white dance for World Café in Negrotown. We make a cross-town passage with him that Kenneth Bearden in his 1999 essay "Monkeying Around: Welty's 'Powerhouse', Blues-Jazz, and the Signifying Connection"—another landmark contribution to the discussion of Welty and race—identified as required by decree under Jim Crow segregation; that is, the black performers are prohibited by southern practices and Jim Crow law from taking their refreshment break at the white dance.

Through this jump, Welty arranges for white readers to literally cross the color line in the course of the story, to move with Powerhouse as he leaves the dance for Negrotown. The force and genius of this technical strategy is that it negotiates a radically changed racial perspective—mirroring what I take to be a change that happened in and to Welty herself as she, a young white woman, riffed on her position in the white Jackson, Mississippi, audience of a Fats Waller performance, attended the evening that she wrote the story, and bit-by-bit imagined her way into an intimacy with the black "artist traveling in the alien world."[15] That is, having found the voice of the initial narrator in herself, Welty also finds she can hear and speak Powerhouse's voice, and in writing the story she moves away from her first, autobiographical, and white location until she discovers the black performer and herself as doubles—artists struggling with their audience. This change—toward intimacy across the color line—is one she simultaneously arranges for those white readers prepared to follow her strategic and tricky shift in point of view. Full of artistic daring, this story is one kind of answer to a trivializing question that Dean Flower poses: "Was her life of 'sheltered daring' (as she put it in *One Writer's Beginnings*) merely sheltered, all daring spent?"[16] The startling daring and considerable risk of this story is a stunning answer to his question. But to see the story as daring, and as a more than adequate answer to the question, we have to acknowledge art as action, with the potential to be a kind of revolt.

The daring in Welty's art is oblique rather than straightforward, which is not at all the same as masked, "hidden," or silent. Welty addresses the risk of the oblique in an oft-quoted passage from "Must the Novelist Crusade?" that I repeat here with a few more lines than are usually cited:

Great fiction . . . abounds in what makes for confusion. . . . It is very seldom neat, is given to sprawling and escaping from bounds, is capable of contradicting itself, and is not impervious to humor. There is absolutely everything in great fiction but a clear answer. . . . We cannot in fiction set people to . . . carrying placards to make their sentiments plain. . . . What we are sensitive to, what we feel strongly about—these become our characters and go to make our plots. . . . A plot is a thousand times more unsettling than an argument which may be answered.[17]

This is Welty clarifying her sense of the gauntlet that she runs as an artist risking indirection, and yet it is also part of a defense of art as action, as having consequences that spawn change. Choosing art to function as action leaves an individual open to the accusation of affecting only feeling rather than policy, but feeling as well as policy creates change.

Welty criticism now is no longer at the point of discovering Welty's relationship to race. It is here turning toward more specific debates. One of these, as the above discussion suggests, is about whether Welty's path on the subject—across the decades of her career—is more about her consistency or her transformations. Certainly Welty lived through decades full of dramatic social upheaval and change. From the 1930s through the 1950s, racism was more than taken for granted as part of Mississippi's social order: it was repetitively, horrifically, and brutally defended as the very basis of cultural and social organization. These decades yielded the 1960s and 1970s, when all the tragedy, grotesquerie, and violence of racist cultural assumptions were revealed to white Americans who had neither faced nor admitted the extent to which they were complicit in them. And while, on the one hand, Welty's early work—every bit as much as her 1960s stories "Where Is the Voice Coming From?" and "The Demonstrators"—attends whiteness, and shows clear understanding both of what whiteness is and how it offends, the events of the 1960s undeniably made Welty more aware. Seeing more clearly her own position as a white woman made her more self-conscious, alert, and arguably more caught in that subject position. It is in interviews given after her 1971 publication of *One Time, One Place*, making public the 1930s photographs she took of black Mississippians before their reproduction in the larger volume *Photographs*, that you can hear her developing caution. A prevailing and established view in Welty studies—that I myself argue and advocate—is that her photographs of black subjects were collaborative in ways that make them remarkable for their time period.[18] But at the same time her comments in a 1989 interview with Hunter Cole and

Seetha Srinivasan suggest a sensitive defensiveness about her position as a white photographer of black subjects. Asked by the interviewers to comment "on how a shy person such as you took some of these daring photographs," her remarks seem to reflect changes in self-conscious awareness that came with the civil rights battles of the 1960s and engendered an emerging sense of how artistic appropriation of others' experiences could be problematic:

> I think my particular time and place contributed to the frankness, the openness of the way the pictures came about. This refers to both the photographer and the subject . . . I was never questioned, or avoided. There was no self-consciousness on either side. I just spoke to persons on the street and said, 'do you mind if I take a picture' and they didn't care. There was no sense of violation on either side. I don't think it existed; I know it didn't in my attitude, or in theirs. All of that unself-consciousness is gone now. There is no such relationship between a photographer and a subject possible any longer . . . Everybody is just so media-conscious . . . Everybody thinks of pictures as publicity or—I don't know. I wouldn't be interested in doing such a book today, even if it were possible, because it would assume a very different motive and produce a different effect. (MC 191)[19]

In this remark, we hear Welty's nostalgic and temporarily idealized version of an unselfconscious past, which of course would have been white unselfconsciousness rather than black, as well as her uneasiness with an increased self-consciousness that made her more wary of her own whiteness as a defining and limiting racial category, one that she had perhaps unconsciously taken for granted in her interactions with black subjects. That is to say, we hear her discomforted self-awareness increasing.

The awareness of whiteness is very much to the point in probing Welty's handling of race. Thadious Davis, exploring another white Mississippi writer's handling of race, writes about Faulkner's depiction of whiteness: "Most impressive about his achievement is not that he created black characters and positioned them within his fictional world of Yoknapatawpha, but rather that he envisioned what Melville represented as 'the whiteness of whiteness.' Faulkner constructed characters who are consciously white, racialized as white, and depicted the construction of whiteness within Southern and American society. As a result, he allowed outsiders to know in ways not otherwise available to them one ongoing narrative of white people in psychological nudity."[20]

A difference between Welty's fiction and Faulkner's is in his entirely explicit and frequent naming of white as specifically white, emphasizing it as an utterly visible racial category. His naming it is an early anticipation of current practice in racial analysis, one that makes apparent both his awareness of whiteness and his apprehension of its agency. Welty does not use that term as we do today, and yet as this collection will repeatedly show, her fictions over and again look at whiteness in ways that have the potential to make its behaviors visible, to expose its social and cultural practices, its assumptions, its voices, its blindness, as well as—as Jay Watson says of Faulkner's fictions—the "conditions that cloak whiteness and hide its dominating effects."[21] This is fiction in which whiteness, hiding "in plain sight,"[22] is made visible to readers who focus on the subject.

How else do her fictions show what Welty knew about whiteness and race? How aware was she? Let me stress three unmistakable implications of her work, and another defined area of debate.

Numerous Welty fictions across her career make the color line as well as white privilege and unawareness culturally visible. Contrary to the nostalgia of her interview remark, the fiction does not at all portray a past that was ideally unselfconscious; rather, it repeatedly makes clear the ignored yet not successfully passed-over awkwardness of the gaping distances introduced between lives lived in shared space but separated by social structure. This material brings forward an emergent debate; that is, whether or not her treatments of marginalized black characters in fictions focusing on white communities successfully point readers toward complex lives obscured by the color line. Certainly the voices and interiority of black characters are restricted in these fictions. Are these black characters then merely accepted and possibly dismissed as marginalized in the Jim Crow segregated South, or are they, as I think they are and as David McWhirter contends in his essay here, allowed to become tantalizing "secret agents"? Namely, are they both withholding lives and obscuring emotional reactions while leaving readers in a position to understand how much white doesn't know and even prefers to leave underground? Also germane to the topic, as Donnie McMahand's essay argues, the black body is itself full of meaning in Welty's fiction, and needs to be seen and read.

Second, her fiction repeatedly shows us that Welty understands race, like gender, to be a performance. Earlier I suggested that Powerhouse, like Fats Waller himself, performs his white audiences' blackface expectations, riffing and putting on the orientalist faces of the black jazzman that are expected as well as authorized by his white audience: "Asiatic, monkey, Jewish, Babylonian, Peruvian, fanatic, devil" (159). Resembling the living jazzmen Fats Waller and Louis Armstrong in their extraordinary moments of outrageous staginess,

Powerhouse builds his performance of and on anticipated masks and materials in ways that yield an inventive and original response to a racial state of affairs. Like Louis Armstrong singing—with grin, grimace, and grace—"What Did I Do to Be So Black and Blue?" he creates and transcends an exaggerated performance of African American racial identity scripted by whiteness that may appeal to enthusiastic white consumption but is also powerfully subversive and expressive. That Welty emphasizes the performance of racial identities—black and white—is also clear in Shelley's journal in *Delta Wedding*. As Jean Griffith points out here, after Shelley names Troy's nonchalance with black men as a convincing performance mimicking and appropriating the white Deltan masculinity to which Troy has—by virtue of his lower class and outsider status—a probationary relationship, it worries Shelley that all her family's men are equally imitative performers of white masculinity: "Suppose a real Deltan only imitated another Deltan. Suppose the behavior of all men were actually no more than this—imitation of other men. But it had previously occurred to her that Troy was trying to imitate her father. (Suppose her father imitated . . . oh, not he!)."[23] Or to take another example of Welty's attention to race as performance, in "The Burning," Miss Myra's and Miss Theo's fantastic performances of the lady—their scripted enactments of whiteness—generate the story's elements of grotesque humor. I would argue that from the earliest outset of her creative play, Welty's comedies are built on and emphasize her knowledge of gender, race, and power as social performances, a humor that perfectly anticipates Judith Butler's 1997 theoretical discussions of "a politics of the performative."[24] As early as Welty's juvenilia and then throughout her career, she mined the comedy innate in and intrinsic to everyday performances that are socially scripted and so familiar; many of her comic characters have the quality of revealing a society in which the performance of race, gender, or power verges on parody. And in this volume, Sarah Ford's essay, "Laughing in the Dark: Race and Humor in *Delta Wedding*," suggests something more: that if we look carefully we see the novel's black characters recognize whiteface and blackface both as performed and as humorously comical, especially when the white characters do not recognize their performance.

Third, Welty clearly recognizes and perceives the implications of white material advantage and of black deprivation. This understanding includes the relationship of material advantage and deprivation to American economic history, to the cycle of race and poverty, to conflicts fostered between black and white working classes, and to an uneasy hierarchy of white classes within the presumed monolith of whiteness. Her photographs *Making a Date* and *Window Shopping*, discussed here by Keri Watson and Mae Miller Claxton, help us see the racially divided economic world surrounding Welty in the 1930s that she chose to frame and focus. And as Patricia Yaeger's essay here demonstrates, "The Burning" frames the history of material possession and nonpossession embedded in southern history, including—within the contexts created first by slavery and then by the appropriating white gaze—the issue of black self-possession. These issues of whiteness and material possession are central as well to *Delta Wedding*, "Where Is the Voice Coming From?," and "The Demonstrators," to name only the most obvious examples.

Making these points, this volume of essays on Welty, whiteness, and race is a dedicated attempt to further develop the currently evolving, provocative conversation and carry it forward. The twelve essays that follow here each approach the topic distinctively. The series opens by examining the subject in light of Welty's biography and then moves, more or less—and to the extent possible with essays treating multiple works—chronologically across her career starting with other early stories—"A Curtain of Green," "Keela," "Powerhouse," "A Worn Path," "Livvie,"—and with her 1930s photography. These are followed by several essays on *Delta Wedding*, a cluster acknowledging that the critical controversy opened by this early novel needs, at last and still, to be deliberated in detail. These *Delta Wedding* essays themselves extend into readings of *The Golden Apples*, "Where Is the Voice Coming From?," and *One Writer's Beginnings*. Then, the final entries of the collection attend "The Burning," "The Demonstrators," and *The Optimist's Daughter*. This collected assembly of discussions simultaneously defines and mediates the field's emerging debates.

Suzanne Marrs in her essay "Welty, Race, and the Patterns of a Life" consolidates and extends what she knows as a Welty scholar and biographer. Writing as a friend as well as a biographer, Marrs describes her own dilemma when, reading through files of correspondence in Welty's home after the writer's death, she finds four letters, all written in the late 1940s to John Robinson, that puzzle and trouble her because Marrs had never heard Welty use a racial slur, and these letters each contain the same distinctive one, "nigger." Marrs assesses her own thoughts about those specific uses, and decides that she needs to follow the pattern of Welty's life in order to choose between her speculations. The evidence she collects follows Welty's interest in the arts of diverse cultures, her disgust with Mississippi politics and leaders, her sense that art can be a particularly meaningful response to injustice, her rueful awareness of the difficulty of having professional relationships across the color line in her home place of Jackson, her fear of violence and reprisal for speaking publicly in the 1960s, and, nevertheless, her increasing definition of a voice opposing oppression, not only directly and indirectly in her fiction, but in protesting gestures made in the realms of action. Moreover, Marrs speculates about the differences between John Robinson and Eudora Welty on the topic, and on the interaction between them. This essay, the logical overture for this collection, collects, consolidates, and sifts Marrs's biographical work of several decades, assembling and reconsidering what we know—because of Marrs's extensive and continuing work— which informs the critical discussions that follow.

In "Parting the Veil: Eudora Welty, Richard Wright, and the Crying Wounds of Jim Crow," Susan Donaldson pictures a dialogue between the works of these two Mississippi writers who, divided by legalized segregation, never met, though born within months of each other and educated in Jackson, Mississippi, schools. Donaldson finds and identifies unexpectedly parallel purposes in their very different work reflecting life under Jim Crow in the 1930s and 1940s. And in her analysis she connects Welty's determination to part "a curtain, that invisible shadow that falls between people, the veil of indifference to each other's presence, each other's wonder, each other's human plight"[25] to the imagery and implications of W. E. B. Du Bois's "sombre veil of color," and its power to wreak psychic damage on black and white alike. This framing leads Donaldson to a fresh reading of the roles of white womanhood and racial interactions in the stories of *A Curtain of Green*, an interpretation that presents Welty's critique as paralleling Wright's in the stories of *Uncle Tom's Children*.

Keri Watson in "Eudora Welty's *Making a Date, Grenada, Mississippi:* One Photograph, Five Performances" considers one of Welty's photographs through its performance in five settings over the decades before its 1989 publication in the volume *Photographs*. Watson argues that these five distinct and effectively politicized performances of *Making a Date* each challenged the status quo of race relations in a particular time and place. "Through her repeated publication and exhibition of one photograph, Welty reached a wide-ranging audience," and "she always put that audience in a position to empathize with her subject." Emphasizing the notion of performance "complicated by the ideology of the photographer, the situation and placement of the image, and the positionality of the viewer," she argues: "No matter how authentic, documentary, or unbiased they may appear, photographs are never static and literal transcriptions of reality." Her discussion demonstrates how Welty's "single contentious image enacts and promulgates numerous meanings . . . for multiple audiences, across time and place . . . to effectively negotiate issues of race."

In "'The Little Store' in the Segregated South: Race and Consumer Culture in Eudora Welty's Writing and Photography," Mae Miller Claxton considers both how civil rights conflicts played out in consumer life and how Welty's photography, prose, and fiction intersect that sphere of racial status quo and change. Claxton traces Welty's interest in all that is implied in the emblematic image of the photo *Window Shopping*, an image that suggests to Claxton a middle-class consumer separated from the contents of the store window by the large plate glass of segregation. She unfolds a politics of shopping as well as the story of a disenfranchised but rising African American middle-class consumer, a developing Saturday world in which black and white customers moved around town in consumer spaces more shared than the segregated spaces of schools, churches, and restaurants. Claxton works with Grace Hale's argument that, on Saturdays, town "commercial districts were the most integrated . . . spaces in southern life," and "that department stores were 'muddled middle' spaces where segregation remained vulnerable." By considering Welty's photographs of African American men and women as well as her stories "A Worn Path," "Livvie," and "Where Is the Voice Coming From?," Claxton reveals Welty's attention to economic stories in which, increasingly, "black consumers threatened the status quo of white society with their access to better education, jobs, and new consumer goods." Considering Gordon Parks's comment that he "picked up a camera because it was [his] choice of weapons against what [he] hated most about the universe: racism, intolerance, poverty," Claxton sees Welty's images and writing as revealing a similarly daring effort toward revisioning.

The next several essays continue Barbara Ladd's 1988 impulse to read *Delta Wedding* by focusing on its black characters. They open the novel variously, but together they are a critically important and revealing response to Trilling's early misreading, and an informing acknowledgment that clarifying this early novel is key to any reading of Welty on race. These controversial essays, sometimes opening and entering new points of debate, are compatible in that as a group they enrich each other's resonant, provocative interpretations.

In "Secret Agents: Welty's African Americans," David McWhirter argues that although Welty's oeuvre includes a handful of stories focused squarely on African American characters, her work more typically locates African Americans as significant but largely inscrutable presences at the margins of her narratives. He suggests that, while she writes mostly about the lives of white Mississippians, Welty also is telling the story of how much whiteness does not account for and does not know. McWhirter uses Gayatri Spivak's discussion in *A Critique of Postcolonial Reason* of "'native' as'. . . the curious guardian at the margin who will not inform."[26] He then shows that Welty's work is replete with such secret agents, black figures whose presence in her stories signal a larger world of knowledge and purpose and motivation. In *Delta Wedding*, this hinted-at life is obvious in and central to the occluded stories of Partheny, Aunt Studney, Man-Son, Root, Big Baby, and of course Pinchy, whose "coming through," celebrated by her African American community, is as mysterious to the reader as it is to the Fairchilds who never ask about it. While discussing *Delta Wedding* and Welty's "The Demonstrators" to establish his interpretative paradigm, McWhirter eventually concentrates on the series of black characters from *The Golden Apples* and from *One Writer's Beginnings*, among them Fannie, the "black sewing woman" who tells "tantalizing" gossipy tales that the child Eudora is sheltered from, but from whom she nevertheless learns to "know that stories are there." Similarly, the African Americans in many of Welty's works paradoxically call our attention to lives and histories that the narratives are not, in any direct way, telling, but that we are led to know are there.

In "Laughing in the Dark: Race and Humor in *Delta Wedding*," Sarah Ford spotlights how, as Ellen puts her coconut cake made from Mashula's famous recipe into the oven, Roxie, sitting on the back porch, "could be heard laughing, two high gentle notes out in the dark." The reader is not told exactly what Roxie is laughing at, and "is also not told if Roxie was actually heard, just that she could be heard, if, that is, anyone is listening." Ford's essay examines the African American characters in *Delta Wedding* and the text's use of humor to peer into their alternative viewpoints. To do that, she notes that while Welty seems to limit point of view to white female characters who ignore the black workers around them, the writer's technique allows the reader access to perspectives a bit beyond these Fairchild women's perspectives. Ford helpfully defines and engages debates concerning how readers are to parse the distance between character and narrator in free indirect discourse. It is this technique and difficulty that seems to produce the extreme divergence in readings of this text. Asserting a distinct clue to follow, Ford highlights the audible but commonly unnoticed humor in the novel's black voices. She shows the text repeatedly pulling back to show black characters all engaging in ironic behaviors that suggest they are laughing at the Fairchild family's rather dense unconsciousness, and she argues that humor and laughter—though not an outright revolt against the rigid race system depicted in the novel—can be a powerful tool in subverting racial hierarchies. As in Charles Chesnutt's *The Conjure Woman Tales*, where a reader can either be schooled by the text into sympathy with Julius and Chesnutt, or miss that invitation entirely and think Chesnutt is writing in sympathy with his white narrator, John, the text of *Delta Wedding* permits a reader to misread or simply miss this humor, but Ford proposes that if a reader is attentive and open, the text itself schools her to find an ironic perspective on whiteness.

In "'I Knowed Him Then Like I Know Me Now': Whiteness, Violence, and Interracial Male Intimacy in *Delta Wedding* and 'Where Is the Voice Coming From?,'" Jean C. Griffith converges on the intersecting issues of race, class, and gender in Welty's early novel and her late short story. Reading across these two fictions featuring white men in violent encounters with black men, she brings into focus a curious blend of startling brutality and odd intimacy that mark male relationships across the color line. These are behaviors in which white men assume they can predict and intervene in black men's actions, a postulation that shapes the hierarchy of male social positions. From that point, she explores the assumption of a white male "responsibility to physically control black men, whether it is socially sanctioned (as in the cases of Troy and George) or outside the law (as in the killer's). Across the [two] works, the responsibility to control black men defines a white man's status relative to other white men." Griffith is interested in boundaries between classes of white men being negotiated against the more generalized idea of whiteness in contrast to blackness. In the novel, similar scenes involving violence, intimacy, paternalism, and social control across the color line cause us to compare and contrast George Fairchild—Delta family paragon—and Troy Flavin—who is "working-class" and "vaguely Irish," an outsider who considers what it means to be a "real Deltan" when he tells Ellen that "by now, I can't tell a bit of difference between me and any Delta people you name . . . it's just a matter of knowing how to handle your Negroes."[27] While Troy—as he negotiates probationary entrance into his fiancé's family—asserts whiteness as easing class, ethnic, and eugenic boundaries, the murderer in "Where Is the Voice Coming From?" attempts a similar strategy in a more recent time, with less success. Moreover, because Welty offers these encounters as seen by white women—in the first case by Dabney and Shelley, and in the second by the murderer's wife as well as by Welty herself as she asks the question, "Where is the voice coming from?," a reader may critically assess not only whiteness and masculinity but also whiteness and womanhood.

In "Bodies on the Brink: Vision, Violence, and Self-Destruction in *Delta Wedding*," Donnie McMahand calls attention to the fallibility of reading the novel's black characters as inscrutable. He argues he is

> not ready to let them go, not without inquiry into the part of their presence that Welty seldom obstructs—their bodies. To see and know these figures more fully, if not completely, the reader must be willing to decipher the signs of their bodies, a challenge that almost every white character in the novel fails even to attempt. Their failure to investigate, to question, casts the black body into a state of strange, unknowable disruptiveness, an ontic force to fear, control, or dismiss but not understand . . . Even as Welty's black characters refuse . . . to tell their stories, their bodies prove less reticent.

McMahand demonstrates how the novel contains and distinguishes between subordinate black bodies that literally disappear from the page—some evaporating into the idyllic atmosphere of the pastoral setting—and those figures whose rebellious acts, furtive or extravagant, coincide with displays of the black body. He maintains that the novel's formation of the Fairchilds' narrow white gaze is dramatized during moments of interracial contact as a literal loss of vision or as genuine mesmerism. Forging a link between Welty's novel and Toni Morrison's *Song of Solomon*, McMahand discusses how these writers similarly expose a strange yet significant slippage between the black character's self-assertion and self-destruction. The essential conflict for many of the black characters in Welty's novel involves a battle for agency, a battle waged against the imposition of the white gaze, positioned not only in the open space of social interaction but also within the black self.

Patricia Yaeger moves ahead to Welty's 1951 avant-garde and experimental Civil War story focalized through the house slave Delilah who will be violently "freed" subsequent to—as well as violated in and after—the burning of her mistresses' plantation house. In this fiction, Welty undertakes black interiority. It is Delilah's crisis of consciousness that records and survives the atrocities consequent to the plantation house's historic upheaval; it is her situation as well as her chronicling ear and eye that simultaneously make us aware of the violence long routine in women's plantation relationships. In "'Black Men Dressed in Gold': Racial Violence in Eudora Welty's 'The Burning,'" Yaeger makes connections across the "riddling quality" of the story's baroque, "difficult, beautiful style," across the writer's belated worry that the story might be "too involved and curlicued around with things," to a critical recognition that the story's overabundance of details precisely corresponds to the economy of things that opens up southern history and "the violent sources of New World plenitude." Yaeger argues that story's "prescience is . . . to create an intricate analysis of race" focused on the "sadistic asymmetries" and "forced deprivation" of Delilah's lack of possession, not only of things but also of her apparent child and of her self. The story, "obsessed with genteel excess, with white people's superabundant goods and objects, which depend on a world of slave labor," is centered in the everyday and nonchalant violence between plantation women, white and black, a violence in defense of things, their care, maintenance, and upkeep. "Thing-obsession unearths a ferocity in the plantation household that transgresses ordinary ideas about white female gentility in the U.S. slave-owning world." And Yaeger decodes the maddening detail of Delilah's encounter with the burned and melted Venetian mirror—which has in its frame "black men dressed in gold"—as "a scene of recognition, grounded in a lifetime of laboring over white people's objects . . . 'Delilah would have known that mirror anywhere.'"

In "Ice Picks, Guinea Pigs, and Dead Birds: Dramatic Weltian Possibilities in 'The Demonstrators,'" Rebecca Mark suggests that, as anyone who likes detective novels knows, it is always a detail that eventually unravels the nature of the crime; the moment a detective sees the missing sock, the broken light, or the moved vase, she is finally able to understand, if not necessarily solve, the mystery. In "The Demonstrators," there are murders, but Mark tells us this is no ordinary detective story; the motives, who actually killed whom, and who is responsible become, through carefully executed details, metaphorical questions asked of the citizens of a racially conflicted America in the 1960s. Mark argues that previous readings of these stories often hide the details that allow a much more devilish and radical story to emerge. This radical revisioning of the story draws on Mark's interest in reading Welty intertextually and through details that are clues to allusions that direct and, in this case, alter her reading of the story.

Julia Eichelberger recognizes that Welty's portrayals of race and racism in twentieth-century Mississippi have, in over sixty years of response, met questioning readers. This readership has not found "evidence of Welty's progressive attitudes in her fictional texts, which rarely portray straightforward resistance to racism," and readers have puzzled over why Welty did not make clearer that she found Mississippi's racial hierarchy reprehensible. To these readers, "scholarly efforts" to trace Welty's opposition to racial injustice amount to "special pleading." In "Rethinking the Unthinkable: Tracing Welty's Changing View of the Color Line in Her Letters, Essays, and *The Optimist's Daughter*," Eichelberger enters that debate, returning to the 1940s letters that perplexed Marrs in the opening essay here, and she writes that she wishes to keep them—the "presence or . . . rarity" of racist language—in mind as she analyzes "other references to race in [Welty's] private . . . and public statements," and in particular as she reads Welty's 1971 novel, *The Optimist's Daughter*, set in 1960s Mississippi. While Claudia Roth Pierpont, in assessing the novel's "seemingly quietist treatment of social upheaval, calls the novel 'morally simplified,'" and Dean Flower "faults its focus on 'the same non-disruptive familial themes that had generated *Delta Wedding*'" (327), Eichelberger argues that *The Optimist's Daughter* "does situate its protagonist's private family memories within the context of Mississippi's history of white supremacy." In particular, one seed of the novel—visible in Welty's letters about a dark-skinned Bombay man who had been in the same New Orleans hospital as her brother—along with the transformation of that incident into her fiction, and the treatment of race in the novel all suggest to Eichelberger "that Welty's attitude toward the color line, which was always progressive compared with most white Mississippians, changed between the 1940s and the 1960s."

These essays respond then to the need to deliberate a controversial topic. And they, as a group, further advance the developing discussion of Welty and her body of work as sensitive to and conscious of issues of race in ways that we might not have expected or previously appreciated.

Notes

1. Trilling, "Fiction in Review," 60–61.
2. Welty, *Collected Stories*, xi. Hereafter cited parenthetically.
3. Marrs, "Metaphor of Race," 697, 707.
4. Ladd, "Coming Through," 541–42, 544.
5. Yaeger, *Dirt and Desire*, 11–12.
6. Gwin's 2010 lecture, available online, is forthcoming as *Remembering Medgar Evers: Writing the Long Civil Rights Movement*.
7. Pierpont, "A Perfect Lady," 101.
8. Flower, "Eudora Welty and Racism," 332, 327.
9. Flower, "Eudora Welty and Racism," 331, 330.
10. Marrs writes, in a personal communication, that this is "a rough estimate of the number of letters, including letters at MDAH, Washington U, Colorado, the University

of Illinois, along with . . . the letters at Maryland, National Library of Canada, Texas, and Millsaps to reach the total" (June 2011).

11. Flower, "Eudora Welty and Racism," 331.

12. For a full biographical discussion of "Powerhouse" and the topic of race, see Suzanne Marrs, "Eudora Welty, the Liberal Imagination and Mississippi Politics."

13. Welty, *Stories, Essays, and Memoir*, 158. Hereafter cited parenthetically. It is especially relevant to notice that when Welty edited her stories for reprinting in *The Collected Stories* (1980), she elected to change a select number of the appearances of the word "nigger" to "Negro." As she told her editor John Ferrone, this word was a "way of speech forty years ago" but now is "throbbing with associations not then part of it" (Ferrone, "Collecting the Stories," 21). Ferrone recalls that at first she

> wanted the word 'nigger' to be deleted from 'Why I Live at the P. O.' In a later letter, she asked to have it deleted wherever it appeared . . . [Later] she decided instead to review the offensive word case by case, because in the end it was dealt with in several ways. In "Why I Live at the P. O." the word was excised, but in "Powerhouse," "Negro man" replaced "Nigger Man," and "Negro" was substituted elsewhere in the stories . . . In a number of instances, where it occurred in speech and was an expression of character, the word was left, as in "Keela, the Outcast Indian Maiden" and especially in "Where Is the Voice Coming From?" the story told though the eyes of Medgar Evers's murderer.

The revisions suggest Welty's increased sensitivity to and self-consciousness about racial issues after the 1960s. When Richard Ford and Michael Kreyling prepared the *Library of America* authoritative text of the stories, they chose to use the original texts, a decision that reestablishes the implications of the descriptor in the narrating white audience member's thoughts, but also opens the need to parse the distance between that narrator and the author. And while the *Library of America* edition carefully restores Welty's original texts, it is then unable to be faithful to her final judgment about the use of the word.

14. Pollack, "Words Between Strangers."

15. This is Welty's phrase in her gloss on "Powerhouse" in her interview with Linda Kuehl, reprinted in Prenshaw, *Conversations*, 85.

16. Flower, "Eudora Welty and Racism," 329.

17. Welty, *The Eye of the Story*, 149–50.

18. I've argued this in numerous presentations including, to name three, at the exhibition *Passionate Observer: Eudora Welty Among Artists of the Thirties*, Mississippi Museum of Art, 2002; in *Colloque Eudora Welty: The Poetics of the Body*, University of Haute Bretagne, Rennes, France, 2002; and in the National Endowment for the Humanities Landmarks in American History and Culture Workshop, "Eudora Welty's Secret Sharer: The Outside World and the Writer's Imagination," 2008. It is a topic I also discuss in *The Body of the Other Woman in the Fiction and Photography of Eudora Welty*, forthcoming.

19. Cole and Srinivasan, "Eudora Welty and Photography: An Interview," in *More Conversations with Eudora Welty*, 188–213.

20. Davis, *Games of Property: Law, Race, and Faulkner's* Go Down Moses, 254.

21. Watson, *Faulkner and Whiteness*, 3–4.

22. Watson, *Faulkner and Whiteness*, ix.

23. Welty, *Delta Wedding*, 285–86.

24. Butler, *Excitable Speech: A Politics of the Performative*.

25. Welty, preface to *One Time, One Place*, 12.

26. Spivak, *A Critique of Postcolonial Reason*, 190.

27. Welty, *Delta Wedding*, 183.

Bibliography

Appel, Alfred, Jr.. "'They Endured': Welty's Negro Characters." In *A Season of Dreams: The Fiction of Eudora Welty*. Baton Rouge: Louisiana State University Press, 1965.

Bearden, Kenneth. "Monkeying Around: Welty's 'Powerhouse,' Blues-Jazz, and the Signifying Connection." *Southern Literary Journal* 31, no. 2 (1999): 65–79.

Butler, Judith. *Excitable Speech: A Politics of the Performative*. London: Routledge, 1997.

Cole, Hunter, and Seetha Srinivasan. "Eudora Welty and Photography: An Interview." In *More Conversations with Eudora Welty*, ed. Peggy Whitman Prenshaw, 188–213. Jackson: University Press of Mississippi, 1996.

Costello, Brannon. *Plantation Airs: Racial Paternalism and the Transformations of Class in Southern Fiction, 1945–1971*. Baton Rouge: Louisiana State University Press, 2007.

Davis, Thadious M. *Games of Property: Law, Race, and Faulkner's* Go Down, Moses. Durham: Duke University Press, 2003.

Ferrone, John. "Collecting the Stories of Eudora Welty." *Eudora Welty Review*, 1 (2009): 181.

Flower, Dean. "Eudora Welty and Racism." *Hudson Review* 60, no. 2 (2007): 325–32.

Gwin, Minrose. *Remembering Medgar Evers: Writing the Long Civil Rights Movement*. Athens: University of Georgia Press, forthcoming.

Hardy, John E. "Eudora Welty's Negroes." In *Images of the Negro in American Literature*, ed. Seymour L. Gross and John E. Hardy, 221–32. Chicago: University of Chicago Press, 1966.

Harrison, Suzan. "'It's Still a Free Country': Constructing Race, Identity, and History in Eudora Welty's 'Where Is the Voice Coming From?'" *Mississippi Quarterly* 50, no. 4 (1997): 631–46.

Kuehl, Linda. "The Art of Fiction XLVII: Eudora Welty." In *Conversations with Eudora Welty*, ed. Peggy Whitman Prenshaw, 74–91. Jackson: University Press of Mississippi, 1984.

Ladd, Barbara. "Coming Through: The Black Initiate in *Delta Wedding*." *Mississippi Quarterly* 41, no. 4 (1988): 541–51.

Marrs, Suzanne. *Eudora Welty: A Biography*. New York: Houghton Mifflin Harcourt, 2006.

———. "Eudora Welty: The Liberal Imagination and Mississippi Politics." *Mississippi Quarterly*, supplement (2009): 5–11.

———. "The Metaphor of Race in Eudora Welty's Fiction." *Southern Review* 22, no. 4 (1986): 697–707.

Pierpont, Claudia Roth. "A Perfect Lady." *New Yorker*, October 5, 1998, 94–104.

Pollack, Harriet, and Suzanne Marrs. *Eudora Welty and Politics: Did the Writer Crusade?* Baton Rouge: Louisiana State University Press, 2000.

———. "'Words Between Strangers': On Welty, Her Style, and Her Audience." *Mississippi Quarterly* 39, no. 4 (1986), 481–507.

Spivak, Gayatri. *A Critique of Postcolonial Reason: Toward a History of the Vanishing Present.* Cambridge: Harvard University Press, 1999.

Trilling, Diana. "Fiction in Review." *The Nation*, May 11, 1946, 578. Reprinted in *Eudora Welty: The Contemporary Reviews*, ed. Pearl McHaney, 60–61. New York: Cambridge University Press, 2005.

Yaeger, Patricia. *Dirt and Desire: Reconstructing Southern Women's Fiction, 1930–1990.* Chicago: University of Chicago Press, 2000.

Watson, Jay, ed. *Faulkner and Whiteness.* Jackson: University Press of Mississippi, 2011.

Welty, Eudora. *The Collected Stories of Eudora Welty.* New York: Harcourt, 1980.

———. *Delta Wedding.* New York: Harcourt, 1946.

———. *The Eye of the Story.* New York: Random House, 1990.

———. *One Time, One Place.* Jackson: University Press of Mississippi, 1971.

———. *Stories, Essays, and Memoir.* New York: Library of America, 1998.

SUZANNE MARRS

Welty, Race, and the Patterns of a Life

When Harriet Pollack asked me to write an essay for this volume, I wondered what more I could say. I had already published three articles dealing with Eudora Welty's treatment of race in her fiction, I had discussed her depiction of black characters in my book *One Writer's Imagination*, and I had explored her attitudes on race in my biography of her. Still, Harriet persisted with her request, and I decided to acquiesce in the hopes of taking a more informal approach, of being free to write not only as a Welty scholar and biographer but also as her friend, of being able to bring information scattered throughout my previous work into a focused essay, of being able to revisit Welty's letters that had puzzled and troubled me, and of even discovering new insights.

What, as her friend, did I know about Welty and race? From the day in 1983 when I met her and throughout the following years when I lived, as I still do, only a few blocks from her Jackson, Mississippi, home, I had a sense of Eudora Welty as the most open-minded of individuals. She was interested in other people and treated them with genuine respect. She responded to absurdities of language or situation with humor, but she was not given to ridicule. Though she would pass judgment on actions or comments she found unwise or unreasonable, though she was predisposed to support liberal Democratic candidates for office, though she actively disliked politicians she deemed corrupt or inept or wrongheaded, I never knew her to judge an individual on the basis of class, creed, or race. I saw that ethnic or racial slurs were anathema to her, and they did not pass her lips. She certainly recognized the continuing existence of a color line, but she rued that fact.

My sense of Eudora was shared by many other Jacksonians. Edwin King, who had been a chaplain at Tougaloo College just north of Jackson during the civil rights movement and who had almost been killed because of his pro–civil rights stance, revered Eudora. He told me of her insistence that a 1963 reading at Jackson's Millsaps College be an integrated event, and he felt that her openness set a model for what we might now call a "postracial" America. Recently, Eudora's longtime friend Patti Carr Black was asked to define the essence of Eudora's character. That essence lay, Patti asserted, in Eudora's rhetorical question: "If you treat everybody *first* as a human being—people you love best, & people you hate most—& people you have yet to understand—isn't that the only way"?[1] Certainly it was Eudora's way, even in old age. The white hairdresser who came to the house to wash and set her hair; the African American women who stayed with her when she could no longer manage alone; the white dentist and doctors who made house calls for Eudora; the journalists and novelists, white and black, who visited her; the white classical musician Milton Babbitt and the African American jazz great Billy Taylor, who both called upon her—all testified to her embracing of them.

In 1998 I began my work on a Welty biography by reading Eudora's letters to her lifelong friend Frank Lyell. Spanning the years 1931 to 1976, the letters reinforced my own sense of Eudora's character and the sense shared by so many others in Jackson. So too, for the most part, did the letters I read next, letters to John Robinson, with whom Eudora had been romantically involved between 1937 and 1952. I was startled, however, to find that in a handful of letters to Robinson written between 1946 and 1948 Eudora used the word "nigger" as a descriptor. Had these letters been written by Eudora in her teens or early twenties, I might have attributed such language to the white culture in which she had been reared and that she later came to question. Had the letters been written at whatever age by Flannery O'Connor or Katherine Anne Porter or William Faulkner, I would not have felt surprise. I well knew that these writers were of their time and place, but I did not think of Eudora in the same way. Still, here were four instances in which she, a woman in her late thirties, used the word: first, to refer to a young person working at a Jackson business called, as Eudora enjoyed pointing out, "Nat'l Hide & Fur"; second, to refer to a dance and to a teenager who by mistake had phoned her from the dance; third, to identify some little boys who asked her to participate in a game with candy as the prize. Last of all, in December 1948, Eudora recalled seeing "a man play Hecate, a nigger man too, in the Negro Macbeth (laid in Haiti)."[2] Over the next seven years of reading the massive Welty correspondence available for research, I would not find another instance of a racial epithet. But what was I to make of the ones I had seen? They might betoken Eudora's failure to escape wholly a southern pattern of expression, or they might be evidence of racist assumptions I had never witnessed in her, or Eudora might have been echoing language used by Robinson, a native of the Mississippi Delta, where the use of the word was pervasive among whites. But other explanations also seem plausible. The fourth instance, for example, by ironically juxtaposing the words "nigger" and "Negro," may first have drawn upon southern racial mythology to define the function of Hecate in Orson Welles's 1936 production of *Macbeth* ("a male ringleader of the forces of darkness, which dominated the play and controlled Macbeth from the very beginning," according to Wendy Smith)[3] and then set that myth in contrast to Eudora's respect for the very real artistic achievements of the play's African American cast. Perhaps there might have been such an implied irony in the earlier uses of the term. Perhaps Eudora was role-playing for an audience of one, John Robinson, who recognized the role and its ironic significance. Certainly, each of the four references came during the years she was writing *The Golden Apples*, a book in which small-town white Mississippi characters typically use the term in speech and in thought and a book in which the term itself becomes a mark of provinciality and cultural blindness. But reading the letters in isolation left me unsure about any of these interpretations. In fact, the letters raised many questions I was not able to answer with confidence. Why did the term appear in letters written in the late 1940s and why during so brief a time span? Why did the term appear in letters to John Robinson and not to Frank Lyell? Why had the term appeared at all given the fact that in 1950 both Eudora and John Robinson told William Jay Smith how offensive they found the title of Ronald Firbank's *Prancing Nigger*? Why in a letter to Robinson later that year had Eudora quoted a shared acquaintance's use of the word? Was this her way of looking askance at a character failing?[4] In 1998, faced with these questions, I trusted that ongoing biographical research would allow me to document the patterns of Eudora's life and to provide a context in which the significance of the Robinson letters might be more adequately understood. Here's what I found.

As a student in New York City and later on visits there in the early 1930s, Eudora's experience was thoroughly cosmopolitan. She loved Romany Marie's restaurant in Greenwich Village, where the clientele might include Isamu Noguchi, Paul Robeson, and Buckminster Fuller. She loved hearing the jazz musicians who played at Harlem's Cotton Club and Small's Paradise. And in 1933 she felt the imaginative and emotional, if not intellectual, pull of Hindu culture as she twice saw Uday Shan-Kar dance. She told her friend Frank Lyell:

"You must see Shan-Kar—I don't know of anything you would like more—he is marvelous—very beautiful—he is continuously divine—really his dances are like the humours of the gods— . . . he has the most enchanting body I have ever seen, he uses it like a voice—I don't know anything about the hindu cosmos but the appeal of all he does is very direct and you are instantly enchanted." Eudora's enthusiastic response to Shan-Kar's creative interpretation of Indian dance anticipated by more than fifty years the words she would use to describe classical Russian ballerina Galina Ulanova: "magical and quite apart from anything, either on stage or on earth."[5]

Away from New York, Eudora's experience involved a similar embracing of diversity. In the 1930s and into the 1940s, though she could not wholly bridge the gap between black and white, Eudora took an active interest in African American life. In doing so, she set herself apart from most of her white Jackson compatriots. She and three friends were the only white people in the audience at a Mamie Smith concert at Jackson's Alamo Theater. By herself, Eudora attended a rural, African American religious service, which she found quite moving. She and a few friends relished attending a street dance in Jackson's black business district—some might point to her calling two little dancing girls "monkeys," but Eudora used that term to describe twice as many white characters as black in her fiction; for her the term seemed to carry a playful, mischievous import. And Eudora photographed African American life in Mississippi. She snapped most of her photographs, as she later reported, "without the awareness of the subjects or with only their peripheral awareness." "The snapshots made with people's awareness," Eudora also recalled, "are, for the most part, just as unposed: I simply asked people if they would mind going on with what they were doing and letting me take a picture. I can't remember ever being met with a demurrer stronger than amusement."[6] Without doubt her privileged status as a white person made it almost impossible for her African American subjects to decline. Still, the most remarkable quality of the Welty photos is the affinity photographer and subject so often seem to feel toward each other. Never are the pictures patronizing; never do they deny the subject's dignity.

Eudora placed this personal pattern of openness in a larger context when, in January 1944, she took exception to Thomas Sancton's article "Race Clash," which had appeared in *Harper's Magazine*. In the article, Sancton, the former managing editor of the *New Republic*, a southerner deemed by scholar Lawrence Jackson to be a preeminent white crusader against racism, and the husband of Eudora's friend Seta, looked back at his participation in a 1936 incident of white provocation against African Americans in New Orleans, an incident he had almost immediately rued and now wrote to deplore. He described an episode of heavy drinking with friends, the group's piling into the car of a businessman named Carter, and Carter's subsequent use of the car to harass a deliveryman on a narrow backstreet in a black neighborhood. This behavior prompted the spontaneous gathering of twenty or thirty angry African Americans, and Sancton's own summoning of the police, who he knew would take the white side in the dispute. Still he declared he was "glad that it happened" because "it taught me something about my Southern world that I could not have found in a book." Eudora felt that the essay was based, as she wrote in a letter to her agent Diarmuid Russell, on "an error in conception" and that there was a note of smugness in it. She sensed that Sancton felt a sort of self-approving joy in confessing and using this incident to indict his "Southern world." Eudora further opined that Tom "was simply drunk and did something few people would have done, drunk or sober," and she contended that this sort of drunken, malicious, and foolhardy white hostility was not typical. It would be impossible to imagine John Robinson "with a thousand drinks in him," she told Russell, having done anything similar, even though he had been "long exposed to the 'dangerous air' of Lake Pontchartrain" and was "not a bosom lover of Negroes."[7] Pushed by the article to think in terms of racial otherness even as she separated herself from Robinson's 1944 views of race, Eudora was somewhat defensive of the white South. She seemed to focus on the report of Carter's violent act, not the issue of Tom's acquiescence to a friend's cruelty or the "white is right" mindset of the police. She was on point, however, in contending that Sancton's error in conception was to suggest both that his own hard-won insight had somehow redeemed the event and that the character-corrupting influence of a Jim Crow system became clearly visible among the privileged only when alcohol removed inhibitions. In her fiction published between 1941 and 1943, she had shown, as an unobtrusive narrator, representative or emblematic abuses of power by quite sober white people across class lines: the kidnapping of a crippled black man by a carnival show boss, the condescension of a white saleswoman to a rural black housewife, the casual cruelty of a rather gentlemanly white hunter who is amused by pointing a loaded gun at an elderly black woman, the banishing of black performers to black cafés. And in her fiction she had also granted black characters the same complexity and mystery she had given their white counterparts, a complexity and mystery that is totally absent in Sancton's stereotypical, if well-intended, January 1944 portraits of

African Americans. But, unlike Sancton, Eudora had not yet taken an editorial stance.

Six months after Eudora had written to Russell about the Sancton essay, John Robinson, in a letter from Italy where he served in the Army Air Corps, requested that she comment on another January 1944 essay, one written by the liberal Mississippian David Cohn. In the *Atlantic Monthly*, Cohn had attempted to explain the mind-set of contemporary southern white men to the nation. Issues of sexuality, economics, and cultural indoctrination, he wrote, had made racism an unalterable part of their identities. In fact, Cohn believed that white southerners would wage a civil war if the federal government sought to dismantle a system of segregation. On the other hand, if "social segregation" were maintained, he believed that the black southerner could achieve "the right to justice in the courts; the right to security in his person and property; the right to a fair share in the distribution of tax money for the purposes of education, health, and public improvements . . . the right to earn a living, to be paid according to his worth and not his color, to be protected in the practice of the professions and skills, . . . [and] to assume his fair share of taxes and other burdens of the community." Cohn then concluded, "No man can view the position of the American Negro without a sore heart, a troubled conscience, and a deep compassion. Nor can one view the position of the Southern whites without sympathy, for they are the sum of their inheritance and their environment, and act according to their lights. Whites and Negroes alike will each have to yield much to the other if American democracy is to survive, and each will have to yield out of conviction rather than compulsion."[8]

This essay, which at times empathized with and at times patronized both southern whites and blacks, which earnestly called for social change but rejected the viability of federally imposed remedies, evoked a qualified response from Eudora. "Yes," she told John, "I read the Cohn article in *Atlantic* & thought it pretty balanced." Perhaps she felt it was a "pretty balanced" portrait of the predominant southern male mind-set. Perhaps it even seemed a balanced portrait of Robinson, who was "not a bosom lover of Negroes." But unlike Cohn, Eudora felt not so much that northerners failed to understand the reasons behind white southern intransigence as that they failed to understand the divergent views held by southern progressives. She complained that her current summer job at the *New York Times Book Review* had been marred by such attitudes: "The other day going down on an elevator someone introduced a girl 'from PM' & me 'from Miss.' & when I said How do you do, *she* said 'Oh you're from *Mississippi* where they persecute the negro & have the highest percentage of illiteracy in the union.' 'Ground floor' said the elevator boy—& that time I was speechless & only in a dumb fury at the unfairness & rudeness & smugness of these people." In fact, though Eudora granted, in what she must have known was an understatement, that there was "just enough truth in the actual situation" to prompt such attacks, she seemed to feel that there were enough southerners of goodwill to promote change over time. She was certainly more hopeful than Cohn. To her the social separation of the races did not seem as unalterable as it did to Cohn. Instead, she told Robinson, "If you treat everybody *first* as a human being—people you love best, & people you hate most—& people you have yet to understand—isn't that the only way, the only basis." Here Eudora clearly called for white southerners to eliminate the sort of behavior Sancton had described in his essay, but she did much more. She asserted the common humanity of all and presumed, in her mention of "people you *have yet* to understand" (italics mine), that interracial understanding would and should grow. It is tempting to suppose that in this passage, which Patti Black in a 2010 speech had used to define Eudora's character, Eudora was also calling for John to embrace racial interaction, not merely a veneer of politeness. Any focus on the personal, however, became political when her letter looked toward an Allied victory in World War II. Anticipating the terms of peace, she implicitly linked the destructiveness of institutionalized segregation to the prospective Allied partition of Germany: "Suppression & tearing apart never do any good," she declared with an eye toward a different future.[9]

Then in the spring of 1945 Eudora learned of the Holocaust. After the Buchenwald concentration camp had been liberated and newspaper accounts of its terrors had been published, Eudora implored John not to "be relating yourselves, requisitioning, to any Germans—to cruel men—It makes me want to cry out. I do cry out."[10] To her it further seemed that the defeat of Hitler's Germany made it imperative to improve race relations at home. A nation built upon suppressing, tearing apart, and destroying the Jewish people had been vanquished. Failure now to reform ourselves, she sensed, would betray the war effort and the liberation being wrought abroad. And such a betrayal seemed in the offing in late August 1945, when Mississippi Senator Theodore Bilbo, for whom anti-Semitism and prejudice against African Americans went hand in hand, declared that he would seek reelection on a platform attacking the Fair Employment Practices Committee and anti–poll tax laws. Eudora had long opposed politicians like Bilbo, and his pursuit of a new term intensified her opposition: the announced platform built upon Bilbo's virulent and outspoken bigotry, and his popularity in Mississippi made Eudora feel that the state was unworthy of its returning soldiers, who had bravely fought against racist regimes. She seemed to believe that Robinson would, in the wake of his European wartime service, share her outrage, and in an August letter to him, she voiced a desire to crusade against such politicians and policies:

> Mississippi is as bad as those things make you believe and a little worse for the lack of even regret among the people here who could have minded or could start now. Yes, a trance—that is what it must be—if trances are that stubborn. What will happen if we let it keep us—want it to keep us—from seeing things as they really are in Mississippi. I think "when the men come back" many times a day and it gives me both hope and dread—thinking then a little hard-headed sense will be brought to bear, and then aching to think what the men will find if we don't come to. I realize of course, and more from what you just said, that all they've seen too is dependent on the individual—I know not to look for them in numbers to have seen at all what you would see and know anyway, but I can't help but think that regardless and regardless, the *hope* is there—and God knows it ought to be *here*, cherished at home and fed some. I've never been a crusader, being a more shy and private person, but I may be now—the way I speak out, and can't sleep from indignation.

The next day Eudora sent similar comments to Diarmuid Russell. "I started reading *A Passage to India* again—the politics in Mississippi make me so sick I have to get some release and there really isn't any against the rage that comes over me—what is going to happen, with things like this and people like that Bilbo—It's too much for me."[11] Significantly, Eudora found an antidote to Mississippi politics in E. M. Forster's 1924 novel, which depicted the evils of racism in India under the British Raj. Reading about a country far from home while at the same time knowing that Forster shared her rage against benighted politics was a source of comfort. Eventually, she would assert that such novels provided not merely a "release" from social ills but a more powerful force for change than the protests of the crusader.

In December 1945, however, Eudora composed an editorial protest rather than relying solely upon her talents as a fiction writer, which in the novel *Delta Wedding* she had just used to depict the daily indignities to which black characters like Parthenia and Aunt Studney were subject. Believing that the press and politicians in her own state were betraying the values for which World War II had been fought, she wrote the *Jackson Clarion-Ledger* to complain, particularly objecting to the paper's coverage of Gerald L. K. Smith's recent visit. While in Jackson, Smith—who according to Walter Goodman was "the country's noisiest anti-Semite"—proclaimed himself opposed not only to "Stalinism" but also to "Internationalism and other forms of alienism" and sought to expand his nationalist movement in the South. Knowing that Smith both blamed Jews for the Great Depression and World War II and denied the reality of the Holocaust, Eudora was offended by the *Clarion-Ledger*'s neutral coverage of his speech. Recognizing the legacy of Nazism and the spirit that would go on to fuel McCarthyism, Eudora asked the editor, "Isn't there anybody ready with words for telling Smith that that smells to heaven to us, that we don't want him, won't let him try organizing any of his fascistic doings in our borders, and to get out and stay out of Mississippi?" She went on to ask, "Is there still nothing we can do to atone for our apathy and our blindness or our closed minds, by maintaining some kind of vigilance in keeping Gerald Smith away?" Eudora concluded her letter by denouncing Smith's ideological pals: "We will get Bilbo and Rankin out when their time, election time, comes, God willing."[12] In her hometown newspaper, the usually circumspect Eudora thus made a forceful and impassioned political statement, a statement for openness, tolerance, freedom of speech and of belief, the very values she had championed in her wartime fiction and would continue to champion. Eudora denounced the isolationism, anti-Semitism, and racism that were the staples of Senator Theodore Bilbo and U.S. Representative John Rankin, recognized that the defeat of Nazism had not destroyed the hatreds it represented, and called for change. In the editorial mode of Thomas Sancton, Eudora sought to "atone for . . . our closed minds" and hoped that Mississippi might prove a more open society than it had in the past.

The Jackson response to Eudora's letter was mixed. "Got some phone calls of approval," she wrote Diarmuid Russell, "and 1 anonymous letter saying I was known as a dirty Communist and to keep my mouth shut." Russell told Eudora that her expression of disgust would "probably have the Klan out for your blood," but she seemed unworried by that prospect.[13] In the coming years she would have more cause for worry.

The desire for cultural diversity Eudora espoused in opposing Senator Bilbo and Gerald L. K. Smith both embraced and extended beyond the African American community. Not surprisingly, she also voiced a concern for the plight faced by Native Americans. In the fall of 1947, after spending two and a half months in San Francisco, she traveled home, making a stopover in Arizona and witnessing the living conditions faced by the Navajo. To Robinson she reported, "The sad thing is the *Indians*"; and to Russell she wrote, "The Indians there though are starving, truly, it is said. People seem to be investigating, but not doing anything about it yet." After reaching Jackson, Eudora continued to be concerned; she wrote to Robinson about the ominous situation that threatened an ancient culture: "You can see ruins—from the train window—of villages, I could hardly believe it—but looked up in a book since coming back and they were ruins when the Spaniards found them in the sixteenth century. And cliff dwellers. It was terrible to see the little huts with Indians living in them now, for in Arizona I read in the local papers how the Navahos are starving and the government will not help. They seemed really to be ending now before people's eyes, the race."[14]

Even as Eudora publicly and privately expressed a desire for inclusiveness and a more just social order, she worried about the difficulties of transforming desire into action. She gave voice to such worries when she and Russell exchanged letters about a possible operetta of *The Robber Bridegroom*. John Bauer, who had helped to establish the Ojai Music Festival in California, had asked to write the libretto and indicated that Bernard Rogers, who taught at the Eastman School of Music, would compose the score. Before long, Rogers demurred, and Bauer had second thoughts about his own involvement as a writer. Still hoping to be the producer, Bauer suggested two other possible librettists— Paul Horgan, the novelist and historian who had studied at the Eastman School, and Langston Hughes, the distinguished poet and dramatist who had played such a central role in the Harlem Renaissance. Eudora approved of both writers but was not interested in personally working on the operetta. Still, the suggestion that she work with Hughes prompted her to face the difficulties of collaborating in Jackson with a black writer. "If I had my wish," she wrote Russell in February 1947,

> I wouldn't have anything to do at all with any libretto, and hope I won't have to. As to the problem of working on it with Mr. Hughes, that couldn't be solved practically if it had to be done in Mississippi, and he probably knows better than I the difficulties. There wouldn't be a place he could stay, or where we could sit together. He sounds like a fine person to write the libretto though, if he wants to set about it on his own. Mr. Horgan too sounds good—but my opinion is a lay one on the whole subject. I don't want to go way back to the Robber Bridegroom and start worrying again on that old piece of work—and hope I won't be asked to—and don't imagine Mr. B. [Bauer] and I would take much of a shine to each other, to make that part

go very smoothly. If a person like Langston Hughes or Paul Horgan takes over a libretto job it should be a good one and not need my meddling. Don't you think so?[15]

Eudora clearly admired Langston Hughes's poetry and was willing to entrust him with her story. She herself did not want to return to an "old piece of work," but if she had wanted to do so in Jackson, she would have been unwilling to expose Hughes and herself to the harassment—or worse—that an interracial meeting of colleagues could have brought down on their heads. There were still no public locations in the city where she and Hughes could have worked together on a libretto; segregation was pervasively and officially in place. Just north of Jackson, the private, African American Tougaloo College, where in the 1950s Eudora attended integrated events, might have provided a haven, but in 1947 Eudora did not know of the possibility. Nor did a private home seem an option. Meetings between an African American man and a white woman, the arrivals at and departures from either the Welty house or another residence, would have been noticed and talked about in Jackson and would have been risky, especially for Hughes.[16] Eudora's hopes that the rigid color line described by David Cohn would weaken over time had not come to pass. The South continued to be dominated not only by a system of Jim Crow laws, but also, as Cohn had written, by an "iron taboo" that absolutely prohibited encounters "smack[ing] of social equality."[17] At some point in the 1940s editor John Woodburn had taken Eudora to dinner at Ralph and Fanny Ellison's apartment; going to the home of this respected writer and his wife had been her first social contact with African Americans, and she and the Ellisons became fast friends. But the Ellisons lived in New York. Jackson presented a greater challenge to black and white interaction.

In 1951 Eudora confronted another such complex problem of cultural interaction when she was at the Ochsner Foundation Hospital in New Orleans where her brother Walter was being treated. There, in a hospital made frigid by an unusual cold wave, one other patient claimed her attention: "A Bombay, India lone soul is in a bed nearby—No one seems to know how or why he has ended up there—A very young, bearded, dignified, wonderful face—Just rests on bended elbows, hands behind head, gazes out over at nothing. And so far from home . . ." Eudora had long felt pulled toward the culture of India—her response to seeing Shan-Kar dance and her admiration for *A Passage to India* may have come to mind when she saw the man from Bombay so alone in a foreign land. When this lone soul was discharged from the hospital, Eudora's dismay for him intensified, and she told Robinson: "His final humiliation: the negro girl (who came to work today in blue uniform over long sleeved plaid wool lumberjack & nun-like cowl which she wore all morning) who brings you water & things like that fixed him up to go & said to a friend, 'I *combed* his hair, *scraped* out de dandruff, *greased* him, *shave* off dat beard, & got him dressed up.' She fixed him to look just like a Negro, of course."[18] Reading this letter in isolation, one might wonder if Eudora equated being made to look like a Negro with being humiliated. But the patterns of Eudora's life indicate that something else is at stake here. From Eudora's perspective, the bearded man from India, bearded for religious reasons, had been reduced by illness and hospitalization to passivity; openly exposed to others' glances, he was at the mercy of their care. Groomed by a hospital worker to fit in New Orleans's African American culture, he had been denied his own. He had not felt able to assert his will. Sensing his despair, Eudora wrote Diarmuid Russell, "I hope his religion takes him back— what about that lost beard?"[19] The man himself appears to have been less hopeful; his gaze "out over at nothing" suggests a truly nihilistic vision. In *The Optimist's Daughter*, a novel written more than fifteen years later, Judge Clinton McKelva as a patient in a New Orleans hospital behaves much as the man from Bombay had, and his daughter Laurel realizes that the judge's "grayed-down, anonymous room might be some reflection itself of Judge McKelva's 'disturbance,' his dislocated vision that had brought him here."[20] That literally dislocated vision has its metaphoric counterpart. The wife he loved deeply has long since died, and at age seventy-one, the remarried judge no longer has a wife he cherishes, only one he can indulge. His daughter lives hundreds of miles away. No longer is he an officer of the court. No longer is he able to tend to his family, his household, his garden. He is tied down in a hospital bed, wholly dependent upon others. The identity and the sense of dignity he has forged over the years are no longer his own. His nihilism results from the same source as the Bombay man's. Looking back to her time in Ochsner's with her brother, Eudora recalled not an issue of race but one of respect and identity. That same concern had been evident in 1949, when Eudora sailed to Europe and found only one passenger in tourist class to be objectionable—she complained to John Robinson that an American woman had used the word "nigger" and had done so within the hearing of "two colored gentlemen." Even beyond their hearing, Eudora herself used the word "gentlemen," granting these fellow shipmates her respect and rejecting cultural stereotyping.[21] Moreover, she seemed to assume now, as she might not have in 1944, that Robinson embraced her views.

Eudora wanted to share this respect for diversity with her young nieces when in 1956 she took them to see the many cultures represented at the United Nations, and at the same time she wanted to share it with the young African Americans studying at Tougaloo College on the outskirts of Jackson. During the 1950s, typically in the company of Millsaps College history professor Ross Moore and his wife, Eudora had frequently attended lectures and plays at Tougaloo, and in 1958 Tougaloo professor Ernst Borinski invited her to address his Social Sciences Forum. According to Millsaps College political science professor John Quincy Adams, Borinski had designed the forum as part of an effort to provide a "model of an integrated society," and Millsaps professors of history, sociology, and political science had been frequent speakers.[22] The invitation for Eudora to speak about her work was a very unusual one for the Social Sciences Forum—her fiction and her creative process seemingly had little to do with the social sciences—but simply by addressing the group, Eudora was issuing a call for integration. In fact, this lecture came only five months after a 1958 furor about the Millsaps College Religious Forum, which had dared to invite integrationists to speak, and her lecture seems almost to have been a response to the clamor raised by local newspapers, a clamor that had prompted Millsaps to close its public events to African Americans and to discourage its professors from teaching or speaking at Tougaloo. Eudora clearly regretted that Millsaps would no longer provide a "model of an integrated society," but she participated in such a model at Tougaloo, even though speaking at Tougaloo involved some personal danger. By 1958, white visitors to Tougaloo might have expected to have their visits monitored by the State Sovereignty Commission or its informers. Eudora's friend Jane Reid Petty recalled that she, Eudora, and others often carpooled when going to Tougaloo, varying the car they took as often as possible so that the sheriff, whom they suspected of recording the tag numbers of white visitors to Tougaloo, would not see a pattern in their visits. Though the possibility of harassment loomed in the offing, neither Eudora nor her friends were deterred from this activity.

Fear did govern a decision she made in 1962 after the courts had ordered the University of Mississippi to accept the enrollment of James Meredith, an African American, and Mississippi governor Ross Barnett demanded that admission be denied. Attorney General Robert F. Kennedy then sent federal marshals to enforce the court order, and riots broke out at Ole Miss. On September 30 students gathered to chant support for Barnett and opposition to Kennedy. As night approached, the students turned violent, throwing rocks, bottles, and metal pipes at the marshals. Marshals responded by firing tear gas into the crowd. By this time, armed segregationists from within and outside the state had joined the students and began firing rifles at the U.S. marshals. The next morning found two men dead, 160 marshals hurt or wounded, buildings damaged, cars still burning on the campus. Eudora was horrified by the violence and by the segregationist stance that Barnett and the university had taken. She told Frank Lyell, "I can't even *start* to go into the Oxford mess—The really depressing thing is that Miss. thinks Barnett is a 100% glorious *hero*. Wish I was in Timbuctu—or Xanadu." Still she was not ready to turn, as she had once before, to editorial commentary. *The New Republic* had sent a telegram requesting her reactions to the "Mississippi crisis," but Eudora did not respond. As she confided to Frank, "They also phoned & said 'Speak for the unheard voices in Miss.['] I said no because (a) I'm a coward—look what they've done to R. McGill (b) it wouldn't help (c) I don't madly admire the *New Rep.* though haven't seen it lately." Speaking out was indeed dangerous. When Ralph McGill's editorials in the *Atlanta Constitution* denounced the Ku Klux Klan bombing of an Atlanta synagogue, "outraged racists responded with death threats, garbage piled on McGill's lawn and abusive telephone calls. Politicians stoked the fires by calling him 'Red Ralph' or nigger-lover Ralph McCoon."[23] This was not the civil war that Cohn had predicted in the 1940s, but battles were being fought. Eudora now elected to choose her battles. Although she feared verbal and physical assaults and called herself a coward, she was not silenced for long. Within a year she was again lecturing at integrated events and publishing timely short stories about racial atrocities. These public opportunities suited her talents better than editorializing.

An opportunity to combine a lecture with fiction arose in 1963 in Jackson when Millsaps College hosted the Southern Literary Festival. Millsaps officials feared racial violence and wanted the Southern Literary Festival to abide by the school's policy of segregation; Eudora, nevertheless, asked that her appearance be open to all, and it was. Her lecture, previously published by Smith College under the title "Words into Fiction," seems detached from any sort of political situation. In it, Eudora acknowledged that a reader may have a conception of a novel that differs from that of the writer, but she contended that this difference "is neither so strange nor so important as the vital fact that a connection has been made between them." The novel, she argued, is "made by the imagination for the imagination." After delivering this address, however, Eudora went on to show her audience the political import a work "made by the imagination for the imagination" could have—she read the story "Powerhouse" to the interracial audience.[24]

Written in 1940 and inspired by a Fats Waller concert Eudora had attended, "Powerhouse" is the story of an African American pianist and his band playing at a segregated dance; it focuses on the white audience's simultaneous fascination with and repulsion by the band leader, Powerhouse, and on the band's ability to find intermission conviviality and refreshments only at a black café. In reading this story at the festival, Eudora took a considerable risk. The narrative voice located in the story's white racist audience might have offended black listeners at Millsaps even as the author's clear identification of Powerhouse as representative of artists like herself might have offended whites. But Eudora trusted in the ability of her listeners, and she might well have expected the story to bring together the two factions attending the lecture and reading.

In "Powerhouse," Eudora suggests that a shared act of imagination can bridge, if only momentarily, the separateness between individuals. Though both Powerhouse's white audience at the dance and his black admirers at the World Café feel separated from him, either by race or by fame, his performances transport them, bringing them "the only time for hallucination," leaving them in a "breathless ring," sending them "into oblivion," or causing them to moan "with pleasure." The requested song that closes the story seems particularly relevant to this issue of communication and imagination. "Somebody loves me," Powerhouse sings and then concludes, "Maybe it's you!" Despite the odds, maybe Powerhouse will have a deep and lasting effect on a member of his audience; the probability seems slight, especially to Powerhouse, who delivers the lyrics, according to the narrator, with "a vast, impersonal and yet furious grimace."[25] Still, the story's very existence suggests that imagination can transcend the boundaries of race. The Fats Waller concert in Jackson brought forth at least one powerfully imaginative response in the form of a story from Eudora Welty.

More than twenty years after writing this story based on the Waller concert, Welty read it to proclaim the destructiveness of segregation and the emancipating effect of imagining oneself into other and different lives. Combining her story with a lecture about the power of the imagination to unite reader and writer was a political act for Eudora, an act of courage and vision, one that would prove to have more impact than her earlier and by then almost forgotten letter to the *Jackson Clarion-Ledger*. John Salter, the professor who led the Tougaloo contingent on April 18, reported that "Eudora Welty gave an excellent lecture, including a reading of one of her short stories—which we could follow as she read since we had brought along several copies of her work. When the evening was over we walked slowly outside. A group of Millsaps students came up and indicated that they were quite glad that we had attended. Other than that, no one appeared to notice us, and that, in its own small way, marked a significant breakthrough in Mississippi." Eudora's part in this breakthrough won her the enduring respect of black students from Tougaloo, and in a February 1985 appearance at Millsaps, Anne Moody, one of those students, recalled how important it was for her to hear Welty read.[26]

Three months later, in the wake of Medgar Evers's assassination and the publication of a story detailing the horror of that event ("Where Is the Voice Coming From?"), Eudora decided she could not at that time undertake what would have been still another symbolic act supporting social change. At the last minute, after much agonizing and with deep regret, she declined to be interviewed by an African American, novelist Ralph Ellison, on national television. And she had cause for agonizing about the consequences of such an interview. As Steven D. Classen has observed, the assassination of Medgar Evers might well have come in response to his appearance on WLBT-TV: "In May 1963 Evers lobbied, as he had many times previously, to appear on local television in an equal-time response to segregationist voices. He did so on May 20. Less than a month later Evers was murdered in his driveway by a man who had watched in the darkness for him to arrive at his Jackson home." And Classen goes on to note that "Mississippians close to Evers and his cause have long speculated, while not necessarily asserting a causal link, on the relationship between Evers's local broadcast appearance and his death. Jackson writer Eudora Welty is among those who have done so, penning a powerful story that places the reader in the point of view of Evers's killer. In Welty's 'Where Is the Voice Coming From?' the assassin is clearly angered and inspired to kill by the sight of a black man's face on television, and he bitterly remarks: 'His face was in front of the public before I got rid of him, and after I got rid of him there it is again—the same picture. And none of me.'"[27] In the wake of writing these lines for her story, Eudora may well have feared that such violence might come her way if she made a nationally televised appearance with a black friend and peer. Certainly, she feared that so public an interview with Ellison would generate a good deal of white hostility, hostility that would affect her ability to hire desperately needed caregivers for her mother, who in August would be coming home from her five-month stint in a convalescent facility, and that might also affect the quality of care her mother received in the future. Eudora must also have recognized that even if the white racists who controlled Mississippi's television stations in the 1960s had decided not to broadcast her appearance with Ellison, they would have reported it to the Sovereignty Commission, a state-sponsored spy agency, which in turn might well have worked in its typical fashion to denigrate and ostracize the Welty women. A desire to shelter her ailing mother from this volatile environment of racial tension and especially from white recrimination thus governed her decision, as she confided to Reynolds Price, not to be interviewed by Ellison. Instead, old friend and dramatic collaborator Hildegard Dolson conducted the interview for the CBS program *Camera Three*. Ellison for a brief time was understandably mystified by Eudora's decision. Shortly after the cancellation, Ellison told Price how open and outgoing Eudora had always been with him, and he worried that he might have in some way unwittingly offended her. Price explained Eudora's situation to him and also told Eudora of Ellison's worries. According to Price, Eudora then wrote to Ellison to explain her deep-seated apprehensions for her mother, and the Welty-Ellison friendship endured.[28]

The *Paris Review*, which had planned to publish the televised interview, was less understanding, and the cancellation threatened to become a cause célèbre when the review decided not to run the interview. Hildy Dolson was offended by the *Paris Review*'s posturing and wrote to Eudora to express her support. "Diarmuid wasn't supposed to tell you that the *Paris Review* people had backed out. But he knew that was the reason I got involved, and as long as he mentioned it, I'll add now that they behaved very badly. Unlike Ralph Ellison, who understood and felt you were right, the *Paris Review* crowd were as snide as a Pink Citizens Avant-Garde Council. For them to take that attitude, on top of your powerful story in *The New Yorker*, was all the more idiotic and infuriating. When Clare Roscom [of *Camera Three*] phoned me, he said it threatened to blow up into a distorted, unpleasant news story, and for that reason he refused to try any of the writers I suggested as being more suitable [as interviewers]. He wanted a friend of yours. And that's what he got—and now enough of that."[29] Eudora's decision not to be interviewed by Ellison was one about which she felt great ambivalence. The prospect of violence and the need to protect her mother were set against her desire to honor a commitment to a friend. She was ambivalent not about racism but about a choice that would leave her unhappy, whatever she decided. Ralph Ellison understood that and respected Eudora.

In December 1964, with her mother back in residence at a Yazoo City nursing home, Eudora delivered a second lecture/reading at Millsaps College, again during particularly tense times. She did not on this occasion have to request unrestricted attendance—Millsaps now welcomed all to its public events—but the previous summer had seen the murders of three civil rights workers in Philadelphia, Mississippi, the firebombing of forty black churches, and the white Citizens' Council's intimidation of whites known to have "moderate" sensibilities, intimidation that had not ceased. In her lecture, entitled "The Southern Writer Today: An Interior Affair," Eudora delivered comments that she would soon publish as "Must the Novelist Crusade?" Here, she rejected an ostensible political purpose for fiction, arguing that "there is absolutely everything in great fiction but a clear answer," that fiction is concerned more with the complexities of human experience than with proposing solutions to human difficulties. But she also asserted, "What matters is that a writer is committed to his own moral principles. If he is, when we read him we cannot help but be aware of what these are. Certainly the characters of his novel and the plot they move in are their ultimate reflections. But these convictions are implicit; they are deep down; they are the rock on which the whole structure of more than the novel rests." The great novel, she argued, is grounded on the bedrock of principle, the very principle for which the crusader speaks. As an example, she offered *A Passage to India*, which she had earlier lauded in a letter to Diarmuid Russell. But this time she asserted that the novel provided not a release from injustice but an enduring revelation of it. It is, she said, a "moral" novel, though not a crusading one: "It deals with race prejudice. Mr. Forster, not by preaching at us, while being passionately concerned, makes us know his points unforgettably as often as we read it . . . The points are good forty years after their day *because of the splendor of the novel.* What a lesser novelist's harangues would have buried by now, his imagination still reveals. Revelation of even the strongest forces is delicate work."[30]

Eudora followed this address with a reading of "Keela, the Outcast Indian Maiden," which, appropriately, examines the complexities of human relationships. The story, written in 1938 and first published in 1940, describes a crippled black man who was once kidnapped into carnival work as a geek called Keela, the Outcast Indian Maiden, and who, notwithstanding the horror of his past, feels nostalgic about the carnival experience, in which he was noticed, whereas now, within his own family, he is not. The story further deals with the guilt felt by Steve, the carnival barker, and with his inability, nevertheless, to overcome the separation of race. Finally, the story depicts a bystander's courting of detachment from the horror and guilt Keela represents.

Complex though it is, however, "Keela" makes an inescapable political and moral statement—the dehumanizing nature of racism is infinitely more grotesque than a carnival sideshow. Certainly, Steve recognizes that by acquiescing to this evil, he has become part of it: "'It's all me, see,' said Steve. 'I know that. I was the one was the cause for it goin' on an' on an' not bein' found out—such an awful thing. It was me, what I said out front through the megaphone.'" On the other hand, his acquaintance Max, the owner of Max's Place, represses any guilt that might be his. "'Bud,' said Max, disengaging himself, 'I don't hear anything. I got a juke box, see, so I don't have to listen.'"[31] Max, in his disengaged state, might be speaking for many white Mississippians in 1964—they did not want to recognize their own complicity with evil, they did not want to accept the guilt they shared with Steve. But in reading this twenty-six-year-old story to her 1964 audience, Eudora drew attention to that guilt, perhaps also recalling her own internal debate about the aborted Ellison interview. She did not ask that her audience become political activists, but she did ask, implicitly, that they refuse to be part of racist activities, that they recognize the humanity and complexity of all individuals. Within three months Millsaps College would announce that African American students were welcome to enroll. In 1965 five students would become the first African Americans to do so.

In 1966 Eudora published "The Demonstrators," a second story focused on the civil rights movement and the racists who opposed it, and with this story she won the praise of Jesse Jackson.[32] But it was 1972 before she was again invited to appear on national television. By then, William Buckley, host of the PBS series *Firing Line*, was eager to ask about the origins of "Where Is the Voice Coming From?," and Eudora's response is instructive: "What I was writing about," she said, "really was that world of hate that I felt I had grown up with and I felt I could speak as someone who knew it, and I didn't think anything else written about things like that *were* anything else but, more or less, tracts." Eudora also told Buckley that this story was not the only one in which she had voiced her opposition to racism. "I assumed," she said to Buckley, "that my whole life I had been writing about injustice, if I wanted to, and

·

love and hate and so on. They are human characteristics which I had certainly been able to see long before it was pointed out to me by what happened in those years. I was always against it, but what I was writing about was human beings. I put it in the form of fiction; that is, in dramatic form. I was writing about it from the inside, not from the outside, and when it was stated from the outside it seemed to me so thin and artificial." Later in the program, Gordon Weaver, one of the panelists who joined Buckley in the interview, asked if the oppressive atmosphere of the South had discouraged its writers from confronting political controversy in their fiction. Eudora's answer was clear. "I didn't feel any avoidance in anything I was doing and I might get just as mad as I could be about things at home and then I would go up to New York and the things that people would say there made me madder and I would feel defensive because there was a great void of ignorance between the two parts of the country. I think a writer, all his life, is aware of all sorts of threatening and menacing things going on. This time was very open and dramatized and the whole world knew about it, but there are always the human threats of people, of injustice and all these other things that go on through your whole life, and you can't run away from that."[33] Though Eudora had at times chastised herself for not being a more conventional activist, though she had sought to avoid a threat to her mother's welfare, she did not believe that writing fiction could ever be a form of aesthetic avoidance for her; on the contrary, she had come to articulate more and more clearly her belief that the artist must create an interior, heartfelt, enduring statement against injustice, including the injustice of race prejudice. Her 1963 decisions to read a story from the 1940s, "Powerhouse," at Millsaps and to write a new story, "Where Is the Voice Coming From?," were based on this belief. So too were the 1964 public reading of her early story "Keela, the Outcast Indian Maiden" and the subsequent publication of new work—the 1965 essay "Must the Novelist Crusade?" and the 1966 story "The Demonstrators." And Eudora went on to reiterate her faith in the social significance of fiction in a 1979 essay, one in which she recalled penning her very first published story, one about a poor white farm couple. "I never doubted," she wrote, "that imagining yourself into other people's lives is exactly what writing fiction is."[34] The act of imaginative identification with other people certainly signaled her transcendence of the artificial and insidious separations of class and race in her native South. In creating Powerhouse from both a performance by Fats Waller and her own mode of performing and in creating Judge Clinton McKelva from the experiences of both a young man from Bombay, who was "so black," and her own brother, who was so white, she rejected stereotypes based on color.[35] And in imagining herself into the lives of characters, black and white, old and young, male and female, she invited readers to make their own imaginative leaps and, in the process, to reject a host of destructive stereotypes. For Eudora, art was not divorced from life but inherently political: it involved fully and powerfully engaging the nature of human relationships.

What then can we say about the patterns of Eudora Welty's life? The biographical record of that life, it seems to me, demonstrates that the Eudora Welty I met in 1983 and the Eudora Welty of the previous five decades were in fact the same person. Of course, as a writer and a person, she had over time changed, grown, and become more self-aware, but the intellect, the honesty, the generosity of spirit, and the embracing of cultures not her own were constants throughout her life. I am persuaded, therefore, that irony or role-playing was involved in Welty's use of the word "nigger" in four letters written to John Robinson between 1946 and 1948. In the late 1930s she had begun to indict racism in her fiction and in 1945 had publicly attacked the racist demagogues Theodore Bilbo, John Rankin, and Gerald L. K. Smith. In the 1950s and 1960s she had gone on to support integrated events in her hometown, most notably at the historically black Tougaloo College and the white, pre-1965, Millsaps College. Moreover, the contrast in her comments about Robinson in 1944 and to him in 1949 indicate that during the interim he seemed, perhaps at least partially because of her influence, to have adopted a somewhat more forward-looking stance. When placed in the context of these patterns, the seemingly inexplicable and anomalous passages in Eudora's letters raise the issue of narrative or epistolary voice. Readers of fiction must attend to shifts in voice; readers of letters can do no less. Though one critic has argued that Eudora Welty was "ambivalent about racism" because she did not embrace "either the importance of racial difference or the historic guilt she was supposed to feel," that conclusion ignores a large body of evidence to the contrary.[36] Eudora made slavery and the Civil War the subject of only one story, but she repeatedly wrote about ongoing racial injustice in both her fiction and her correspondence. She saw people, whatever their race, as individuals, but she also valued the cultural diversity represented by Arizona's Navajo, India's Shan-Kar, and Mississippi's African American citizens. She was ambivalent about the wisdom of decisions she had made, about choosing when to defy and when to avoid danger, about the conflicting demands of crusading and of writing, and about a home state she both loved and took to task, but she did not feel ambivalent about racism. The patterns of Eudora Welty's life make that perfectly clear.

Notes

I gratefully make the following acknowledgments for materials quoted in this essay.

> Letters by Eudora Welty from the Eudora Welty Collection housed in the Mississippi Department of Archives and History reprinted by permission of Eudora Welty, LLC, copyright © Eudora Welty and used courtesy of the Mississippi Department of Archives and History.
> Letters from Diarmuid Russell reprinted by permission of Pamela Jessup, copyright © Diarmuid Russell and used courtesy of the Mississippi Department of Archives and History.
> Passages excerpted from my book *Eudora Welty: A Biography*. Copyright © 2005 by Suzanne Marrs. Reprinted by permission of Houghton Mifflin Harcourt Publishing Company. All rights reserved.
> Passages excerpted from my book *One Writer's Imagination: The Fiction of Eudora Welty*. Copyright © 2002 by Louisiana State University Press. Reprinted by permission of Louisiana State University Press.

1. Patti Carr Black, quoting a letter from Eudora Welty to John Robinson, [July 13, 1944].

2. Welty to Robinson, [November 8, 1946], [June 29, 1947], [November 19, 1947], [December 1, 1948].

3. Wendy Smith, "The Play That Electrified Harlem," 2.

4. William Jay Smith, personal conversation with author, June 2, 2002; Welty to Robinson, [September 2?, 1950].

5. Eudora Welty to Frank Lyell, [January 1933] filed in envelope dated October 15, 1932; [April 30, 1959].

6. Welty to Robinson, September 12, 1942; Eudora Welty, *One Time, One Place*, 3–4.

7. Thomas Sancton, "Race Clash," 135; Eudora Welty to Diarmuid Russell, January 13, 1944. Lawrence Jackson discusses Sancton's crusade against racism in his book *The Indignant Generation*, 149–66.

8. David L. Cohn, "How the South Feels," 50, 51.

9. Welty to Robinson, [July 13, 1944].

10. Welty to Robinson, May 1, [1945].

11. According to historian Leonard Dinnerstein, "Theodore Bilbo of Mississippi liked the nice Jews of his state but railed against the 'kike Jews' of New York." In his book *Take Your Choice: Separation or Mongrelization*, Bilbo associated Jews, particularly ethnologist Franz Boas, with civil rights agitation, writing that "for some reason which has never been publicized, this German Jew [Boas], a newly arrived immigrant,

wanted to destroy the racial stock which had carved this mighty nation out of a wilderness" (160). Welty to Robinson, August 23, [1945]; Welty to Russell, August 24, [1945].

12. "Bilbo and Rankin Get Blessings of Former Huey Long Chieftain," December 20, 1945; Walter Goodman, *The Committee*, 181; Eudora Welty, "Voice of the People," December 28, 1945.

13. Eudora Welty to Diarmuid Russell, Sunday [late December 1945]; Diarmuid Russell to Eudora Welty, January 2, 1946.

14. Welty to Robinson, [November 6, 1947]; Welty to Russell, November 12, [1947]; Welty to Robinson [November 13, 1947].

15. Welty to Russell, February 9, [1947].

16. Tougaloo professor Ernst Borinski arrived at Tougaloo for the fall semester of 1947 and met Eudora sometime in the early 1950s—both dates were too late for him to have facilitated a Welty/Hughes meeting on campus. Thanks to Millsaps College emeriti faculty members Charles Sallis, a historian of the South, and T. W. Lewis, a religious studies professor, both lifelong Mississippians, for discussing Tougaloo and the racial dynamics of 1947 with me. Both Sallis and Lewis stressed that an interracial meeting between a black man and a white woman, as colleagues, would have been more dangerous for the man than the woman.

17. Cohn, "How the South Feels," 49.

18. Welty to Robinson, January 28, [1951], February 1, [1951].

19. Welty to Russell, [February 1951].

20. Eudora Welty, *The Optimist's Daughter*, 14–15.

21. Welty to Robinson, [October 22, 1949].

22. John Quincy Adams Papers.

23. Welty to Lyell, [October 17, 1962]; Jack Nelson, "Ralph Emerson McGill," 54.

24. Eudora Welty, Personal conversation with author, and R. Edwin King, Personal conversations with author; Eudora Welty, "Words into Fiction," 144, 145.

25. Eudora Welty, "Powerhouse," 159, 167, 169, 170.

26. John R. Salter, *Jackson, Mississippi*, 102; Edwin King arranged for Moody to speak at Millsaps, attended the lecture with her, and told me of her comments about Welty's importance to the Tougaloo contingent (June 19, 1997).

27. Steven D. Classen, *Watching Jim Crow*, 3–4. Thanks to Ralph Eubanks for calling my attention to Classen's book.

28. Welty's 1963 correspondence with Russell and with Mary Lou Aswell (Welty Collection, Mississippi Department of Archives and History, Jackson, Mississippi) suggests a July decision by Welty; Reynolds Price, Personal conversation with author. The interview with Hildegard Dolson aired on Sunday, August 18, 1963.

29. Hildegard Dolson to Eudora Welty, August 23, [1963].

30. Eudora Welty, "Must the Novelist Crusade?" 149, 152–53, 154.

31. Eudora Welty, "Keela, the Outcast Indian Maiden," 51, 50.

32. Jesse Jackson to the editor, *New Yorker*, November 27, [1966].

33. William F. Buckley, 101, 100, 108–9.

34. Eudora Welty, "Looking Back at the First Story," 755.
35. Welty to Russell, [February 1951].
36. Dean Flower, "Eudora Welty and Racism," 331.

Bibliography

Adams, John Quincy. Papers and Audio Tapes. Faculty Papers, Series F. Millsaps College Archives. Jackson, Mississippi.

Bilbo, Theodore. *Take Your Choice: Separation or Mongrelization*. Poplarville, Miss.: Dream House Publishing, 1947.

"Bilbo and Rankin Get Blessings of Former Huey Long Chieftain," *Jackson Clarion-Ledger*, December 20, 1945.

Black, Patti Carr. Address at Northminster Baptist Church. Jackson, Mississippi, summer 2010.

Buckley, William F. "'The Southern Imagination': An Interview with Eudora Welty and Walker Percy." *Conversations with Eudora Welty*, ed. Peggy W. Prenshaw, 92–114. Jackson: University Press of Mississippi, 1984.

Classen, Steven D. *Watching Jim Crow: The Struggles over Mississippi TV, 1955–1969*. Durham: Duke University Press, 2004.

Cohn, David L. "How the South Feels." *Atlantic Monthly*, January 1944: 47–51.

Dinnerstein, Leonard. "Antisemitism in American Politics." Tom Paine.common sense. Accessed 22 February 2004. www.tompaine.com/feature2.cfm/ID/3475.

Dolson, Hildegard. Letter to Eudora Welty, August 23, [1963]. Eudora Welty Collection, Mississippi Department of Archives and History, Jackson, Miss.

Flower, Dean. "Eudora Welty and Racism." *Hudson Review* 60, no. 2 (2007): 325–32.

Goodman, Walter. *The Committee*. New York: Farrar, Straus, and Giroux, 1968.

Jackson, Jesse. Letter to Editor, *New Yorker*, November 27, [1966], Eudora Welty Collection, Mississippi Department of Archives and History, Jackson, Miss.

Jackson, Lawrence. *The Indignant Generation: A Narrative History of African American Writers and Critics, 1934–1960*. Princeton, N.J.: Princeton University Press, 2010.

King, R. Edwin. Personal conversations with author, March 20, 1997; April 7, 1997; June 19, 1997.

Marrs, Suzanne. *Eudora Welty: A Biography*. New York: Harcourt, 2005.

———. *One Writer's Imagination: The Fiction of Eudora Welty*. Baton Rouge: Louisiana State University Press, 2002.

Nelson, Jack. "Ralph Emerson McGill: Voice of the Southern Conscience," review of *A True Legend in American Journalism*. *American Journalism Review* 24.6 (July/August 2002): 54–55.

Price, Reynolds. Personal conversation with author, October 25, 1998.

Russell, Diarmuid. Letters to Eudora Welty, January 2, 1946; June 17, 1963. Eudora Welty Collection, Mississippi Department of Archives and History, Jackson, Miss.

Sancton, Thomas. "Race Clash." *Harper's Magazine*, January 1944: 135–40.

Salter, John R. *Jackson, Mississippi*. Hicksville, N.Y.: Exposition Press, 1979.

Smith, Wendy. "The Play That Electrified Harlem." *Civilization* 3, no.1 (1996): 38–43. Accessed May 28, 2011. http://memory.loc.gov/ammem/fedtp/ftsmth00.html, 1–4.

Smith, William Jay. Personal conversation with author. June 2, 2002.

Welty, Eudora. "Keela, the Outcast Indian Maiden." In *A Curtain of Green*. 1941. Reprint, New York: Library of America, 1998. 48–56.

———. Letters to Diarmuid Russell, January 13, 1944; August 24, [1945]; Sunday [late December 1945]; February 9, [1947]; November 12, [1947]; [February 1951]. Eudora Welty Collection, Mississippi Department of Archives and History, Jackson, Miss.

———. Letters to Frank Lyell, [January 1933]; [April 30, 1959]; [October 17, 1962]. Eudora Welty Collection, Mississippi Department of Archives and History, Jackson, Miss.

———. Letters to John Robinson, September 12, 1942; [July 13, 1944]; May 1, [1945]; August 23, [1945]; [November 8, 1946]; [June 29, 1947]; [November 6, 1947]; [November 13, 1947]; [November 19, 1947]; [December 1, 1948]; [October 22, 1949]; [September 2?, 1950]; January 28, [1951]; February 1, [1951]. Eudora Welty Collection, Mississippi Department of Archives and History, Jackson, Miss.

———. "Looking Back at the First Story." *Georgia Review* 33 (1979): 751–55.

———. "Must the Novelist Crusade?" In *The Eye of the Story*. New York: Random House, 1978. 146–58.

———. *One Time, One Place*. New York: Random House, 1971.

———. *The Optimist's Daughter*. New York: Random House, 1972.

———. Personal conversation with author (spring 1997).

———. "Powerhouse." In *A Curtain of Green*. 1941. Reprint, New York: Library of America, 1998. 158–70.

———. "Voice of the People." *Jackson Clarion-Ledger*, December 28, 1945.

———. "Words into Fiction." In *The Eye of the Story*. New York: Random House, 1978. 134–45.

SUSAN V. DONALDSON

Parting the Veil

Eudora Welty, Richard Wright, and the Crying Wounds of Jim Crow

Using a camera in Depression-era Mississippi, Eudora Welty told biographer/ critic Hermione Lee in 1988, introduced her to a world far beyond the confines of her sheltered Jackson upbringing and, to a great extent, the subject matter for her future fiction. Photography, she noted, "taught me so much, about coming upon people I didn't know and taking this minute from their lives. But I had to go to fiction from photography. That's the only way you can really part the veil between people, not as images, but in what comes from inside, in both subject and writer."[1] She was if anything more precise and passionate about that ambition at the end of her famous essay "One Time, One Place," which prefaced her 1971 collection of photographs taken largely of poverty-stricken Mississippians living under the strictures of segregation in the 1930s. "I knew this, anyway," she concludes in that essay, "that my wish, indeed my continuing passion, would be not to point the finger in judgment but to part a curtain, that invisible shadow that falls between people, the veil of indifference to each other's presence, each other's wonder, each other's human plight."[2]

The reference to parting the veil is highly significant, especially for a talented photographer and writer strongly drawn to documentary photography in the 1930s — despite her demurral in "One Time, One Place" that the book was more of "a family album" than "a social document."[3] For Welty's photographs shared with some of the greatest documentary art produced in the period the impetus to know and record the Depression's economic and social divisions and, in the eloquent words of Elizabeth Abel, "to reweave the social fabric by making its increasingly divided fragments more fully visible."[4] But perhaps even more to the point, the reference to parting the veil between human beings, and thereby making them visible to one another, echoes to a striking degree W. E. B. Du Bois's language in *The Souls of Black Folk* to evoke the psychic damage, indi-

48

vidually and collectively, wrought by institutionalized segregation on black and white alike. For African Americans "the sombre veil of color" as Du Bois defined it split one's very sense of self and created the burden of double consciousness, "this sense of always looking at one's self through the eyes of others." For white Americans, in turn, the veil rendered their fellow human beings invisible and utterly barred from any viable communal exchange or reciprocity. "In a world," Du Bois warned, "where it means so much to take a man by the hand and sit beside him, to look frankly into his eyes and feel his heart beating with red blood; in a world where a social cigar or a cup of tea together means more than legislative halls and magazine articles and speeches,—one can imagine the consequences of the almost utter absence of such social amenities between estranged races, whose separation extends even to parks and street-cars."[5]

Tracing the consequences of Jim Crow segregation—of whole communities rendered invisible, of stories never told, exchanged, and heard, of selves diminished and withered by the dictates of state-mandated racial separation—was a crucial subtext in Welty's photographs and fiction of the 1930s and early 1940s, particularly in her first collection of short stories, *A Curtain of Green*, published in 1942 and generally hailed by critics as yet another example of southern Gothic, which offered a collective portrait, in the words of one reviewer, of "the demented, the deformed, the queer."[6] For what *A Curtain of Green* presents is something very like a panoptic cellblock of human beings confined in separate stories and isolated from one another by a racially fissured society policed in the name of protecting idealized white southern womanhood. In this respect, Welty's first book parallels to a stunning degree portraits of the emotional damage wrought by Jim Crow in the earliest fiction and nonfiction published by her fellow Mississippian Richard Wright, who like Welty was deeply involved with documentary art at roughly the same time.

Richard H. Brodhead has already pointed out the "strange symmetries" linking the lives and art of the two most famous products of Mississippi's capital city Jackson, born within seven months of each other but separated by the institutionalized segregation that roughly paralleled their lives and careers. Among the most admirable insights Brodhead has to offer in his analysis is his strong objection to "a polarized account of Welty as white privilege and Wright as black deprivation."[7] Overlooked in his examination, though, is the strongest bond between two Mississippians separated in life and writing by that "veil" of color so forcibly deplored by Du Bois: their fierce critique in common—and often complementary—of Jim Crow's dehumanizing regime of surveillance and the damage it had inflicted on white and black alike, their indictment of the violence required to maintain white privilege and white blindness, and their startlingly similar strategy of resisting Jim Crow's regime of surveillance and parting the "veil" between white and black. Ultimately, what they both posed as an alternative to Jim Crow's white gaze of surveillance and the objectification it required was something like a "third eye," in the words of anthropologist Fatimah Toby Rony—a way of looking back and resisting the eye of power and even posing the possibility of dissolving the distance between white and black, self and other.[8] The parallels in their writing during the 1930s and early 1940s, in fact, reveal something like an opaque, covert dialogue between two Mississippians on either side of the color line who never even exchanged words directly but who in many respects collaborated in compiling a complex and powerful indictment of the damage wrought by a racially obsessed society.

Raised and educated in the rigidly segregated neighborhoods and schools of Jackson, Welty and Wright, arguably Jackson's most famous native son and daughter, never once seemed to cross paths in their long and productive careers.[9] Nevertheless, their first publications—Welty's *A Curtain of Green* (1942) and Wright's *Uncle Tom's Children* (1936, 1937, 1938) and *12 Million Black Voices* (1941)—pursue highly similar and even complementary negotiations with the crisis of meaning and the acute sense of loss they saw arising from the cultural traumas imposed by Jim Crow. They both exposed and responded to sites of injury inflicted by a highly fissured society resulting in, as Ron Eyerman argues in his book *Cultural Trauma*, "a dramatic loss of identity and meaning, a tear in the social fabric."[10] In doing so, they brought to visibility and hearing alternative voices and identities—those buried and silenced by the official history and rhetoric of white supremacy and by the "sombre veil of color" that W. E. B. Du Bois saw as so destructive to white and black alike. By giving prominence to the social wounds struck by Jim Crow, Welty and Wright together—on opposite sides of the veil, to be sure—managed to create something like an intertextual space allowing for a reformulation of the very boundaries between self and other and the creation of "a dynamic space of mutual recognition," which Holocaust studies scholar Eric L. Santner sees as the only genuinely productive response to trauma.[11]

From the earliest stages of his career, in fact, Richard Wright frankly identified his writing as the most potent political weapon he could wield to protect himself against the wounds inflicted by Jim Crow. In *American Hunger*, the second portion of *Black Boy* set in Chicago, Wright poignantly traces his rising ambition to express the pain and emotional deprivation bequeathed to him and African Americans in general by a racially obsessed society—"that constant sense of wanting without having," he wrote, "of being hated without reason."[12] For him the anguished silencing and wrenching isolation imposed by segregation were strangely evoked by the surrealistic scenes he witnessed every day as an orderly in a Chicago research hospital—the silent wailing of dogs used as test animals whose vocal chords were slit by medical researchers, and the sudden and eerie glimpse of two separate lines of women hospital employees marching down a corridor, one line of white women dressed in impeccably white uniforms and one line of black women dressed in rags and armed with brooms, mops, and cleaning chemicals. "I wondered what law of the universe kept them from being mixed," Wright wrote.[13] Indeed, the hospital itself, which confined Wright and his three fellow African American orderlies to its underground corridors, seemed to symbolize all too clearly the deprivations—loneliness, invisibility, incarceration—imposed by racial separation.

The experience helped crystallize Wright's yearning to break free of that imposed loneliness by finding and creating an audience and community for the stories he felt impelled to tell, poetry and fiction that he saw "linked white life with black, merged two streams of common experience." Only through his writing could he break the veil of color and begin "to reveal the vast physical and spiritual ravages of Negro life" as well as "the kinship between the sufferings of the Negro and the sufferings of other people." In writing he could give voice to his own wounds caused by Jim Crow—the "racial hate" that "had been the bane of my life"—and render legible the disorderly and damaged lives of the rebels against Jim Crow he came to know as a member of Chicago's radical John Reed Club, like Ross, a southern-born black Communist waiting to be tried for "inciting to riot."[14] Above all, in writing he could reveal all those stories hidden behind the color line that African Americans themselves could not tell and that white Americans had refused to hear or acknowledge.

Welty was also impelled to reach across those barriers of racial hatred, but she was considerably more reticent than Wright, both in her fiction and in her public statements about the cost wrought by institutionalized segregation and about the civil rights movement in general. Late in life, though, she freely acknowledged that her work as a junior publicity agent coupled with the camera she was learning to use in the early 1930s provided her with both protection for an admittedly shy person and, in her own words, "a hand-held auxiliary of wanting-to-know" that gave her entrée into African American life not usually open to white Mississippians.[15] "It was," as she told Jonathan Yardley in a 1973 interview, "a matter of getting to see something of the state. I'd never seen any of it before, except on family car trips. I hadn't realized anything about the life here . . . I went to every county seat in the state. It was a—I almost said 'heart-opener'—a real eye-opener."[16] By 1934, in fact, Welty seriously began to pursue the possibilities of a career in photography, motivated in part, according to her biographer Suzanne Marrs, by her rising interest in black life in Mississippi. Her experiments with a series of cameras, beginning with a 2½ × 4½ Kodak Eastman six-16, led her to apply to study with famed documentary photographer Berenice Abbott in 1934, and in her application she singled out the "particular studies of negroes" she was undertaking with a future book in mind—but pointedly dissociated her project from the sentimentalized and condescending photography of African Americans that Doris Ulmann had produced for Julia Peterkin's nostalgic book on Gullah culture titled *Roll, Jordan, Roll*, published that same year.[17] By the next year Welty was negotiating with publisher Harrison Smith to publish a collection of fiction and photographs focusing on African American culture tentatively titled "Black Saturday," but Smith regretfully turned down the project and cited as reasons the publication of Peterkin's illustrated book and the unlikelihood of marketing a similar book during the Depression. Just a few years later, though, Welty succeeded in having an exhibition of her photographs mounted at the Camera House, Inc., on East 60th Street in New York City.[18] Not until 1971 would Welty succeed in collecting and publishing those early photographs—to great critical acclaim—in her photographic album of Depression-era Mississippi entitled *One Time, One Place*.

Yet even at the height of the civil rights movement, Welty preferred to let her fiction speak for itself, as she vehemently declared in her famous and much misinterpreted essay eventually titled "Must the Novelist Crusade?" It is telling, though, that when she was asked to speak before integrated Millsaps College audiences in 1963 and 1964—years of appalling racial violence in Mississippi— she read two stories, "Keela, the Outcast Indian Maiden" and "Powerhouse," written nearly three decades earlier, that revealed the "shock" of recognition— her own term—experienced in those youthful photographic encounters with black Mississippians living under Jim Crow.[19] Considering the fact that Welty chose these two stories to read at civil rights events, one concludes that the "shock" she felt was the kind of confrontation with the color line—and the violence with which racial separation was maintained—that Richard Wright depicted with obsessive force throughout the whole of his career.

"Keela, the Outcast Indian Maiden" is shaped by that "shock" of recognition like no other piece of fiction in Welty's first published collection of stories, *A Curtain of Green*, the very title of which alludes opaquely to the veil of color draped between white and black. The story itself emerged from Welty's earliest ventures into the hidden corners of segregated Mississippi during her brief time working and traveling for the Works Progress Administration. Suzanne Marrs notes in her biography of Welty that sometime in the mid-1930s the apprentice writer heard a report "about a little Negro man in a carnival who was made to eat live chickens," and from that kernel emerged a powerful short story which suggests nothing so much as a shattering discovery of white privilege based on black powerlessness and exploitation.[20]

The story is told from the perspective of a small elderly African American man named Little Lee Roy who is unexpectedly visited in his backcountry home by two white men, one of whom, Steve, a former carnival barker, seems to be in search of penance. With a certain amount of glee and good humor, Little Lee Roy listens to the man named Steve obsessively recount his tale of working as a barker for a carnival sideshow featuring an attraction dubbed "Keela, the Outcast Indian Maiden," who ate live chickens for the entertainment of paying customers. To the other white man named Max, who apparently has shown Steve where Little Lee Roy lives, the former barker explains how he came to discover that Keela was really a tiny, crippled African American man kidnapped from his home by a traveling show and forced to growl, make threatening gestures, and eat live chickens in his imposed guise of an Indian maiden. As a barker, Steve takes the performance at face value, until one man in the audience steps forward, offers his hand to Keela across the barrier ostensibly protecting the audience, and reveals Little Lee Roy as the victim he is—of both the carnival and the white spectators whose avid stares evoke the dehumanizing effects upon those who serve as objects of a racialized gaze.

For Little Lee Roy that moment of revelation is one of liberation—from the sideshow, from the spectators, and in many respects from the very memory of "de ole times when I use to be wid de circus," as he tells his disinterested children later—times safely relegated to a now-distant past for him.[21] But for Steve it is a discovery that traps him in multiple retellings of the incident, as though each telling is an unsuccessful attempt to purge himself forever of that searing memory when he discovers both his sense of whiteness and his own culpability in the exploitation of a fellow human being. Beyond his repetitive telling of the tale, though, Steve has no idea what to do, and even going to see Little Lee Roy produces no satisfactory results. In the end, Steve suggests, as Peter Schmidt has eloquently argued, yet another avatar of Quentin Compson denying his hatred of the South at the end of *Absalom, Absalom!*[22] From the perspective of Dominick LaCapra in *Writing History, Writing Trauma*, this sort of storytelling, endlessly repeating itself, exemplifies a "depressed, self-berating, and trauma-tized self, locked in compulsive repetition, . . . possessed by the past, [facing] a future of impasses."[23]

The vocabulary of trauma theory, in fact, as developed by practitioners like LaCapra and Cathy Caruth over the past two decades, appears to be all too relevant to elucidate repetitive patterns of suffering and pain of the kind that Welty traces in this story and others and that Wright recounts again and again. Caruth herself resorts to an elusive phrasing that half-reveals, half-withholds in her explanation of the affect, representation, and experience of trauma. By her lights trauma "is always the story of a wound that cries out, that addresses us in the attempt to tell us of a reality or truth that is not otherwise available." By way of explanation, she resorts to a brief literary allusion in Freud's *Beyond the Pleasure Principle*—to Torquato Tasso's *Gerusalemme Liberata* (1581), in which the epic's hero unknowingly kills his disguised beloved in a duel and then inad-vertently repeats that action in a magic forest when he strikes his sword against a tree. The tree in turn begins to bleed as the voice of his lost beloved, impris-oned within the tree, reproaches him for wounding her yet again. From Ca-ruth's perspective, the story illustrates a number of paradoxes about trauma, not the least of which is the importance of defining trauma not so much as the wound itself as "the response," Caruth says, "to an unexpected or overwhelm-ing violent event or events that are not fully grasped as they occur, but return later in repeated flashbacks, nightmares, and other repetitive phenomena."[24]

To a striking degree, Steve's sudden encounter in "Keela, the Outcast Indian Maiden" with the realities of whiteness and blackness—along with his difficul-ties in recounting those realities—suggests something like a half-articulated response to the kind of trauma Caruth describes: a crying wound seeking ad-dress and audience but only with partial success. His encounter and his com-pulsive retelling of it also evoke something like an inversion of the "stock scene of racial discovery" that scholars including Michael Cooke, Priscilla Wald, and Shawn Michelle Smith see as shaping so much of twentieth-century African American literature, from Du Bois's *The Souls of Black Folk* and James Weldon Johnson's *Autobiography of an Ex-Coloured Man* to Zora Neale Hurston's *Their Eyes Were Watching God*, Richard Wright's *Native Son*, and Ralph Ellison's

Invisible Man.[25] Smith in particular marshals Lacanian theory to excellent effect by examining Du Bois's own description of his first shocked recognition of the color line and its shattering effect on the individual psyche. In the very first chapter of *The Souls of Black Folk*, Du Bois writes:

> It is in the early days of rollicking boyhood that the revelation first bursts upon one, all in a day, as it were. I remember well when the shadow swept across me. I was a little thing, away up in the hills of New England, where the dark Housatonic winds between Hoosac and Taghkanic to the sea. In a wee wooden schoolhouse, something put it into the boys' and girls' heads to buy gorgeous visiting-cards—ten cents a package—and exchange. The exchange was merry, till one girl, a tall newcomer, refused my card,—refused it peremptorily, with a glance. Then it dawns upon me with a certain suddenness that I was different from the others; or like, mayhap, in heart and life and longing, but shut out from the world by a vast veil.[26]

Smith aptly describes this scene as an inversion—and a racialized one at that—of Jacques Lacan's mirror stage of ego formation, when the infant suddenly misrecognizes its reflection in a mirror as an idealized, whole self. Resorting to William James's three-part definition of the self as constituted by the "material me, the spiritual me, and the social me," Smith argues that Du Bois's discovery of double consciousness—through that scene of shocked recognition—hinges on others' perception of the self in the constitution of individual identity. His account of double consciousness—of always looking at oneself through the eyes of others—emerges, according to Smith, from the social self's first direct encounter with the color line. "This violent negotiation," Smith declares, "proves shocking and transformative, and its effects reverberate back to and disrupt the very foundations of one's initial, idealized misrecognition of self as image in the (Lacanian) mirror stage. Indeed, for Du Bois, double consciousness results from an *inverted* mirror stage brought about by a classmate's racialized rejection of him."[27]

Richard Wright would explore that moment of racial discovery again and again throughout his work, but it was in his first book—and its opening chapter on "The Ethics of Living Jim Crow: An Autobiographical Sketch"—that he exposed with obsessive urgency the pain and the raw wounds inflicted by each bruising encounter with the color line. In the first section of "The Ethics of Living Jim Crow," Wright recounts his "first lesson in how to live as a Negro" during his early childhood in Arkansas. A battle with cinders fought between small black and white boys in his neighborhood leaves him bloodied and his mother horrified—but not because of his physical injuries. Beating him within an inch of his life, his mother compounds each blow with the singular lesson that he was never again to fight with white children. The aftermath for the bruised and bloody child was even more painful: "All that night I was delirious and could not sleep. Each time I closed my eyes I saw monstrous white faces suspended from the ceiling, leering at me."[28] This initial encounter with hostile white faces and eyes is followed by an account of an early job, significantly enough, with a white optical company that ends with threats of violence against Richard for failing to measure up to the exacting standards of those hostile white eyes always scrutinizing him. Yet another job stint is punctuated by Wright's witnessing a brutal beating by his white bosses of a black woman, and additional sketches feature the physical dangers awaiting vulnerable black boys under constant surveillance when they do not respond with lowered eyes, ready smiles, and exaggerated courtesy before any white woman who might be in their vicinity.

Several years later, in the originally published version of his autobiography *Black Boy*, Wright would remember how vast was the distance stretching between the white world and his isolated, impoverished childhood and how vital it was for him to learn laboriously the complicated web of racial etiquette protecting him from white violence. "I had to feel and think each tiny item of racial experience in the light of the whole race problem," he wrote, "and to each item I brought the whole of my life. While standing before a white man I had to figure out how to perform each act and how to say each word."[29] Above all, he had to remember the proper demeanor to maintain before any white woman, whose symbolic status as the reason and justification for white supremacy required absolute obeisance and whose very presence reverberated with danger for African Americans. Even in a hotel frequented by white prostitutes, upon whom he had to wait in his capacity as bellboy, the possibility of crossing that line of color was fraught with danger. "Your presence awoke in them no sense of shame," Wright recalled in the fifth sketch of "The Ethics of Living Jim Crow," "for you were not regarded as human. If they were alone, you could steal sidelong glimpses at them. But if they were receiving men, not a flicker of your eyelids could show."[30]

It was in the collection's opening story, "Big Boy Leaves Home," though, that Wright exposes just how devastating those scenes of racial discovery could be—and how completely intertwined they were with cultural narratives of the surveillance and violence required for the putative protection of white womanhood, narratives invoked time again as the central rationale for segregation itself. For the title character, Big Boy, learns the lessons and dangers of falling under those measuring and hostile white gazes when he and his friends are discovered skinny-dipping by a white woman. Desperate for escape from the imminent danger she represents, Big Boy stands within three feet of the woman and repeatedly beseeches her for his clothes. Her only response is to scream for her husband, who summarily shoots two of the boys in the group. The scene underscores Big Boy's utter vulnerability—nakedness and all—in the presence of the white woman, and its emotional charge is surpassed only by the horrifying lynching scene that inevitably follows. With the exception of the first murder scene in Wright's 1942 novel *Native Son*, where Bigger Thomas suffocates a white woman to escape detection by her blind mother, no other text in Wright's work illustrates as nakedly the power of a white woman to destroy a black man in a segregated society mandating her "protection."

Big Boy discovers, in short, what it means to be black in a Jim Crow world. To be black means to be at the mercy of the murderous white gaze surveying any infractions of the color line and of its accompanying myths of white womanhood requiring protection. To be black means to be subject to the extraordinary violence wielded to police the color line and to guard those myths of white womanhood—as Big Boy learns watching a third friend burned alive by a festive white mob to the accompaniment of singing white women. Big Boy initially appears all but helpless as he witnesses the horrifying scene from a nearby hiding place, but he takes action when he strangles one of the mob's tracking dogs with his bare hands and then flees the scene altogether—yet another person joining the cresting wave of African Americans fleeing north to escape the white gaze and its imperative of violently enforcing the "etiquette" required by Jim Crow.

Nowhere does that imminent threat of death and ever-present racial violence loom so ominously and powerfully in Welty's first two collections of short stories, *A Curtain of Green* (1941) and *The Wide Net* (1942), although, to be sure, Welty's early stories do display sudden eruptions of violence: the inexplicable suicide in "Clytie" of poor demented Clytie Farr, who plunges headfirst into a rain barrel, seeking a face that will finally respond to her; the impulsive and dreamlike stabbing in "Flowers for Marjorie" of a pregnant woman by her desperate, unemployed husband, no longer able to distinguish fantasy from reality; the gang rape inflicted on a young woman in "At the Landing" who wanders from her confining home. One story in particular, though—the title piece "A Curtain of Green" in Welty's first short-story collection—does focus on a near-encounter with death that parallels with unsettling force the terrifying confrontation with and recognition of the mythic white woman, whose cultural stature is maintained through constant surveillance and brutal violence.

Among the most opaque and puzzling of the stories in *A Curtain of Green*, the title story focuses on the furious energy of an unkempt, grief-stricken widow named Mrs. Larkin, who married into the first family of the town Larkin's Hill and who, since the death of her husband the summer before, has confined herself to her lush and overgrown garden. There she digs, hoes, and plants in frantic haste and confusion without any regard for her own appearance, her unsightly flowerbeds, or her bewildered neighbors, to whom the garden resembles "a sort of jungle, in which the slight, heedless form of its owner daily lost itself." Indeed, that "jungle" that Mrs. Larkin so furiously cultivates provides her with something like the protection afforded white women by the "sombre veil of color"—a barrier of sorts against the ordinary catastrophes of life. But catastrophe has already befallen the grief-stricken woman. What preoccupies her in the midst of her ceaseless labor is the sudden accident—a falling chinaberry tree—that ended her husband's life and her own sense of order and security. There in the garden, awaiting the daily summer rain, she feels sudden terror, "as though her loneliness had been pointed out by some outside force whose finger parted the hedge." In her panic and her anger, she turns to the only other person in that lush greenery—a black boy named Jamey who works in her garden—and on him she prepares to vent her rage, fear, and vulnerability with the hoe she raises as a weapon. Absorbed and whistling, Jamey in all his young vulnerability seems to her an unaccountable reminder of her own susceptibility to hurt and danger, "so helpless was she, too helpless to defy the workings of accident, of life and death, of unaccountability." Aiming the hoe at Jamey's head, she also directs toward him all her anger at her loss and her exposure to pain, grief, and harm as she asks herself, "Was it not possible to compensate? To punish? To protest?" But then the rain abruptly begins, and Mrs. Larkin lowers her hoe and sinks to the ground as Jamey turns to look at her.[31]

The story's point of view then shifts to Jamey, who runs to her side in the rain to rouse her and then looks "in awe at the unknowing face, white and rested under its bombardment." Looking at her, he suddenly remembers "how something had filled him with stillness when he felt her standing there behind him looking down at him, and he would not have turned around at that moment for anything in the world." He recalls as well "the noise of the windows next door being shut when the rain started . . . But now, in this unseen place, it was he who stood looking at poor Mrs. Larkin." Having been pondered with half-murderous intent by Mrs. Larkin's increasingly agitated gaze—and probably watched by white neighbors from their windows—Jamey suddenly acquires the power to look back, and at a white woman at that. After briefly calling out her name, he abruptly leaves the garden and the story altogether, and in doing so appears to have quitted a narrative all too familiar in a segregated society—that of a white woman from whom a glance and a word can serve as a death sentence to a black man.[32]

But then it is precisely that narrative, along with the power and authority of white southern ladies to police a rigidly defined racial hierarchy, that "A Curtain of Green" rigorously interrogates. Mrs. Larkin may belong to the first family of Larkin's Hill, but her status is no protection against misfortune or mortality, and her sudden impulse to behead her hired laborer is a measure of her misplaced sense of entitlement—and the security afforded by whiteness. In that moment of rage she briefly sees in the hapless Jamey not just an object on which to vent her grief and anger but a reminder of her exposure to the tragedies of human life against which the mythology of white southern womanhood was supposedly erected to protect her.

In a curious manner of speaking, "A Curtain of Green" encapsulates the volume's sometimes satirical and humorous, sometimes angry critique of white southern ladies whose confidence in their sense of social and racial privilege blinds them to the poignant humanity of those relegated to subordinate status by virtue of class and race. The stories in Welty's first collection may be populated, as her first reviewers observed, by figures on the margins of small southern towns—like carnival hucksters, sideshow geeks, traveling salesmen, backwoods farmwives, troubled schoolgirls, impoverished recluses, and musicians—but those marginal figures are nearly always policed by white southern ladies who take it upon themselves to guard and maintain the rigidly defined racial and social hierarchies of their small southern towns. More often than not these guardians of white southern womanhood are revealed in *A Curtain of Green* as comic bunglers incapable of living up to their own high standards—like Mrs. Watts, Mrs. Carson, and Aimee Slocum in "Lily Daw and the Three Ladies," the volume's opening story. They decide to pack off a slow-witted and much abused local girl named Lily Daw to the Ellisville Institute for the Feeble-Minded of Mississippi, only to learn that Lily has her own plans, including marriage to a fast-talking xylophone player. Welty's ladies also have a marked tendency to talk themselves into the kind of high-minded, self-complacent isolation that characterizes the manic narrator of "Why I Live at the P. O.," who finds she can only maintain her sense of dignity and self-worth within the confines of the second-smallest post office in the state of Mississippi.

Perhaps even more to the point, though, the ladies who charge through the stories of *A Curtain of Green* as self-designated custodians of social and racial order are revealed to be singularly blind to the realities that surround them—even though they appear to assume the responsibility of monitoring and maintaining that order. They may succeed—at least partially—in relegating the residents of their towns to their respective social and racial categories as anomalies, oddities, and outcasts, and indeed, so many of the central figures in *A Curtain of Green* are each confined to separate stories that resemble nothing so much as isolated panoptic cell-blocks. But from time to time Welty's ladies inadvertently reveal just how little they do see. In "Petrified Man," the habitués of the beauty parlor expend considerable time and energy analyzing the attractions of a traveling sideshow come to town—its pygmies, Siamese twins, and in particular its petrified man, supposedly turning to stone for all to see. Left unsaid is the emotional violence wrought by their avid gazes upon those attractions, figures on the margin who find themselves fixed like pinned butterflies under the panoptic gaze of white women who take for granted their status as the central rationale for a segregated and highly regimented society. Their easy self-complacency is quickly punctured when one of the beauty salon customers suddenly equates the petrified man on display with a wanted poster of a serial rapist reproduced in a scandal sheet magazine. However much the women in the salon pride themselves on their vigilant surveillance of their world and its possible dangers, they have all—with one exception—revealed themselves to be singularly blind to one of those dangers precisely because it has been curtained off and confined for their viewing pleasure according to the dictates of a segregated society. It is a story, finally, that slyly satirizes the misplaced faith of white women in Jim Crow's economies of visibility and invisibility, designating what can be seen and unseen and structured by what Robyn Wiegman has referred to "segregation's tenuous geometry of public gazes."[33]

Elsewhere in Welty's writing and photography, that blindness is measured by the emotional violence it wreaks upon black and white alike, as in the poignant story of Clytie Farr in "Clytie," a half-deranged southern lady whose family has fallen on hard times and become something of a scandal in their small community of Farr's Mill. Clytie and her family now live precariously under the domineering presence of her equally mad sister Octavia, who tries to reclaim a small measure of their lost social status by cutting off all ties with the community, including the former black servant for whom their invalid father cries. Clytie herself is reduced to roaming the streets, parroting her sister's commands, cursing in the garden, and finally seeking surcease from her crippling sense of abandonment by drowning herself in a rain barrel, where she finally discovers a face she recognizes, her own. In a manner of speaking, she is as much a victim of her sister's imperious gaze as is the black servant who is summarily turned away at the door.

To a great extent, Richard Wright parallels Welty's critique of white blindness and all the violence wrought by the white gaze in both *Uncle Tom's Children* and his pioneering phototext *12 Million Black Voices*. In photograph after photograph chosen from the Farm Security Administration files with Edwin Rosskam, *12 Million Black Voices*, brings attention to workers and dancers performing for a distant and seemingly all-powerful white gaze. It was in his earlier book *Uncle Tom's Children*, though, that he set himself to a task paralleling Welty's own in *A Curtain of Green* and in her Depression-era photographs: revealing the limits of that white gaze and its dependence on unremitting violence for the maintenance of a rigidly hierarchical racial order. In the first three stories of *Uncle Tom's Children*, white violence exerted to reestablish white order frequently results in black violence responding to and defining the limits of white power in moments of confrontation. Nowhere is that fissuring of white power stressed more forcefully than in the last story, "Bright and Morning Star," which focuses on the transformation of a mother's religious piety into militant activism and which concludes with her death at the hands of a white mob whose very act of murder reveals the limited reach of their power: their failure to make her betray her comrades. "Yuh didn't get what yuh wanted!" Sue exults at the moment of her death. "N yuh ain gonna nevah git it! You didn't kill me; Ah come here by mahself."[34]

All of Wright's protagonists in *Uncle Tom's Children* are armed with similar revelations of the ultimate limits of white power and of the agency they acquire with those revelations, and with that knowledge they all resort to a range of strategies to test the limits and weaknesses of Jim Crow's scopic regime. The most traditional of those strategies is the one resorted to by Big Boy in the first story, in which he finds something like temporary invisibility in makeshift kilns away from the lynch mob that pursues him. But he also resorts in the end to the time-honored course of flight through the aid of a truck ride north, and significantly enough, the story ends at dawn as Big Boy begins to find some measure of safety in his own migration north.

In the following story, "Down by the Riverside," the protagonist, named, poignantly enough, Mann, tests instead the possibilities of confrontation and violence, however reluctantly, in his desperate attempt to get his pregnant wife to a hospital in the midst of a flood as dangerous to whites as it is to African Americans. He kills once in self-defense and comes close a second time—but it is not until he tries to outrun his tormentors that he is summarily shot. Even more directly confrontational, though, is the aggrieved husband Silas in "Long Black Song," who discovers the ambiguous and disturbing sexual encounter his wife has with a white traveling salesman, kills the salesman, and then stoically faces down the mob that condemns him to death by fire. As Silas's wife looks on in horror and full awareness that he has stoically sought out his own death, he dies in many respects on his own terms—by killing as many of his opponents as possible.

These suicidal embraces of vengeance, violence, and death, however, are not the only alternatives to escape and flight pondered in Wright's stories. The recourse to violence is countered in "Fire and Cloud," the collection's original concluding story, with the possibilities of renewal and redefinition found in the resources of community, and it is those possibilities that the story's protagonist, a minister frantically seeking to aid his starving congregation, finds when he joins forces with Communist activists in a protest demonstration. Within the ranks of white and black armed with both religious belief and political commitment, he finds a new sense of self among many and an alternative to that crippling sense of diminishment fostered by the ever-present threat of lynching.

What all these protagonists have in common is their determination to look back at the white gaze, an act of defiance and resistance that anthropologist Fatimah Tobing Rony refers to as "the third eye." Making a distinction between the eye of the gazer and the eye of the one gazed upon, Rony builds her theory of the third eye on W. E. B. Du Bois's famous description of the origin of double consciousness as the "sense of always looking at one's self through the eyes of others" or of seeing "darkly as through a veil." The third eye, for Rony, is a "racially charged glance" that disregards both the power bestowed on the one who gazes and the victimization of the one gazed upon in order to "see the very process which creates the internal splitting, to witness the conditions which give rise to . . . double consciousness." Rony turns to both Du Bois and to Frantz

Fanon to ponder the possibilities of looking back at the dominant eye of power and surveillance, foregrounding its underlying process of objectification, and dissolving the distance between self and other. "The third eye," Rony maintains, "turns on a recognition: the Other perceives the veil, the process of being visualized as an object, but returns the glance. The gesture of being frozen into a picturesque is deflected." Looking back at power, Rony declares, the third eye represents an alternative to both the eye of power and to objectification by "demanding sovereignty over one's own image." It is a strategy Rony sees characterizing the work of African American women in particular—Josephine Baker, Zora Neale Hurston, Toni Morrison, and Elizabeth Alexander—all of whom follow the lead of early ethnographic subjects in films and photographs who stare back at the camera and question its authority through parody, open resistance, contestation over context, and even silence.[35]

So too do Wright's protagonists in *Uncle Tom's Children* stare back—as does Wright himself in his experimental folk history *12 Million Black Voices*. In that pioneering phototext, Wright took as his charge to unearth, catalog, and mourn the multitude of racial injuries suffered by men, women, and children living behind the veil—in his words, "to place within full and constant view the collective humanity whose triumphs and defeats are shared by the majority," to foreground a subjugated, buried, and silent history defined by racial injuries that had become founding traumas for African American identity, "the basis," Dominick LaCapra observes of founding traumas, "for collective or personal identity, or both."[36] Hence the text of *12 Million Black Voices* brings attention again and again to the shuttered gaze of its implicitly white readers. To those readers, Wright declares, ". . . you usually take us for granted and think you know us, but our history is far more than you suspect, and we are not what we seem." Indeed, what the readers do not see—or hear, for that matter—is the wound inflicted by the process of racialization and the division imposed by Jim Crow—"an uneasily tied knot of pain and hope whose snarled strands," Wright declares, "converge from many points of time and space."[37]

To a startling extent, then, Wright anticipates Caruth's description of trauma as a story in which the voice crying out does so through the wound itself, unowned, unclaimed, wholly other, but nonetheless demanding, Caruth declares, "a listening and a response" and, perhaps even more emphatically, "a plea by an other who is asking to be seen and heard, this call by which the other commands us to awaken."[38] Wright's direct address to the reader suggests something of this crying out as well as a demand to respond despite the barriers erected by segregation and official designations of race. The first-person plural to which Wright resorts in 12 *Million Black Voices*, he observed in an interview, was experimental, tentatively ventured for a projected series of novels covering African American history, which he saw as "a more minute examination of the 'Bigger Thomas' type—that is, the cultural disinherited, the marginal man living in an emotional no-man's-land."[39] It was for those voices that Wright made his plea to an audience distanced by segregation to see and to hear, to breach the veil imposed by Jim Crow.

Such pleas would have resonated strongly with Welty, who charted her own preoccupation with seeing, hearing, and responding from the expeditions she made throughout Mississippi and who came to define both her photography and her writing as the most effective weapons to overcome the barriers imposed by segregation. Writing of that experience in "One Time, One Place," she observes that she learned the value of waiting for "the moment in which people reveal themselves"; and the reward was one of her most famous photographs, *Woman of the 1930's*, one that shows a black woman looking back at her white photographer, subject to subject, engaged in mutuality, recognizing each other's subjectivity—and interdependence (fig. 1). "When a heroic face like that of the woman in the buttoned sweater . . . looks back at me from her picture," Welty added, "what I respond to now, just as I did the first time, is not the Depression, not the Black, not the South, not even the perennially sorry state of the whole world, but the story of her life in her face."[40] To that story Welty's photograph gives precedence—her acknowledgment and recognition of that "third eye"—precisely because it acknowledges her subject's sense of agency and evokes a moment of recognition linking photographer and subject. In doing so, the photograph suggests something very like that reconstitution of identity and boundaries—between whiteness and blackness, self and other— which scholars like Eric Santner see as a crucial part of responding seriously to trauma.

Among other things, the photograph ultimately suggests something like that interdependence of whiteness and blackness, self and self, that Wright emphasizes at the end of 12 *Million Black Voices* and that evokes something of that "empathetic unsettlement" which Dominick LaCapra sees as the ethical imperative to take in negotiating representations of traumas and wounded histories, an imperative resisting the assertion of subjectivity at the cost of objectifying.[41] "We black folk, our history and our present being," Wright declares at the end of the volume's text, "are a mirror of all the manifold experiences of America.

Fig. 1. Eudora Welty, *Woman of the 1930's.* Reprinted by permission of the
Mississippi Department of Archives and Russell & Volkening as agents for the author.
Copyright © by Eudora Welty, renewed by Eudora Welty, LLC.

What we want, what we represent, what we endure is what America *is*. If we black folk perish, America will perish." To tell that story, ultimately, to excavate a history rendered silent and invisible, is to bridge the no-man's-land between white and black constructed by Jim Crow, to underscore the ultimately illusory nature of legislated racial separation. "Look at us and know us," Wright concludes, "and you will know yourselves, for *we* are *you*, looking back at you from the dark mirror of our lives!"[42] To do so, the ending of 12 *Million Black Voices* implies, is to resolve cultural trauma by incorporating it into the project of re-formulating identity and boundaries, to "repair," in Ron Eyerman's words, "the tear in the social fabric."[43]

The alternative to incorporating trauma into that project of reconstituting self and meaning, Eric Santner argues, is "narrative fetishism," by which he means "the construction and deployment of a narrative consciously or unconsciously designed to expunge the traces of trauma or loss that called that narrative into being in the first place."[44] Welty herself explores something of this response to cultural trauma to devastating effect in "Where Is the Voice Coming From?" Representing Welty's own intensely felt response to Medgar Evers's 1963 assassination, the story is written in the first-person voice of the killer Welty maintained she knew all too well from living in Mississippi, and what is most striking about that voice is its insistence on removing from sight and hearing a civil rights leader whose very existence is interpreted by the narrator as threatening.[45] After the nameless narrator shoots the man he claims he knows even in the dark, he tells the corpse of the victim: "There was just one way left, for me to be ahead of you and stay ahead of you, by Dad, and I just taken it." To himself he declares, "I was on top of the world myself. For once." But what the narrator learns by watching television news accounts of the murder—and here Suzan Harrison has offered a wonderfully shrewd analysis of the story—is that whatever sense of visible self he retains will be forever linked with, and displaced by, the man he wanted to remove from sight and hearing: "His face was in front of the public before I got rid of him, and after I got rid of him there it is again—the same picture. And none of me." What the murderer is left with to fortify his sense of self is the fact of the murder. "Anyway I seen him fall," he concludes. "I was evermore the one."[46]

For Welty the viable alternative to the death-dealing, rigidly fortified narrative response of "Where Is the Voice Coming From?" is "Powerhouse," written two decades earlier and included in *A Curtain of Green*, long before segregation had fallen under siege. An astonishing story on many counts, "Powerhouse" represents an unexpected response to a Fats Waller concert for a white audience that Welty attended in segregated Jackson in the early 1940s. In "Powerhouse," Welty declared, "I tried to turn the impromptu, frantic and abandoned playing together of a jazz pianist and his musicians into an exchange in words—something with its own rhythmic beat and crazy references, in the same onrush of performance." At the time she wrote the story, she added, ". . . I felt I was outside musical qualifications; it was a sort of combustion; I was writing about a demon." The story reads, in fact, like something akin to demonic possession, an ever-accelerating frantic tale told from the perspective of the white audience avidly watching Powerhouse but a perspective nonetheless shaken loose, "floating around somewhere," Welty notes, "in the concert hall."[47]

From the start, if anything, Powerhouse, like Welty's photograph of the woman who looks back with that "third eye," defies any prospect of being fixed in place by his white listeners. "You can't tell what he is," his white audience briefly ponders. "Negro man?—he looks more Asiatic, monkey, Jewish, Babylonian, Peruvian, fanatic, devil" (131). The wilder and stranger he appears, the more closely the audience watches him—but no more closely than Powerhouse watches back, returning gaze with gaze and looking "down so benevolently upon all our faces."[48]

Given the request to sing "Somebody Loves Me," Powerhouse sings chorus after chorus until "his mouth gets to be nothing but a volcano." Looking out on his audience, he sings, "Somebody loves me! Somebody loves me, I wonder who?" His final cry, directed at his audience and his putative narrators, long since relieved of their narrative responsibility, rings out with the certainty and conviction that Welty herself felt in "parting the veil" between subject and subject: ". . . Maybe it's you!" Crossing the lines in Jim Crow Mississippi between white and black, audience and performer, that last line tells his listeners that he sings them as well as himself, that his cries from the wounds delivered by racism are theirs as well as his, and that his story is as much theirs as his—for he has, after all, made their narrative his own just as their storytelling of listening to his music initially assumes his story to be theirs.[49]

It is a story, finally, reaching over those barriers established by Jim Crow segregation that came close to trapping Welty in the 1950s and 1960s, when her preoccupation with ensuring good nursing care for her mother kept her confined within the barriers of segregation and far more reticent about her support for the civil rights movement than many of her readers would have liked.[50] "Powerhouse" suggests a disavowal of traditional white southern representations of African Americans designating the lines between white subject and racialized object and ultimately a rethinking and reconstitution of the boundaries between self and other, whiteness and blackness, and those who have the power to gaze and those who insist upon the right to gaze back.

Welty herself was all too aware of the power wielded by Jim Crow's regime of surveillance, but she was also keenly attuned to the possibilities of looking back at power and resisting its relentless drive toward objectification. It was this knowledge that enabled her to part that troubling veil between her and Mississippians of color even in the 1930s and early 1940s, when the authority and power of Jim Crow seemed unassailable. With that third eye looking back and resisting the eye of power, she was able to scrutinize, satirize, and expose the myths of white womanhood and privilege undergirding legalized segregation, and the final result in her earliest fiction and photography was a passionate indictment of Jim Crow and the damage it wrought through the power to look and categorize. It was an indictment that complemented as well the portrait of racial trauma that Wright had been displaying in his earliest writing, for both writers portrayed just how devastating and damaging each bruising encounter with the color line could be for white and black alike. For Welty those encounters signaled the price to be paid for white privilege and white power—everlasting guilt for the violence by which the color line was maintained and at the same time blindness to the vulnerability of power that depended on the exploitation of others for existence. For Wright, each encounter with the color line and the eye of power meant a diminishment and estrangement of self amid suffocating silence and invisibility. But in their art and perhaps in their lives as well, these two Mississippi writers discovered just how empowering the third eye could be in its capacity to subvert, expose, and block the objectification and dehumanization intended by the white gaze of Jim Crow.

Notes

1. Lee, "Eudora Welty/1988," 151.
2. Welty, preface to *One Time, One Place*, 12.
3. Welty, preface to *One Time, One Place*, 9.
4. Abel, *Signs of the Times*, 183.
5. Du Bois, *The Souls of Black Folk*, 5, 147, 150.
6. Qtd. in Peterman, "A Curtain of Green," 104.
7. Brodhead, "Two Writers' Beginnings," 105, 118.
8. See, in general, Fatimah Tobing Rony's *The Third Eye*.

9. For biographies of Welty and Wright, see Marrs, *Eudora Welty*, and Michel Fabre, *The Unfinished Quest of Richard Wright*. See also Marrs's invaluable *One Writer's Imagination*.

10. Eyerman, *Cultural Trauma*, 2.

11. Santner, "History beyond the Pleasure Principle," 153.

12. Wright, *Black Boy (American Hunger)*, 314.

13. Wright, *Black Boy*, 356.

14. Wright, *Black Boy*, 375, 395, 435, 391.   .

15. Welty, *One Writer's Beginnings*, 84.

16. Yardley, "A Quiet Lady in the Limelight" (1973), 6.

17. Marrs, *Eudora Welty*, 42. Pearl Amelia McHaney discusses the cameras Welty used in the 1930s and 1940s in her essay "The Observing Eye," in *Eudora Welty as Photographer*, 8–9.

18. Smith to Eudora Welty, April 2, 1935; and Robbins to Eudora Welty, March 18, 1937, Eudora Welty Collection.

19. Welty, preface to *One Time, One Place*, 12. Suzanne Marrs discusses at length Welty's participation in interracial events and discussions at Tougaloo College and Millsaps College in the late 1950s and early 1960s in *One Writer's Imagination*, 169–78. For an excellent overview of Welty's political concerns in her fiction, nonfiction, and everyday life, see Harriet Pollack's fine introduction to *Eudora Welty and Politics*, 1–18. See also the ten essays included in that collection, among the best criticism published on Welty to this day.

20. Qtd. in Suzanne Marrs, *Eudora Welty*, 53.

21. Welty, "Keela, the Outcast Indian Maiden," in *Stories, Essays, and Memoir*, 56.

22. Schmidt, *The Heart of the Story*, 196.

23. LaCapra, *Writing History, Writing Trauma*, 66.

24. Caruth, *Unclaimed Experience*, 4, 91.

25. The phrase is Michael Cooke's and is examined at length by both Priscilla Wald and Shawn Michelle Smith. See Cooke, *Afro-American Literature in the Twentieth Century*; Wald, *Constituting Americans*, especially 181–92; and Smith, *Photography on the Color Line*, 25–42.

26. Du Bois, *The Souls of Black Folk*, 4.

27. Smith discusses Du Bois's indebtedness to William James in *Photography on the Color Line*, 26–31.

28. Richard Wright, "The Ethics of Living Jim Crow," in *Uncle Tom's Children*, 3, 5.

29. Wright, *Black Boy*, 231.

30. Wright, "The Ethics of Living Jim Crow," 11.

31. Welty, "A Curtain of Green," in *Stories, Essays, and Memoir*, 131–32, 133, 134.

32. Welty, "A Curtain of Green," 136.

33. Wiegman, *American Anatomies*, 41.

34. Wright, "Bright and Morning Star," in *Uncle Tom's Children*, 215.

35. Rony, *The Third Eye*, 4, 213, 216. The reference to Fanon is to *Black Skin, Black Masks*.

36. Wright, *12 Million Black Voices*, xix–xx; and LaCapra, *Writing History, Writing Trauma*, 81.

37. Wright, *12 Million Black Voices*, 10, 11.

38. Caruth, *Unclaimed Experience*, 9.

39. Edwin Seaver, "Readers and Writers" (1941), in *Conversations with Richard Wright*, 44–45.

40. Welty, preface to *One Time, One Place*, 11.

41. LaCapra, *Writing History, Writing Trauma*, 78.

42. Wright, *12 Million Black Voices*, 146.

43. Eyerman, *Cultural Trauma*, 4. See also Santner, "History beyond the Pleasure Principle," 152.

44. Santner, "History beyond the Pleasure Principle," 144.

45. See Marrs's discussion of the story's background in *Eudora Welty*, 303–4.

46. Eudora Welty, "Where Is the Voice Coming From?" In *Stories, Essays, and Memoir*, 729, 730, 732. See Suzan Harrison's fine reading of the story, "'It's Still a Free Country,'" 631–46.

47. Qtd. in Marrs, *One Writer's Imagination*, 25.

48. Welty, "Powerhouse," in *Stories, Essays, and Memoir*, 158, 159.

49. Welty, "Powerhouse," 160; see also Pollack, "Words Between Strangers," 60–69.

50. See Marrs's discussion in *One Writer's Imagination*, 175–76; and in *Eudora Welty*, 304–7.

Bibliography

Abel, Elizabeth. *Signs of the Times: The Visual Politics of Jim Crow*. Berkeley: University of California Press, 2010.

Brodhead, Richard H. "Two Writers' Beginnings: Eudora Welty in the Neighborhood of Richard Wright." *Yale Review* 84 (April 1996): 1–21; rpt. in *The Good of This Place: Values and Challenges in College Education*. New Haven, Conn.: Yale University Press, 2004.

Caruth, Cathy. *Unclaimed Experience: Trauma, Narrative, and History*. Baltimore, Md.: Johns Hopkins University Press, 1996.

Cooke, Michael. *Afro-American Literature in the Twentieth Century: The Achievement of Intimacy*. New Haven, Conn.: Yale University Press, 1984.

Du Bois, W. E. B. *The Souls of Black Folk*. 1903. Introd. Donald B. Gibson. Reprint, New York: Penguin Classics, 1989.

Eyerman, Ron. *Cultural Trauma: Slavery and the Formation of African American Identity*. New York: Cambridge University Press, 2001.

Fabre, Michel. *The Unfinished Quest of Richard Wright*. 2nd ed. Trans. Isabel Barzun. Urbana: University of Illinois Press, 1993.

Fanon, Frantz. *Black Skin, White Masks*. 1952. Trans. Charles Lam Markmann. Reprint, New York: Grove Press, 1967.

Goldfield, David R. *Black, White, and Southern: Race Relations and Southern Culture, 1940 to the Present*. Baton Rouge: Louisiana State University Press, 1960.

Griffin, Farah Jasmine. *"Who Set You Flowin'?" The African-American Migration Narrative*. New York: Oxford University Press, 1995.

Hale, Grace Elizabeth. *Making Whiteness: The Culture of Segregation in the South, 1890–1940*. New York: Pantheon, 1998.

Harrison, Suzan. "'It's Still a Free Country': Constructing Race, Identity, and History in Eudora Welty's 'Where Is the Voice Coming From?'" *Mississippi Quarterly*, special Eudora Welty issue, ed. Albert J. Devlin, 50 (Fall 1997): 631–46.

JanMohamed, Abdul W. *The Death-Bound Subject: Richard Wright's Archaeology of Death*. Durham, N.C.: Duke University Press, 2005.

Kinnamon, Keneth, and Michel Fabre, eds. *Conversations with Richard Wright*. Jackson: University Press of Mississippi, 1993.

LaCapra, Dominick. *Writing History, Writing Trauma*. Baltimore, Md.: Johns Hopkins University Press, 2001.

Lee, Hermione. "Eudora Welty/1988." In *More Conversations with Eudora Welty*, ed. Peggy Whitman Prenshaw, 146–53. Jackson: University Press of Mississippi, 1996.

Marrs, Suzanne. *Eudora Welty: A Biography*. New York: Harcourt, 2005.

———. *One Writer's Imagination: The Fiction of Eudora Welty*. Baton Rouge: Louisiana State University Press, 2002.

McHaney, Pearl Amelia. "The Observing Eye." In *Eudora Welty as Photographer*, ed. Pearl Amelia McHaney, 1–24. Jackson: University Press of Mississippi, 2009.

Norrell, Robert J. *The House I Live In: Race in the American Century*. New York: Oxford University Press, 2005.

Peterman, Gina D. "A Curtain of Green: Eudora Welty's Auspicious Beginning." *Mississippi Quarterly* 47 (Winter 1992/1993): 91–114.

Pollack, Harriet. "Words Between Strangers: On Welty, Her Style, and Her Audience." In *Welty: A Life in Literature*, ed. Albert J. Devlin, 54–81. Jackson: University Press of Mississippi, 1987.

Pollack, Harriet, and Suzanne Marrs, eds. *Eudora Welty and Politics: Did the Writer Crusade?* Baton Rouge: Louisiana State University Press, 2001.

Rampersad, Arnold, ed. *Richard Wright: A Collection of Critical Essays*. Englewood Cliffs, N.J.: Prentice Hall, 1995.

Ritterhouse, Jennifer. *Growing Up Jim Crow: The Racial Socialization of Black and White Children, 1890–1940*. Chapel Hill: University of North Carolina Press, 2005.

Rony, Fatimah Tobing. *The Third Eye: Race, Cinema, and Ethnographic Spectacle*. Durham, N.C.: Duke University Press, 1996.

Santner, Eric L. "History beyond the Pleasure Principle: Some Thoughts on the Representation of Trauma." In *Probing the Limits of Representation: Nazism and the Final Solution*, ed. Saul Friedlander, 143–54. Cambridge, Mass.: Harvard University Press, 1992.

Schmidt, Peter. *The Heart of the Story: Eudora Welty's Short Fiction*. Jackson: University Press of Mississippi, 1991.

Seaver, Edwin. "Readers and Writers" (1941). In *Conversations with Richard Wright*, ed. Keneth Kinnamon and Michel Fabre, 44–45. Jackson: University Press of Mississippi, 1993.

Smith, Lillian. *Killers of the Dream*. New York: W. W. Norton, 1949.

Smith, Shawn Michelle. *Photography on the Color Line: W. E. B. Du Bois, Race, and Visual Culture*. Durham, N.C.: Duke University Press, 2004.

Wald, Priscilla. *Constituting Americans: Cultural Anxiety and Narrative Form*. Durham, N.C.: Duke University Press, 1995.

Welty, Eudora. "A Curtain of Green." In *Stories, Essays, and Memoir*, ed. Richard Ford and Michael Kreyling, 3–179. New York: Library of America, 1998.

———. *One Time, One Place: Mississippi in the Depression—A Snapshot Album*. 1971. Reprint, Jackson: University Press of Mississippi, 1996.

———. *One Writer's Beginnings*. William E. Massey Sr. Lectures in the History of American Civilization, 1983. Cambridge, Mass.: Harvard University Press, 1984.

———. Papers. Eudora Welty Collection. Department of Mississippi Archives and History, Jackson, Mississippi.

———. *Photographs*. Foreword by Reynolds Price. Jackson: University Press of Mississippi, 1989.

———. *Stories, Essays, and Memoir*. New York: Library of America, 1998.

Wiegman, Robyn. *American Anatomies: Theorizing Race and Gender*. Durham, N.C.: Duke University Press, 1995.

Wright, Richard. *Black Boy (American Hunger): A Record of Childhood and Youth*. Introd. Jerry W. Ward Jr. 1944, 1945. Library of America Restored Text. New York: HarperPerennial, 1993.

———. *Native Son*. 1940. Introd. Arnold Rampersad. Restored Text by the Library of America. New York: HarperPerennial Classics, 1993.

———. *12 Million Black Voices*. Photo direction by Edwin Rosskam. New York: Thunder's Mouth Press, 1941.

———. *Uncle Tom's Children*. New York: Harper & Row / Perennial Library, 1938.

Yardley, Jonathan. "A Quiet Lady in the Limelight" (1973). In *More Conversations with Eudora Welty*, ed. Peggy Whitman Prenshaw, 3–13. Jackson: University Press of Mississippi, 1996.

KERI WATSON

Eudora Welty's *Making a Date, Grenada, Mississippi*

One Photograph, Five Performances

A black man and woman conversing on a sidewalk dominate the tightly cropped black-and-white photograph (Eudora Welty, *Making a Date, Grenada, Missis- sippi*, ca. 1930–35; fig. 2). Her light dress and his rolled up shirtsleeves, as well as the open transom windows behind them, give the impression of a hot summer day. The woman faces us, holding her left pinky finger to her right nostril and her right arm across her body, creating an off-putting and discomfiting stance that grabs the viewer's attention. Does her seemingly colloquial gesture convey once understood, now lost meaning, or is she just scratching her face? Is she signaling us to lower our gaze, or is she defiantly challenging us to go ahead and stare? The hem of her once nice, now stained and outdated crepe dress, caught in the summer breeze, is snagged awkwardly on her hose, and its bod- ice is torn to reveal white underlining. This light spot at her neckline creates a place for the eye to rest and, combined with his bright shirt and the tears in his pants, as well as her light-colored shoes, makes a pyramidal construction that keeps the viewer's eye focused uncomfortably on the pair and their poverty. Whereas the viewer is absorbed in creating a scenario for this couple, the man is interested only in the woman and ignores the viewer, even while we voyeuris- tically observe his crumpled fedora protruding from his back pocket and the soles of his shoes collapsing under his jaunty pose. His right hand rests on his hip and his left arm bends at the elbow, which directs our attention back to the woman and her off-putting yet compelling comportment. The pair is depicted in sharp focus, pushed to the foreground and tightly framed by a fluted column and a wall of storefronts receding into the distance. A plate-glass window of- fers two reflections, although it is difficult to make them out. Could one be a trace of the photographer? Does the reflection invite viewers to enter the scene and thus acknowledge their complicity with the photographer—the taker of

Fig. 2.   Eudora Welty, *Making a Date, Grenada, Mississippi*, ca. 1930–35.
Reprinted by permission of the Mississippi Department of Archives and
Russell & Volkening as agents for the author. Copyright © by Eudora Welty,
renewed by Eudora Welty, LLC.

images? The hatless and somewhat disheveled young woman obviously sees the photographer (and by extension the viewer), with whom she engages, but why does she not lower her hand or adjust her dress? Just as we are intrigued by her, she is interested in the young white woman taking her picture.

The photographer is Eudora Welty, who after completing a year at Columbia University's Business School in 1931, returned to her parent's home on Pinehurst Street in Jackson, Mississippi, and without any formal training began creating an extensive photographic archive of her home state's African American population. Employing a handheld Kodak camera with bellows, probably a No. 2A Folding Autographic Brownie that used 116 film and produced eight 2½ × 4½ inch negatives per roll, Welty went out into the streets of her home state and snapped candid shots of her black neighbors.[1] Just over two million people lived in Mississippi in 1930, 51 percent of whom were black.[2] Yet of the 209 photographs housed at the Mississippi Department of Archives and History that Welty took between 1931 and 1935, 74 percent feature African Americans.[3] They are primarily street scenes of blacks interacting with one another and in some cases the photographer. While Welty's photographs have been compared to those produced by the Farm Security Administration, it should be emphasized that Welty, working in the early 1930s and independently of any federal or local agency, was documenting the social landscape of Mississippi before the Historical Section of the Resettlement Administration.[4] Furthermore, of the printed photographs taken in the South between 1935 and 1942 by Roy Stryker's team of now-famous photographers, only 10 percent contain discernable black figures, making Welty's concentration on black subjects unique.[5] Why did she train her lens on Mississippi's African Americans, how did she find an audience for her photographs, and how do her images compare to those created by other photographers working at the time? What is it about the medium of photography that made it uniquely suited to Welty's investigation of issues of race?

Whereas Welty's fiction receives significant and sustained attention, her photographs have not garnered the scholarly consideration they deserve, despite the efforts of Patti Carr Black, Suzanne Marrs, Pearl McHaney, and Harriet Pollack, among others.[6] Building on their research and employing social and performance theories, I endeavor to examine Welty's photographs as unique cultural manifestations—as independent objects that simultaneously record a historical moment and exist across time. As Harriet Pollack has suggested, Nicolas Natanson's *The Black Image in the New Deal: The Politics of FSA Photography* provides a sociohistorical context for understanding Welty's images.[7]

In it, he identifies five stereotypes that characterize images of African Americans from the 1930s and 1940s: poor yet contented, rhythmic and unrestrained, hard-gambling and hard-praying optimists, noble primitives, and extreme and pitiful victims.[8] Welty's images deviate from these normative constructions of African Americans. She took primarily unposed photographs of 1930s black Mississippians, working independently without the guidance of a Stryker shooting script. This is not meant to imply that the resulting images are amateurish, only that Welty had no institutional authority to take them. Yet in their taking, she laid claim to the right—she endowed a certain power onto the act.[9] When she asserted this privilege, she enacted what Judith Butler termed "the political promise of the performative."[10] Because the performative needs to maintain conventional power, convention itself has to be reiterated, and in this reiteration it can be expropriated by unauthorized usages and create new historical trajectories.[11] Welty photographed a marginalized group—Great Depression–era black Mississippians—and thus began the insurrectionary process of overthrowing established codes of legitimacy vis-à-vis the visibility that photographs provide those photographed. As I will demonstrate, the simultaneous replication and usurpation of normative values is present in Welty's images as well as their varied instances of publication and exhibition. Following Natanson and Butler, I argue that Welty's photographs are consciously constructed portraits that enact sharp social commentary and provide a legitimating venue for her subjects.

This paper considers one of Welty's photographs—*Making a Date, Grenada, Mississippi*—and its performance and reception in five discrete circumstances: in the early 1930s in Welty's unpublished manuscript "Black Saturday"; in 1934 in an art exhibit held in Jackson; in 1935 on a page in Lincoln Schuster's *Eyes on the World: A Photographic Record of History-in-the-Making*; in 1936 in a one-woman exhibition of photography in New York City; and in 1971 in the publication of Welty's photo-book *One Time, One Place: Mississippi in the Depression, a Snapshot Album*.[12] Study of this image illustrates the ways in which Welty furthered the politicized performance of photography and challenged normative raced relations. Individual photographs represent nonrepeatable events, but photographs exist in reproducible format, allowing them complex diachronic lives that engender multivalent readings. Or as Alan Trachtenberg succinctly notes, "They have a life of their own which often resists the efforts of photographers and viewers (or readers) to hold them down as fixed meanings."[13] As Roland Barthes elaborates, "The Text [photograph] is plural . . . [it] is not a co-existence of meanings but a passage, an overcrossing; thus it answers not to an interpretation, even a liberal one, but to an explosion, a dissemination."[14] Following Barthes, Jan Goggans insightfully reminds us that photographs perform a dialogic exchange between the photographer, the subject, and the audience.[15] The photographer takes the picture, the subject assumes subjectivity in the moment of being photographed by using pose to assert and construct identity, and viewers, operating across time, fill in meaning, or animate the event. Susan Sontag has eloquently and famously argued that photographs involve a certain degree of aggressive appropriation.[16] As she writes, "In deciding how a photograph should look, in preferring one exposure to another, photographers are always imposing standards on their subjects . . . There is an aggression implicit in every use of the camera."[17] Despite the power photographers inherently wield over their subjects, I argue that Welty actually legitimated her subjects through their presentation in photographs. Study of *Making a Date, Grenada, Mississippi*, ca. 1930–35, illustrates how a single contentious image enacts and promulgates numerous meanings, both ideologically and ontologically, for multiple audiences, across time and place, and thus demonstrates how photography is a fluid medium that allowed Welty to effectively negotiate issues of race.

1. "Black Saturday," 1930s

By 1935 Welty had amassed hundreds of negatives and prints of Mississippi's black population.[18] She decided to try to publish these photographs with a collection of her short stories after seeing Julia Peterkin and Doris Ulmann's *Roll, Jordan, Roll*, which she disliked because of its sentimental, romanticized portrayal of South Carolina's Gullahs.[19] As she wrote Berenice Abbott, "I have photographed everything within reason or unreason around here, having lately made a study of negroes [*sic*], with an idea of making a book, since I do not like Doris Ulmann's pictures."[20] Welty named her resulting manuscript "Black Saturday," saying, "I used the subject of Saturday because it allowed the most variety possible to show a day among black and white people, what they would be doing, the work and the visit to town and the home and so on."[21] In other words, with "Black Saturday" Welty attempted to accurately depict race relations in her local environment, but these associations are constantly in flux. Because she captured her subjects in photographs that exist across time, these relationships and our understanding of them are not constant, but subsist in a constantly morphing reiteration, one dependent on changing sociopolitical circumstances.

Between 1933 and 1937, Welty stalwartly sought publication of her unique photographs, including *Making a Date*. Describing her early struggles, she said, "I tried to sell those pictures to fiction editors . . . Once a year for three or four years I carried around two bundles [one of pictures, one of short stories] under arm on my two-weeks' trip to New York, and carried them home again."[22] In 1935 Welty pitched "Black Saturday" to publishers Harrison Smith and Robert Haas in New York.[23] Smith rejected the manuscript, writing, "I am sorry to say that we have decided not to take it. The photographs are excellent and, together, present an engaging picture. But in view of Julia Peterkin's book [*Roll, Jordan, Roll*] last year, and the general unwillingness of the public to buy many books at all, we feel too doubtful about a sale which would satisfy you or justify ourselves in adding "Black Saturday" to our list."[24] In 1937, after the publication of several of her short stories in literary magazines and the successful publication of Margaret Bourke-White and Erskine Caldwell's *You Have Seen Their Faces*, Welty again sought publication of "Black Saturday," sending her manuscript to Harold Strauss at Covici-Friede. He rejected the manuscript, citing marketability as the main issue. As he writes, "The book sellers would not be able to classify your volume at all, nor to find the proper counter for it. The short stories themselves offer untold publication difficulties. Combined with photographs, the difficulty is insuperable."[25] Welty also sent her manuscript to Whit Burnett at Story Press, who likewise cited prohibitive publication costs.[26]

I challenge publishers' insistence that marketability and classification prevented publication of "Black Saturday." Book sales steadily increased after 1936, dozens of photo-texts, including *Roll, Jordan, Roll* and *You Have Seen Their Faces*, were published in the 1930s, and "Black Saturday" is easily classifiable as a photographic book—the most popular genre of the era. Photographic magazines like *Life* and *Look* were prevalent, and the public enjoyed viewing the world through pictures; this was the "Golden Age" of Hollywood. As William Stott notes, "A documentary motive was at work throughout the culture of the time: in the rhetoric of the New Deal and the WPA arts projects; in painting, dance, fiction, and theater; in the new media of radio and picture magazines; in popular thought, education, and advertising."[27] Welty's photographs both fit within and work against this tradition.

Welty took humanistic portraits of African Americans, primarily women and children, not poor whites, like the predominant output of the FSA. Welty's images, taken independently and free from the conventions and demands of a federal agency, seem informal when compared to those created for the FSA file. When viewed in the context of the early 1930s and in contrast to those of FSA photographers working in Mississippi (Arthur Rothstein, Ben Shahn, Walker Evans, Dorothea Lange, Russell Lee, and Marion Post Wolcott), they illustrate how her work neither confirms contemporary expectations nor presents propagandistic views popular at the time. Welty created formally interesting compositions without treating people like arrangements of positive and negative space. Furthermore, she created an intimacy with her subjects that was exceptional for the period. In the mid-1930s, candid photographs of black southerners like *Making a Date, Grenada, Mississippi*, which show people in ragged clothing, conversing naturally on the street, were rare. More familiar were pictorialist images like Gertrude Käsebier's *Black and White* (1902) and James Latimer Allen's *Madonna and Child* (ca. 1930), or photographs like Edward Steichen's *Ripe Corn*, which was the cover image for the inaugural issue of *U.S. Camera Magazine* (1934). Käsebier's photograph imitates nineteenth-century painting in both style and content. The image is in soft-focus to emphasize the romanticism of the subject, a black housekeeper hanging white linens to dry on the line. Like Jean-François Millet, whose paintings ennoble and idealize mid-nineteenth-century French peasantry, Käsebier freezes her subject in a constructed and romanticized antebellum past. Although created in 1902, the laundress looks as if she has been lifted from Eastman Johnson's *Old Kentucky Home* (1859). The woman, wearing an outdated prairie-style dress and long gingham apron, smiles broadly for the camera, and the valuation of the photograph emphasizes the contrast between black and white—both in the image and in society. Here, the black woman's body is a cipher for slavery's antiquated ideas, both marking and masking the racial strife and inequality of Reconstruction. Allen's image, while ostensibly celebrating his black subject through the creation of a Virgin Mary and Christ Child vignette, is a posed construction of sentimentality. Steichen's photograph, on the other hand, is in the ethnographic tradition of the overerotized and supersexualized Other. Following Natanson, Käsebier's image is of the poor yet contented trope, Allen's follows the suggestion of blacks as hard-praying optimists, and Steichen's photograph, perhaps most egregiously, presents a black woman as a sexualized primitive, erotically yielding the bounty of the earth. Welty's photograph does not conform to these stereotypes. Instead, her candid image of a couple on a street corner is realistic yet cryptic, and interesting precisely because of its ambiguity.

It seems obvious to me that a tremendous market existed for photographic books in the 1930s; the question instead was the marketability of a book of photographs of African Americans that did not adhere to stereotypical expectations. Unlike *Roll, Jordan, Roll,* which presents peculiar and sentimental portraits in the tradition of Edward Curtis's "vanishing race" trope, and *You Have Seen Their Faces,* which offers politicized and biased views of southerners, Welty's African American subjects are not contrived victims but multifaceted individuals. Because it did not fulfill the expectations of northern publishers, readers, or viewers, "Black Saturday" was not published during the 1930s, and with her growing success in fiction, Welty began to concentrate her professional ambition on writing. We do not have the binders she shopped to publishers, and it is reasonable to assume that as she published her stories and took more photographs, the composition of "Black Saturday" evolved. Yet we do have Welty's archive of photographs taken in Mississippi during the 1930s. It was not destroyed; instead, she neatly and conscientiously kept her files of negatives and prints. Her photographs later provided inspiration for characters and scenes in her stories and novels, and, as I will show, she continued to seek publication and exhibition of these extraordinary images. Yet in each instance of reception, their meaning changed.

2. A Local Exhibition, Mississippi Art Association, 1934

The first time *Making a Date, Grenada, Mississippi* was shown to the public was probably in a local art exhibit held in Jackson in July 1934. Sponsored by the Mississippi Art Association, which was formed in 1901 to support and promote the artwork of Mississippians, the exhibition was billed as "an unusual exhibition and one of peculiar local interest."[28] The show included photographs by both Welty and Hubert Creekmore as well as watercolor paintings by William Hollingsworth Jr. Creekmore was a close friend of Welty's, and they often photographed their surroundings and each other as well as attended events around town together. Hollingsworth, for his part, had recently returned to Jackson after graduating from the School of the Art Institute of Chicago.[29] Shortly after moving back to Mississippi, black culture became his primary subject.[30] He often visited the Farish district of Jackson, home to the city's black population, to find inspiration for his genre scenes of African American life. Despite forced segregation under Jim Crow, the lives of black people became mainstays in Hollingsworth's and Welty's art, and although they rarely intermingled socially with blacks, they seem to have been drawn to represent the lives of Mississippi's black citizens.[31]

Whatever their motivations, this group exhibit, offering works of different subjects in diverse media by local artists, was well received by the Jackson community. Promoted with luncheons and open houses, the show was marketed to Jackson's society-crowd and complemented the city's construction of itself as cultured and cosmopolitan. In an article dedicated to the photography portion of the exhibit, the *Daily Clarion-Ledger* wrote, "Some charming still-life arrangements, bits of landscape and rare flowers are among the subjects photographed as well as portrait studies, and the composition in each is very unique."[32] Describing the artists and their techniques, the paper wrote, "These pictures were made with a small kodak and then enlarged. All who are interested in pictures are invited to view this exhibit," which features work by "two of Jackson's young people, [who] have beautifully demonstrated the artistic possibilities of photography."[33]

Welty's image provided viewers with an unusual opportunity. Some of the only precedents for photographs of Mississippi's African Americans were studio portraits, like those of Henry Norman and Richard Henry Beadle.[34] Norman, working in the late 1800s, created artfully staged portraits of Natchez's black community, and Beadle, an African American, operated a thriving studio in Jackson's Farish district. Another Mississippian, J. C. Coovert, worked documenting rivers, floods, and cotton culture in the late nineteenth century.[35] His *Flood Waters at Greenville* (1883) documents displaced African American farmers. Unlike these precedents, Welty's photographs are not staged studio portraits or documents of natural disasters; they are genre scenes of everyday black southern life, and they offered the local audience a new way of interacting with African Americans and visualizing their regional identity.

Jackson's white viewers would not have been at all exceptional if they constructed their identity both in coordination with and in opposition to black Mississippians. Societal norms and race relations depended on an oppositional conception of identity. At the same time, the audience at this show, through their voyeuristic appreciation and potential ownership of Welty's photographs, could also own its subject. This interaction between viewer and subject would have been further enhanced by the presence of the plate-glass window in *Making a Date*. Localized viewers could effortlessly place themselves in its reflection and become the taker of the image.[36]

Welty had been in Jackson for three years, taking photographs and working various jobs, including society columnist for the *Memphis Commercial
Appeal* and newspaper columnist and feature photographer for the *Daily Clarion-
Ledger*, when this exhibit was held. Not finding a publisher for "Black Saturday," Welty sought other ways to bring her photographs to the attention of the
public. Combining her images with that of fellow artists gave her an exhibition opportunity while also providing feedback, sales opportunities, and confidence.[37]

3. *Eyes on the World*, 1935

The next time *Making a Date, Grenada, Mississippi* appeared, it was to a national audience in Lincoln Schuster's *Eyes on the World: A Photographic
Record of History-in-the-Making*. Released in June 1935, *Eyes on the World* is
an oversized 301-page coffee-table book, filled with over 350 black-and-white
photographs drawn from a range of source material.[38] Its goal, as described
by the publisher in the foreword, was "to provide a photographic record of
history-in-the-making for the entire year 1934 and the first part of 1935."[39] The
book, divided into seven sections of varying lengths and well received in the
press, covered topics including world politics, the New Deal, and popular culture. A *New York Times* reviewer, reiterating the belief that photographs present
infallible representations of reality, declared, "One thing stands out from the
book as a whole: the camera is going to make it easy for the historian of manners when he comes to resurrect our times."[40] Any ease the camera provides
the historian is equally abated by its insistence to complicate, however, because
as Trachtenberg reminds us, "Between an exposed photographic plate and the
contingent acts whereby people read that inscription and find sense in it lies
the work of culture."[41] In other words, the understanding of any image is complicated by the ideology of the photographer, the situation and placement of
the image, and the position of the viewer. No matter how authentic, documentary, candid, or unbiased they may appear, photographs are never static and literal transcriptions of reality. This tension between authentic evidence and constructed fiction is at the heart of every photographic image. The camera and its
resulting images both enable and frustrate our understanding of the past.

A diverse group of photographers contributed to *Eyes on the World*, including Edward Steichen, Robert Disraeli, and Margaret Bourke-White. Steichen,
who had been a leader in both the pictorialist and straight photography move-

ments before embracing photography's commercial applications, is described in the afterword as a frankly commercial photographer who "exalts commercialism and decries art for art's sake."[42] Alternately, Disraeli and Bourke-White were both members of New York's Photo League, a cooperative of socially committed amateur and professional photographers. The text explains that Disraeli's "candid shots have been widely used for magazine and book illustration and advertisements" and that his "recent book of photo-micrographs, *Seeing the Unseen*, has been hailed as an extraordinary piece of work."[43] Bourke-White, billed as "one of America's most famous industrial photographers," is lauded for her work for *Fortune* as well as her photo-mural projects.[44] Welty does not receive a biography in the text, but one can imagine that she was excited by the inclusion of her photograph in such a major publication.

Located on the lower right-hand corner of page 261, the now cropped, five-by-three-inch photograph shares the page with three other photographs and has been retitled by the editors *Pickup—Deep South*. This cropping and retitling illustrates the ways in which a photograph's "framing" changes or at least augments its meaning. The particularized place of Jackson has been replaced with the generalized "Deep South," forcing Welty's couple to represent all of black southern life. Furthermore, a pickup artist is someone (usually a man) who is skilled in attracting and seducing the opposite sex, perhaps with somewhat sleazy one-liners, whereas "making a date" more simply implies arranging a future romantic meeting. Additionally, the photograph is oddly placed on a page titled "A Pause in the Day's Occupation." The other photographs, one of a middle-aged man titled *Window-shopping in New York*, another of an accordion player and singer surrounded by onlookers titled *Impromptu Concert—Paris*, and one, *Les Halles—morning*, that shows peasant women in an outdoor market carrying baskets of bread, offer specific yet stereotypical views of life in different geographical areas. People on break in New York and Les Halles shop, those in Paris enjoy music, and those in Mississippi seduce. The facing page features two photographs, one above the other. The top image, *They're Off*, shows the start of a horse race; the lower photograph, *Rodeo*, depicts a man wrestling a bull. These images—and some more than others—seem tangentially related to a culture of commodity exchange. Because of the cropping, placement, and retitling, the viewer of the image in *Eyes on the World* surely interpreted the couple's interaction as sexualized. Although the introduction to the book instructs the reader that "the camera will not lie, and cannot flatter or defame . . . The art and science of photography . . . reveal[s] human beings of flesh and blood as they really are, and not merely as they are made to seem in the banal poses of the studio," it seems apparent that a photograph's meaning is anything but fixed.[45] Photographs are always put to some purpose, especially when selected by an editor, cropped, arranged, captioned, and placed among other images.

Welty's photograph is one of only seven in the book that feature African Americans, and three of these are part of a single photomontage, *Workers of the World Unite*. Contributed by the Film and Photo League, the image shows a black man in a suit holding a hand-drawn poster depicting the blue eagle of the National Recovery Act above a depiction of the hanging of Euel Lee and the lynching of George Armwood. Lee, who was convicted of killing a white family of four in 1931 and executed in 1933 in eastern Maryland, was the first black man to successfully secure appeals in two trials. Days after Lee's execution, Armwood was accused of raping an elderly white woman in a neighboring town. Before a trial could take place, a mob overtook the jail and lynched him. Their images are flanked by the words "We Will Never Forget." Another photograph in the montage shows a black demonstrator holding a "Free the Scottsboro Boys" sign. This page is filled with contentious and highly charged subject matter of a racial and timely nature, whereas the next image in the book of a black person is a headshot of blues vocalist and actress Ethel Waters commended for her performance in the musical review *As Thousands Cheer*. The remaining photographs of black Americans all appear in the same section as Welty's image. One, captioned *Man Power*, shows the glistening backs of ten black men working on a boat; another, *Of Human Bondage*, shows a black woman working a plow in which a black man takes the place of the mule. Collaged over the photograph, a newspaper headline reads, "League to Renew Drive on Slavery." On the opposite page, Margaret Bourke-White's *Men against the Sea, Newport Yacht Races for the America's Cup* depicts black sailors performing physical labor. Using Natanson's categories, the subjects of these images are presented as agitators, spectacles, laborers, victims, and noble primitives. Welty's photograph could be viewed alternately as reinforcing stereotypes of southern blacks or as opposing them. Reception would have been influenced equally by the viewer's identity— black or white, southern or northern. With so many images, often several to a page, however, it is difficult to ascertain what kind of sustained looking Welty's photograph may have received, but that viewing was certainly influenced by its caption, title, size, placement, context, and the circulation of the book. Our full understanding of its meaning is simultaneously enhanced and frustrated as *Eyes on the World* conveys multiple meanings for varied viewers across time. The significance of *Making a Date / Pick-up—Deep South* and its connotations are transformed as viewers, cultural contexts, and race relations change.

4. One-woman Show, Lugene Photographic Galleries, New York City, 1936

When *Making a Date* was shown publicly a third time, the title was changed again. An enlarged twelve-by-eight-inch matte print, now titled *Encounter* and listed without the location in which it was taken, was shown at Welty's one-woman show at Lugene Photographic Galleries on Madison Avenue in New York City, March 31 through April 15, 1936.[46] Welty exhibited forty-five photographs, including still lifes and landscapes, but primarily she showed her images of black Mississippians, like *The Date* and *Madonna with Coca Cola*. The gallery advertised her as a provincial curiosity with limited experience, showing pictures of the quaint southern cultural landscape. The catalog introduced the exhibit to its cosmopolitan audience, presenting "Miss Welty" as "a native of Jackson, Mississippi—in the heart of the share-cropper country. Working with only the crudest of equipment and without much experience in the darkroom, she was able to produce this interesting exhibit which we have the distinction of presenting to the public for the first time."[47]

Because of location and cultural context, *Making a Date* (or *Encounter*) carried different connotations for this audience. New York visitors who saw Welty's work would likely have been familiar with trends in contemporary photography and would very possibly have also visited the Julien Levy Gallery, which was located next door.[48] Opened in 1931, while Welty was a student at nearby Columbia, the Levy Gallery exhibited photographers including Alfred Stieglitz, Edward Steichen, Paul Strand, Eugène Atget, and André Kertész. In 1936 the gallery was showing work by Henri Cartier-Bresson, Walker Evans, and Manuel Alvarez Bravo. One can imagine gallery goers visiting exhibits by photography's leading practitioners and then seeing these amateurish images made under "crude" conditions by a provincial young woman.

Photography was gaining recognition as a high art form at this time, and the date of Welty's exhibit coincides roughly with important photography shows at the Museum of Modern Art including Beaumont Newhall's *Photography*

1839–1937 and Walker Evans's *American Photographs*.[49] Viewers may also have been familiar with Francis Benjamin Johnston's *Hampton Album*, Lewis Hines's child labor images, some of which included black subjects, or James VanDerZee's portraits of affluent African Americans, but most photographs of African Americans taken prior to 1930 were either studio portraits or ethnographic images, and photographs of African Americans by white Americans were exceedingly uncommon. Furthermore, reception was influenced by historical events. The year 1936 was an important one for photography. The FSA was now underway and busy promoting New Deal farm policies and recording the American social landscape, and viewers may have been familiar with some of these images through publications like *Life*, *Look*, and *Fortune* magazines. Although they primarily presented poor whites, when they did show African Americans they were dissimilar to Welty's production, which were taken outside the strictures of a government agency. FSA images, like Dorothea Lange's *A Plantation Owner, Clarksdale, Mississippi, June 1936*, Marion Post Wolcott's *Taking the Cotton from the Truck into the Gin through a Large Metal Suction Tube, Hopson Plantation, Clarksdale, November 1939*, and Ben Shahn's *A One-legged Man Sitting in Front of a Building, Natchez, October 1935* generally presented propagandistic images that fall neatly into the categories delineated by Natanson. These images depicted African Americans as hardworking victims and were intended to elicit an emotional response from the viewer that would generate public support for New Deal programs designed to alleviate the suffering of sharecroppers and reform the southern plantation system.[50] Yet Welty's photograph, while not of this trope, is equally political in nature, if not more so, in its refusal to sensationalize southern life. Her subjects assert their independence, pride, and humanity, not their conformity to pre-established stereotypes and expectations of subservience. They must have seemed quite unusual when exhibited, for not only did Welty train her lens on black Americans, but she exhibited them as people, not as sociological data, political victims, or wealthy curiosities.

Welty's photograph and its reception are influenced by titling, style of exhibition, location, and viewers. New York viewers may have been familiar with trends in contemporary photography, and they most certainly brought preconceptions about southerners and race relations to bear upon their understanding of Welty and her images. Because of the variance in circumstances and presentation, *Making a Date* carried different meanings for the New York audience than it had in Jackson or in *Eyes on the World*.

5. *One Time, One Place*, 1971

Finally, in its fourth public reception and the fifth instance presently under examination, Random House published *Making a Date, Grenada, Mississippi* under its original title in 1971 in Welty's *One Time, One Place: Mississippi in the Depression, a Snapshot Album*. Now an established and award-winning writer, Welty was finally in a position to put forward her photographs the way she intended them to be seen and to publish a version of "Black Saturday," her manuscript rejected thirty-five years before. She chose one hundred of the photographs she took in the 1930s and organized them into four categories that correspond to four sections in the book: "Workday," "Saturday," "Sunday," and "Portraits." She replaced the short stories she had included in the "Black Saturday" manuscript with a five-page introduction.

Making a Date, Grenada, Mississippi is located on page 63 of *One Time, One Place*, across from a similar image, *Making a Date for Saturday Night, Jackson, Mississippi,* and now measures 7 × 4¼ inches. Here, it is not presented as *comparandum* to her fiction as it seemingly would have been in the rejected "Black Saturday" manuscript. Nor is it photojournalism as it was in *Eyes on the World*. Nor is it now high art produced by a provincial for a New York audience as it was in the Lugene exhibition. Neither is it presented with a selection of images in diverse media by other artists as it was in the local group show in Jackson. Now it appears in Welty's own book of photographs. She included it in the "Saturday" section, which is dedicated to images of people at leisure. From the vantage point of over three decades, Welty writes in the introduction, "In taking all these pictures, I was attended, I now know, by an angel—a presence of trust. In particular, the photographs of black persons by a white person may not testify soon again to such intimacy. It is trust that dates the pictures now, more than the vanished years."[51] The unusual quality of Welty's photographs was apparent to reviewers, the *New Yorker* exclaiming, "[It] is a little book as nearly perfect as can be," and "Miss Welty's pictures achieve their double distinction as works of art and as important documents in history."[52] The *Brooklyn Library Journal* wrote, "In its graceful pictures of black people from another age Eudora Welty's collection recalls Frances B. Johnston's beautiful *The Hampton Album;* but Welty's photographs seem deliberately less composed, the beauty more captured than planned."[53] The *New Republic* remarked, "This book, with its one hundred photographs, reveals her to be no Walker Evans or Cartier-Bresson, but nevertheless a thoroughly competent amateur—a person who knew how to get along with, *be* with, the black and white people of her state, and a person who back then, even as later on, had the mind, the sensibility of a poet, and the heart of an exceedingly kind human being."[54] The *New Republic*'s critic compares Welty to two of photography's leading practitioners and emphasizes her humanity. Both Evans and Cartier-Bresson are noted for the objectifying distance they create between their subject and the lens—a distance that confirms their status as professionals. Welty, on the other hand, now marketed as an amateur, avoids violation of her subjects.

Taken together, the images included in *One Time, One Place* create a pictorial narrative that emphasize character and place, and reintroduce a subject now palatable to a post–civil rights era audience. The viewing public of the early 1970s, having absorbed the shock of Robert Frank's photographs presented in his landmark *The Americans* (1959), which provided a snapshot view of American life in the 1950s, was equipped finally to appreciate Welty's casual, humanistic depictions of African Americans. *One Time, One Place*, which presents images of Mississippi life in the 1930s, emphasizes the idea of the "snapshot," terminology that accompanies discussions of the new documentary or social landscape movements as celebrated by Museum of Modern Art director of photography John Szarkowski and exemplified in the work of Robert Frank, Garry Winogrand, and Lee Friedlander, but that was conspicuously missing from the initial conception of "Black Saturday." Was this language consciously employed to fulfill consumer and critical interest in the "snapshot aesthetic" celebrated by contemporary photographers? Are her images really snapshots, as she insists in interviews and as the public seemed to expect? Tina Rathborne, writing for the *Harvard Crimson,* thought they were: "The photographs are more than anything snapshots, where the need to record, and more, the fear of losing dominates the impulse. That they are snapshots throws the emotion behind the subjects into a peculiarly desperate emphasis, which a more professional rendition might have mitigated in favor of a better whole. The effect is heartbreaking—the lighting, the blurring, the posing—one knows one is looking backward through a great deal of time onto a period about which our guilt and our sentimentality hang about equal."[55] By 1971 race relations in the United States had changed, as had the conception of photography and its meaning. The deliberate inclusion of the term "snapshot" situated Welty's imagery in opposition to the FSA's propagandistic production and in line with contemporary discourse, further evincing the photograph's fluidity and how it could be put to different purposes at different times and places to convey multiple meanings.

In conclusion, examination of Welty's *Making a Date, Grenada, Mississippi*, ca. 1930–35, in five places across thirty-five years exemplifies how a single photograph encourages flexible mediations, enacts politicized performances, and creates varied impressions. Like the interaction captured between the photograph's two subjects, those subjects and the photographer, and the photograph and its many viewers, the interpretation of the photograph is dependent on its shifting position and the multiplicity of its presentations. Through her repeated publication and exhibition of one photograph, Welty created an image that could be read in multiple ways by a diverse and wide-ranging audience. She placed her photograph with publishers, local Mississippians, a national book readership, and New York City gallery goers, and she always put that audience in a position to empathize with her subject. She was not interested in the perfectly composed photograph but in the sincere, intimate, and revealing image, and she accomplished her task of creating an archive of black Mississippians and of bringing those images to the attention of the public, all without resorting to nostalgia or romanticism. This is a testament to both her vision and the peculiar nature of her enduring medium—photography.

Notes

An abbreviated version of this article was first presented at the American Literature Association Conference, Boston, 2009, in a session organized by the Eudora Welty Society, "Welty at 100: New from the Archives." I am grateful to the conference participants and members of the Eudora Welty Society for their support and suggestions. I am especially indebted to Harriet Pollack for her careful reading of the text.

1. Marrs, *The Welty Collection*, 77–145.

2. Economic Research Department of Mississippi Power and Light Company, *Mississippi Statistical Summary of Population 1800–1980*, Feb. 1983, MDAH.

3. Photographs, MDAH.

4. Kidd, *Farm Security Administration Photography;* Black, "Back Home in Jackson"; O'Connor, "Framing Time in Expressive Spaces"; Miller, "Finding a Voice: Eudora Welty's Photography and Fiction."

5. Natanson, *The Black Image in the New Deal*, 17–26.

6. In 1977 Black organized *Welty*, an exhibition juxtaposing Welty's 1930s photographs with excerpts from her fiction, for the Old Capitol in Jackson. In 1995 she curated *Eudora Welty, Other Places*. Originally exhibited at the Mississippi State Historical Museum in Jackson, she presented viewers with Welty's photographs of New Orleans and New York City taken between 1936 and 1939. Both exhibits are available as traveling exhibitions from the Museum of Mississippi History, a division of the MDAH. In 2002 with René Paul Barilleaux, deputy director for programs at the Mississippi Museum of

Art, Black curated *Passionate Observer: Eudora Welty among Artists of the Thirties*. *Passionate Observer* was exhibited at the Mississippi Museum of Art in Jackson, Mississippi, April 6–June 30, 2002, before it traveled to fifteen other museums in the United States.

For scholarship on Welty's photographs, see Marrs, *Eudora Welty: A Biography; The Welty Collection: A Guide;* "Eudora Welty's Photography"; "Eudora Welty's Enduring Images"; Marrs and Pollack, "Seeing Welty's Political Vision in Her Photographs"; McKenzie, "The Eye of Time"; Meese, "Constructing Time and Place"; and McHaney, *Eudora Welty as Photographer*.

7. Pollack has developed this argument about Natanson's categories and the representation of race in Welty's photography in a series of presentations at the Mississippi Museum of Art during the exhibition *Passionate Observer: Eudora Welty Among Artists of the Thirties* (2002); in *Colloque Eudora Welty: The Poetics of the Body*, University of Haute Bretagne, Rennes, France, 2002; in the National Endowment for the Humanities Landmarks in American History and Culture Workshop, *Eudora Welty's Secret Sharer: The Outside World and the Writer's Imagination* (2008); in her Society for the Study of Southern Literature session "Welty in Black and White," and in lectures at Bucknell University, Millsaps and Dickinson Colleges. For a fuller examination of how Natanson's types enable us to situate Welty's photographs in opposition to contemporary photographic practice, see Pollack, *The Body of the Other Woman in the Fiction and Photography of Eudora Welty*, forthcoming.

8. Natanson, *The Black Image in the New Deal*, 17–26.

9. Butler, *Excitable Speech*, 147.

10. Butler, *Excitable Speech*, 158.

11. Butler, *Excitable Speech*, 147.

12. This study is interested in the various publications and exhibitions of *Making a Date* up to its inclusion in Welty's photo-book *One Time, One Place* in 1971. *Making a Date* may be familiar to the reader from later publications and exhibitions, including but not limited to: *Photographs* (1989); *One Time, One Place* (1996); Pollack and Marrs, *Welty and Politics* (2001); and "Eudora Welty in New York: Photographs of the Early 1930s" at the Museum of the City of New York and the Mississippi Museum of Art (2008–09).

13. Trachtenberg, *Reading American Photographs*, xv.

14. Barthes, *Image, Music, Text*, 35.

15. Jan Goggins, "Performing Class, Performing Gender: Dorothea Lange's Migrant Women," 20th Annual Conference on American Literature, American Literature Association, Boston, Mass., May 21–24, 2009.

16. Sontag, *On Photography*, 4.

17. Sontag, *On Photography*, 6–7.

18. The Eudora Welty Collection, MDAH

19. Black, "Back Home in Jackson," 35.

20. Black, "Back Home in Jackson," 35.

21. Cole and Srinivasan, "Eudora Welty and Photography," xviii.

22. Bernard Kalb, "The Author," *Saturday Review*, April 9, 1955, 18.

23. Harrison Smith to Eudora Welty, April 2, 1935, MDAH.

24. Smith to Welty, April 2, 1935.

25. Harold Strauss to Eudora Welty, November 1, 1937, MDAH.

26. Whit Burnett to Eudora Welty, February 24, 1938, MDAH.

27. Stott, *Documentary Expression and Thirties America*, 4.

28. Black, *Art in Mississippi*, 172; "Miss Welty and Mr. Creekmore Display Unique Art Studies," *Daily Clarion-Ledger*, July 8, 1934, 13; and "Work by William Hollingsworth Shown at Municipal Club Room," *Daily Clarion-Ledger*, July 22, 1934, 9.

29. Welty, *On William Hollingsworth, Jr.*, 23. This review was originally published in 1958 in the *Jackson Clarion-Ledger* in response to the posthumous exhibition of Hollingsworth's paintings at the Municipal Art Gallery.

30. Welty, *On William Hollingsworth, Jr.*, 23.

31. Perhaps they were influenced by the American regionalism movement and the desire of artists at that time to paint their local surroundings. See Black, "Back Home in Jackson," 39; and O'Connor, "Framing Time," 61.

32. "Miss Welty and Mr. Creekmore," *Daily Clarion-Ledger*, 13.

33. "Miss Welty and Mr. Creekmore," *Daily Clarion-Ledger*, 13.

34. Black, *Art in Mississippi*, 157, 159.

35. Black, *Art in Mississippi*, 159.

36. Lacan, "The Mirror Stage," 1285. Lacan has argued that one's sense of self or identity is created externally through the confrontation with one's reflection. In this model, one's self is constituted in and constructed through recognition of the Other. For further discussion on establishing subjectivity through the recognition of another/object, see Sartre, *Being and Nothingness,* and Butler, *Gender Trouble.*

37. In addition to the exhibition at the Jackson Municipal Art Club, Hollingsworth and Welty exhibited their work at the 1936 Mississippi State Fair (where Welty also took numerous photographs). Welty's photograph *Watermelon on the Courthouse Grounds, Pontotoc* won first prize in the genre category. Hollingsworth won a third-prize ribbon for a landscape, and second prize for a portrait. See "Jackson Leader in Art Awards: Professionals Claim Spotlight in Fine Art Exhibits Here," *Daily Clarion-Ledger*, October 23, 1936, 12.

38. Schuster, *Eyes on the World*, 292–93. Photographs were culled from individual photographers, photographic agencies, newsreel companies, magazines, book publishers, newspapers, and press associations.

39. Schuster, *Eyes on the World*, n.p.

40. John Chamberlain, "Books of the Times," *New York Times*, June 28, 1935, 19.

41. Trachtenberg, *Reading American Photographs*, 6.

42. Schuster, *Eyes on the World*, 295.

43. Schuster, *Eyes on the World*, 295.

44. Schuster, *Eyes on the World*, 294.

45. Schuster, *Eyes on the World*, n.p.

46. The titles were most likely changed by the curator, perhaps in conjunction with Welty, as two titles appear written in pencil on the back of the original prints—one in

Welty's hand and another in an unknown hand. Thanks to Forrest Galey at the MDAH for bringing this to my attention.

47. "Eudora Welty," catalog of Lugene exhibit, MDAH.

48. Thanks to Pearl McHaney for bringing this to my attention.

49. The exhibition catalog is in Welty's collection of books. Thanks to the staff at the Eudora Welty House for sharing their inventory with me.

In 1937 the Museum of Modern Art presented its first survey of photography, *Photography 1839–1937*, under the direction of Beaumont Newhall, who was selected to head the museum's newly created department of photography in 1940. Featuring works by Paul Strand, Edward Weston, Eugène Atget, William Henry Fox Talbot, Julia Margaret Cameron, Matthew Brady, and Timothy O'Sullivan, the exhibit traced the historical development of photography in its first one hundred years.

50. The Library of Congress catalog has 2249 negatives taken in Mississippi between 1935 and 1940. RA/FSA photographers sent to Mississippi include Arthur Rothstein, Carl Mydans, Ben Shahn, Marion Post Wolcott, Russell Lee, Dorothea Lange, and Walker Evans. See Black, *Documentary Portrait of Mississippi*. As Stuart Kidd points out in "Visualizing the Poor White," the RA/FSA was formed to remedy poverty among white rural southerners.

51. Welty, *One Time, One Place*, 6.

52. Brendan Gill, "The Inconstant Past," *New Yorker*, December 25, 1971, 66, 67.

53. John Alfred Avant, review of *One Time, One Place*, *Library Journal of the Brooklyn Public Library*, 1972, n.p.

54. "In Brief: *One Time, One Place* by Eudora Welty," *New Republic*, February 12, 1972, n.p.

55. Tina Rathborne, "One Time, One Place: A Mississippi Album," *Harvard Crimson*, December 1, 1971, n.p.

Bibliography

Agee, James, and Walker Evans. *Let Us Now Praise Famous Men*. Boston: Houghton Mifflin, 1941.

Barthes, Roland. *Image, Music, Text*. Trans. Stephen Heath. New York: Hill and Wang, 1977.

Black, Patti Carr. *Art in Mississippi: 1720–1980*. Jackson: University Press of Mississippi, 1998.

———. "Back Home in Jackson." In *Passionate Observer: Eudora Welty Among Artists of the Thirties*, ed. René Paul Barilleaux, 32–55. Jackson: Mississippi Museum of Art, 2002.

———. *Documentary Portrait of Mississippi: The Thirties*. Jackson: University Press of Mississippi, 1982.

Butler, Judith. *Excitable Speech: A Politics of the Performative*. New York: Routledge, 1997.

———. *Gender Trouble: Feminism and the Subversion of Identity*. New York: Routledge, 1999.

Caldwell, Erskine, and Margaret Bourke-White. *You Have Seen Their Faces*. New York: Modern Age Books, 1937.

Cole, Hunter, and Seetha Srinivasan. "Eudora Welty and Photography: An Interview." In *Eudora Welty: Photographs*, ed. Eudora Welty and Reynolds Price, xiii–xxviii. Jackson: University Press of Mississippi, 1989.

Frank, Robert. *The Americans*. New York: Pantheon Books, 1959.

Kidd, Stuart. *Farm Security Administration Photography, the Rural South, and the Dynamics of Image-making, 1935–1943*. Lewiston: Edwin Mellen Press, 2004.

———. "Visualizing the Poor White." In *A Companion to the Literature and Culture of the American South*, ed. Richard Gray and Owen Robinson, 110–29. Malden, Mass.: Blackwell, 2004.

Lacan, Jacques. "The Mirror Stage as Formative of the Function of the I as Revealed in Psychoanalytic Experience." In *The Norton Anthology of Literary Criticism*, ed. Vincent B. Leitch, 1285–1290. New York: W. W. Norton, 2001.

Marrs, Suzanne. *Eudora Welty: A Biography*. New York: Harcourt, 2005.

———. "Eudora Welty's Enduring Images: Photography and Fiction." In *Passionate Observer: Eudora Welty Among Artists of the Thirties*, ed. René Paul Barilleaux, 9–31. Jackson: Mississippi Museum of Art, 2002.

———. "Eudora Welty's Photography: Images into Fiction." In *Critical Essays on Eudora Welty*, ed. W. Craig Turner and Lee Emling Harding, 280–96. Boston: G. K. Hall, 1989.

———. *The Welty Collection: A Guide to the Eudora Welty Manuscripts and Documents at the Mississippi Department of Archives and History*. Jackson: University Press of Mississippi, 1988.

McHaney, Pearl. *Eudora Welty as Photographer*. Jackson: University Press of Mississippi, 2009.

McKenzie, Barbara. "The Eye of Time: Photographs of Eudora Welty." In *Eudora Welty: Critical Essays*, ed. Peggy Whitman Prenshaw, 386–400. Jackson: University Press of Mississippi, 1979.

Meese, Elizabeth. "Constructing Time and Place: Eudora Welty in the Thirties." In *Eudora Welty: Critical Essays*, ed. Peggy Whitman Prenshaw, 401–10. Jackson: University Press of Mississippi, 1979.

Miller, Allison Mae. "Finding a Voice; Eudora Welty's Photography and Fiction." PhD diss., University of Georgia, 1998.

Natanson, Nicholas. *The Black Image in the New Deal: The Politics of FSA Photography*. Knoxville: University of Tennessee Press, 1992.

O'Connor, Francis V. "Framing Time in Expressive Spaces: Eudora Welty's Stories, Photographs, and the Art of Mississippi in the 1930s." In *Passionate Observer: Eudora Welty Among Artists of the Thirties*, ed. René Paul Barilleaux, 56–84. Jackson: Mississippi Museum of Art, 2002.

Pollack, Harriet, and Suzanne Marrs, eds. *Eudora Welty and Politics: Did the Writer Crusade?* Baton Rouge: Louisiana State University Press, 2001.

Sartre, Jean-Paul. *Being and Nothingness: A Phenomenological Essay on Ontology*. Trans. Hazel E. Barnes. New York: Washington Square Press, 1993.

Schaffner, Ingrid, and Lisa Jacobs. *Julien Levy: Portrait of an Art Gallery*. Cambridge: MIT Press, 1998.

Schuster, Lincoln. *Eyes on the World: A Photographic Record of History-in-the-Making*. New York: Simon and Schuster, 1935.

Sontag, Susan. *On Photography*. New York: Picador, 1973.

Stott, William. *Documentary Expression and Thirties America*. Chicago: University of Chicago Press, 1973.

Trachtenberg, Alan. *Reading American Photographs: Images as History, Mathew Brady to Walker Evans*. New York: Hill and Wang, 1989.

Welty, Eudora. *On William Hollingsworth, Jr.* Jackson, Miss.: University Press of Mississippi, 2002.

———. *One Time, One Place: Mississippi in the Depression, a Snapshot Album*. New York: Random House, 1971.

MAE MILLER CLAXTON

"The Little Store" in the Segregated South

Race and Consumer Culture in Eudora Welty's
Writing and Photography

In the last decade, historians such as Ted Ownby and Grace Elizabeth Hale have examined issues of race in segregated Mississippi using the lens of consumer culture.[1] In the introduction to *American Dreams in Mississippi: Consumers, Poverty, and Culture*, Ownby claims that access to goods and money connects to the American dream of abundance, a democracy of goods, and freedom of choice.[2] While white Mississippians had increasing access to consumer goods throughout the twentieth century, access for black Mississippians was limited. In the 1930s, when Eudora Welty began photographing shopping districts in small towns, stores acted as microcosms of society. Black and white often shopped in the same spaces but with strict rules about how economic and social transactions could take place. By the 1960s, African Americans realized that their dollars gave them economic power. Boycotts of white-owned department stores and other places of business directly impacted the civil rights movement of the 1960s. With the increasing buying power of the African American middle class, white store owners began to compete for African American business. They walked a fine line, offering enough incentive to African American customers to get their business while still maintaining the strict social and physical boundaries supporting the status quo of segregation.

While scholarship on Eudora Welty's writings has increasingly focused on race and politics, few scholars have paid attention to Welty's portrayal of the store as a kind of stage set where scenes of discrimination were played out. As a woman from the upper middle class, Welty had access to the main streets of small towns in Mississippi, where she carried her camera and documented African Americans buying and selling on Saturdays. As a writer, she portrays interactions between whites and African Americans in their roles as consumers. Considered together, Welty's photographs and writings act as dual

Fig. 3.   Gordon Parks, *Department Store, Mobile, Alabama, 1956.* Courtesy of the Gordon Parks Foundation.

narratives focusing on key questions relating to race in segregated Mississippi: Who is allowed to come into the store, and how does the consumer exercise her right to participate in American consumer culture and, ultimately, the American dream?

Images by *Life* magazine photographer Gordon Parks and Welty directly connect issues of race to consumer culture. In 1956 Parks visited Alabama on an assignment to cover segregation in the Deep South. In his photograph entitled *Department Store, Mobile, Alabama, 1956*, a beautifully dressed mother and child stand under a neon sign reading "Colored Entrance" (fig. 3).[3] The woman and her child are obviously shoppers, economic contributors to the consumer culture of the town, but they are second-class citizens in this segregated society, their roles clearly illuminated in the neon sign pointing them to a separate entrance.

Eudora Welty captured an image with a similar narrative in her photograph entitled *Window Shopping/Grenada/1930* (fig. 4).[4] An African American woman, dressed in her Saturday go-to-town best, stands outside a store window, chin in hand, contemplating the contents in the window. While the messages in Parks's photos are more obvious, Welty's subject remains mysterious. Given this time period in Mississippi, could this woman walk into this store, try on the clothes, and make a purchase? If she were welcomed in this store, would she have the means to buy the merchandise? While Parks's photo clearly portrays the injustice of segregation, Welty's image forces the viewer to ask more complex questions about the consumer and store portrayed in her image. The plate glass of the store window suggests a physical separation between the woman and the items in the store window, like the separate door in Parks's photo. Welty's photo, however, suggests other societal barriers beyond physical doors and store windows, such as poverty and lack of opportunity. In her writings and her photographs, Welty displays segregated Mississippi through the store window.

In the time period between 1865, at the end of the Civil War, and the 1930s, when Welty began writing and taking photographs, consumer culture became increasingly important as industrialism produced more and more goods and created a distribution system to get them to consumers (Ownby 82). In the late nineteenth and early twentieth centuries, African Americans who worked as sharecroppers or tenant farmers on a plantation would commonly have shopped for their basic needs at a commissary owned by the plantation owner. These stores would carry items such as farm implements and goods,

Fig. 4. Eudora Welty, *Window Shopping/Grenada/1930*. Reprinted by permission of the Mississippi Department of Archives and Russell & Volkening as agents for the author. Copyright © by Eudora Welty, renewed by Eudora Welty, LLC.

basic foodstuffs and work clothing. The storeowner controlled the purchasing power of the customers, determining prices, allowable debt, and choice of goods, mostly necessities for the home or the farm. Plantation owners did not necessarily view their establishments as stores and themselves as storekeepers (Ownby 70). African American farmworkers would have been separated even from these practical goods by economic forces that limited the cash in their possession.

General stores provided an alternative to the plantation commissary and introduced consumers to the world of advertising. According to Hale, these stores were "the stage upon which many southerners first encountered the new branded items with their colorful packaging, collectible trade cards, and eye-catching outdoor signs."[5] Beauty products were sold although many women were still making their own clothes from cloth bought at the local store. A culture of advertising began to impact all Americans via radio, print media, and signs. Welty's photographs from the 1930s vividly portray this pervasive culture.

Although advertising creating consumer desire began to reach the African American as well as the white population, African American customers faced overt discrimination as patrons of general stores. The stores provided more freedom of choice but certainly not access to the American dream of abundance and a democracy of goods (Ownby 1–2). Ownby insists that they "were not settings for racial equality" (72). Customers were identified by race in store ledgers, and stores were largely owned and patronized by white men. African Americans were often harassed and made to feel unwelcome (Ownby 72–73). They were also expected to abide by certain codes of behavior. The mostly white storekeepers, for example, required African Americans to wait until all of the white customers were served and often sold them poor-quality goods (Hale 172–73). Stores became "muddled middle" spaces, as Hale describes them, where the buying power of African Americans began to increase even as their access to these physical spaces was limited (9).

As a child growing up in Jackson, Mississippi, Welty first learned important lessons about consumer culture in a small store in her neighborhood. She vividly describes her experiences in an essay entitled "The Little Store," hastily characterized by Ownby as a "tribute to shopping" (145). Although she does not connect race directly to her experiences, Welty introduces readers to segregated Mississippi in her description of racist advertising and in the absence of African Americans in her narrative. As a middle-class white child, she was welcomed into this space and initiated into a land of "enchantment."[6] As Welty describes it, the Little Store exemplifies consumer culture as part of the American dream. Welty experienced abundance in the rows of glass jars filled with candy and the Cracker Jack boxes stacked up to form a tower. She could choose whatever she wanted with her leftover nickel.

This "enchanted" world had a darker side. Welty talks about the brand names and advertising she encountered in the store, specifically mentioning "the Gold Dust of the Gold Dust Twins that the floor had been swept out with." According to the *Chicago History Journal* website, Gold Dust products were advertised by the Gold Dust twins, two highly stereotypical African American children surrounded by gold coins. The tag line was "Let the Twins Do Your Work."[7] African Americans, as shown by the Gold Dust Twins, were intended for manual labor. As a child, even as she experienced the "enchantment" of consumerism in the Little Store, Welty was also initiated into racism as she viewed the destructive stereotypes of African Americans used in advertisements.

African Americans could be seen in the advertising in the Little Store, but they were not likely present as consumers. Segregation limited the interaction of whites and blacks in neighborhoods. African Americans would likely have had their own "little stores," probably with higher prices. Most white people in Jackson knew few African Americans even though African Americans accounted for 43 percent of the population. As Susan Donaldson states in her essay here, Richard Wright and Welty never met, although he was only six months older than Welty and the valedictorian at Smith Robertson, Jackson's black high school, while Welty attended nearby Central High.[8] While Welty enjoyed and benefited from her use of the local public library, Wright could not enter and searched trashcans in white neighborhoods for books and magazines.[9] Like most of white society in Jackson, Welty grew up separated from the African American population. Asked in an interview whether she heard stories from black people growing up, Welty replied that she "never saw black people [as a child] except in a white household as a servant or something . . . I never heard black people talking among themselves."[10] Welty emphasizes that she both "knew" African Americans growing up and did not know them, due to their limited roles in white society.

The absence of African Americans in "The Little Store" and in Jackson's white society meant that their stories were not told. Welty suggests in her essay that the store also came to represent untold stories and unexplained violence (822). She ends her essay with a claim that in her trips she learned about disturbing stories being silenced: "With the loaf of bread and the Cracker Jack prize, I was bringing home ... early news of people coming to hurt one another, while others practiced for joy" (826). Something had happened at the Little Store, some act of violence to the family that lived behind the upstairs windows over the store. The children of the neighborhood, however, were not permitted to know the story: "At the point where their life overlapped into ours, the story broke off" (826). Very likely, the violence and abuse suffered by African Americans at this time were also kept from her, a part of the untold, silenced stories that her experience with the corner grocery readied her to listen for. Welty told some of those stories in her writings and photographs.

By the 1930s, stores in small towns and cities would have offered more buying opportunities for African Americans and whites alike. At the same time, these settings created the need for shared space. Welty photographed downtown areas in small towns near Jackson such as Canton and Grenada. In *Courthouse town/Grenada/1935*, Welty vividly captures Grenada's downtown stores from the courthouse lawn.[11] Large signs advertise the Jitney Jungle and Dyre Drug Co. along with Jno. T. Keeton Cotton and Anderson Clayton and Co. Cotton. Men lounge on benches advertising "Spotless Dry Cleaners" and "City Lumber Co." The signs remind viewers of the most important product bought and sold in Grenada in the 1930s, cotton, grown and harvested largely by African Americans working as tenant farmers and sharecroppers. In Grenada, along with other small Mississippi towns, the success or failure of the cotton crop directly impacted the buying power of consumers in the town.

Seventy miles away from Grenada, in the town of Indianola, Hortense Powdermaker documented life for African Americans during the same period Welty was taking photographs and publishing her first stories. As a courthouse town, Indianola, or "Cottonville," as Powdermaker calls it, was an important economic center for the entire county: "On Saturdays, both white and colored tenants come to shop, to look about, to gossip with their friends. This is their chance to enjoy a social time after the week's work, and the Negroes especially make the most of it. Wagons and old automobiles loaded with people drive in. Men and women crowd the dry goods stores, merely looking around if they are not able or ready to buy."[12] Powdermaker lists the businesses surrounding the courthouse and notes that most African Americans make purchases in white-owned stores, although there is a small "Negro business center," in addition to a few small shops in houses "across the tracks" (10–11).

Powdermaker's observations provide some answers to the questions suggested by Welty's photograph of the woman looking in the store window. This woman likely filled an important role as a consumer in her small town. Especially during the Depression, shopkeepers would have worked very hard to keep her business. Very likely, she would have been welcomed into this store. However, she might or might not have been allowed to try on clothes, she would not have been addressed as Miss or Mrs., and she would not have been waited on until after every white customer had been served. Most certainly, her ability to buy would have been impacted by wages of $1.50–$3.00 a week as a housekeeper/cook. If she took in laundry, she would have been paid $.50–$1.25 for a washing, depending on the size of the load (117). A teacher might make about $22 a month for five months of the year (135). Welty's window shopper might have had physical access to the goods in the window but very limited economic access. It is not surprising that she stands outside considering the goods, perhaps viewing them with longing.

In her story "A Worn Path" (1941), Welty describes a white-controlled consumer culture strained across the color line, but she also emphasizes her character Phoenix Jackson's successful navigation of a segregated white society in order to achieve her goal.[13] Phoenix, an ancient African American woman, undertakes a long journey to fetch medicine for her sick grandson. Her primary world is the pine trees, the animals, and the seasonal rhythms of nature, and she negotiates this familiar world successfully. Welty sharply contrasts this rural landscape and Phoenix's more metropolitan and commercialized destination, Natchez. She describes Phoenix's entrance into the town: "There ahead was Natchez shining. Bells were ringing. She walked on" (176). Natchez is portrayed as a kind of wonderland, a fantasy world with its red and green electric Christmas lights crisscrossing overhead, "and all turned on in the daytime" (176). In fact, the unfamiliar electric lights confuse Phoenix, whose world is dictated by the daily circumnavigation of the sun. Welty writes, "Old Phoenix would have been lost if she had not distrusted her eyesight and depended on her feet to know where to take her" (176). The streets are paved so that vehicles can negotiate them more successfully, and electric lights wastefully provide light even during the day. It is also the Christmas shopping season, when people are encouraged to spend money with lavish advertisements, decorated store windows, and other promotions. Money is clearly a necessity in this environment. Phoenix stops a white woman carrying an armful of brightly wrapped presents and asks her to lace up her shoes. The woman "gave off perfume like the red roses in hot summer" (176). This perfumed woman represents the white consumer culture of the city as she participates in the Christmas buying season.

Just as Phoenix negotiates the natural world successfully to get to Natchez, she shows a surprising ability to negotiate the consumer culture of the city. Society defines her as a "charity case" and provides her with the medicine for her grandson free of charge, but Phoenix knows that money takes on more importance in an urban setting and has already taken a nickel from the threatening hunter she meets on the Natchez Trace. The attendant at the doctor's office also offers her a few pennies since "It's Christmas time" (179). "'Five pennies is a nickel,' said Phoenix stiffly" (179). With these two nickels, Phoenix goes to the store to buy a toy for the child, something that will delight him. She thinks, "He going to find it hard to believe there such a thing in the world. I'll march myself back where he waiting, holding it straight up in this hand" (179). Unlike Welty's account of visiting the Little Store of her childhood, Phoenix's grandson does not experience the magic of the rows of candy and the tower of Cracker Jack boxes. He does, however, experience the love and sacrifice of his grandmother, who is willing to take this long journey on his behalf.

In "A Worn Path," Welty sharply contrasts white and African American participation in consumer culture. In 1930s Mississippi, African Americans' political and economic opportunities were limited, at best. Phoenix was born a slave and lives out in the country. She tells the nurse, "I never did go to school, I was too old at the Surrender" (178). Although she does participate in consumer culture in the story, Phoenix's economic power is severely limited by her race. However, she manages to negotiate the consumer culture of Natchez, where she obtains the money she wants and gains access to goods she desires.

Welty's story "Livvie" (1942) explores more complex issues of consumer culture, race, and gender.[14] Livvie is a commodity herself, metaphorically "purchased" in an arranged marriage in which a sixteen-year-old black girl is married to "a colored man that owned his land and had it written down in the courthouse" (276). Welty writes, "Where she came from, people said an old man did not want anybody in the world to ever find his wife, for fear they would *steal* her back from him" (276, emphasis added). Welty describes their relationship in economic terms. Livvie brought nothing with her when she married Solomon except for a picture of the white baby of the family she worked for back in Natchez. Most likely, her family was too poor to have photographs made.

Solomon has taken Livvie far from civilization. There are no stores, but consumer culture reaches even this far into the country. Welty mentions Natchez several times as the closest town, but Livvie and her husband live twenty-one miles up the Old Natchez Trace. Welty describes the house: "It was a nice house.

It was in a place where the days would go by and surprise anyone that they were over. The lamplight and the firelight would shine out the door after dark, over the still and breathing country, lighting the roses and the bottle trees, and all was quiet there" (278). They live open to the earth and the quiet woods surrounding them.

It seems an idyllic world, but their haven has been bought with the hard work of Solomon's tenant farmers, who work in the fields as Livvie keeps the house neat. Welty writes, "Livvie knew she made a nice girl to wait on anybody" (278). Like Solomon's tenants, Livvie works for her husband, even though the working conditions are pleasant. And even in its natural setting, the house contains symbols of consumer culture such as Solomon's pocket watch, indicative of artificially imposed time rather than natural time. There is also a "houseful of furniture," including an organ in the front room, a lace bedspread, a Bible, and "a trunk with a key," all trappings of the middle class (276–77). Solomon himself is described as a rich king on his iron bed "with the polished knobs like a throne" (276), his picture with the "fan of hair over his forehead like a king's crown" (279), and his "little gold smile" (280). As Solomon has grown old, Livvie has become more of a maid serving her master than an equal wife. Paradoxically, Welty describes a black master and proprietor, rather than a white one, living off the labor of African Americans. Solomon has bought into the white middle-class value system.

"Civilization," with its ubiquitous consumer products, intrudes on this rural haven as Solomon lies near death. Livvie looks out her window to see a "white lady" coming up the path: "Marvelous to see, a little car stood steaming like a kettle out in the field-track—it had come without a road" (282). "Miss Baby Marie" is a large woman wearing a big hat, and she sells cosmetics, perhaps the item least needed by Livvie. She "brought out bottle after bottle and jar after jar, which she put down on the table, the mantel-piece, the settee, and the organ" (282). Livvie has never tried cosmetics, but she picks up a lipstick that smells like chinaberry flowers. "'It's purple,' Livvie breathed" (283). Miss Baby Marie urges her to try the lipstick and tells her that it costs two dollars. Livvie explains that she doesn't have any money of her own: "My husband, he keep the *money*" (284). Miss Baby Marie gathers up all of the jars "for both black and white" and tells Livvie that she cannot take eggs as payment (284–85). She warns Livvie that she won't come back again because her house is so far out, but she asks to see Solomon. Miss Baby Marie whispers, "What a beautiful quilt! What a tiny old, old man!" (284). Livvie tells her that she still does not have any money "and never did have," but Miss Baby Marie replies, "And never will?" (284). Both realize that Solomon is dying, and Livvie will soon have his money.

Miss Baby Marie represents the first interloper into the home carefully defended against outsiders, surrounded with bottle trees meant to keep evil spirits as well as seductive temptations from coming into the house. Livvie walks out on the Old Natchez Trace, a road built for moving products and people, including slaves, back and forth across the newly acquired Louisiana Purchase.[15] Welty, we know, was fascinated with the history of the Natchez Trace, and she comments in an interview that in her work for the WPA, she read primary sources concerning planters, outlaws, and other frontier personalities.[16] An article entitled "The Forks of the Road Slave Market at Natchez," by Jim Barnett and H. Clark Burkett, pinpoints Natchez as a center for slave trading with an important slave market linked to the Natchez Trace. Huge numbers of slaves were transported to this market, where some were loaded onto ships for New Orleans. Livestock and other articles were also sold here. As a center for consumer culture, Natchez remains connected to its history as a center for the slave trade.[17]

In Natchez during the time of slavery, African Americans were the commodities bought and sold. Welty connects this history with a more recent consumer culture available to African Americans as Livvie meets Cash McCord, who has "been to Natchez" and wears new clothes from head to toe, "ready for Easter" (286). Livvie soon realizes that Cash must have stolen the money for his fine clothes from Solomon. As they, too, look at Solomon lying in bed, the old man awakes and begs forgiveness for taking her away from her family "and from all the young people [who] would clamor for her back" (289). As if in exchange for the time he has stolen from her youth, he offers Livvie his silver watch.

With Miss Baby Marie and Cash as symbols of consumer culture, Welty does not depict commodities negatively or positively, but she does depict their impact on her characters. In contrast to Cash, wearing his fine clothes bought with stolen money, Welty depicts Solomon as equally fixated on money but valuing land ownership, silver watches, and young wives. Livvie will have to choose between Cash's and Solomon's (somewhat) opposing values, but she will at least have her own money to buy (or not) a lipstick next time Miss Baby Marie drives her car up the Old Natchez Trace.

Like Miss Baby Marie, who sells to "both black and white," Mississippi storeowners needed African American and white customers, and these stores were increasingly places where the two races mixed. Grace Elizabeth Hale notes that

"Saturday afternoons in commercial districts were the most integrated times and spaces in southern life" (182). While races might be separated in schools, churches, restaurants, and other spaces, the ritual of Saturday shopping "belonged to all southerners as black and white, middle-class and poor, men and women crowded into towns" (182). Department stores were spaces where segregation became vulnerable.

Middle-class white women were expected to maintain strict codes of behavior in their interactions with African Americans on Saturdays. Dee Cole Grantham provides an eyewitness perspective on segregation and consumer spaces in Indianola, Mississippi, where she grew up in the 1940s and 1950s. Since her father owned a dry-cleaning business, she experienced both sides of the counter. On Saturdays, she explained in an interview, businesses were open as late as 10:00 PM as people crowded into town for shopping and entertainment. Grantham confirmed that there was indeed mixing, but there were still strict rules for behavior. White people were waited on first, and African Americans always had to give way on crowded sidewalks. African American men would not approach white women.

Grantham grew up working at her family's downtown dry-cleaning business patronized by both whites and African Americans. She remembered that pants cost 50 cents to dry-clean, and dresses cost 85 cents, a sizeable amount given the hourly wages paid at the time for most jobs. African American customers would come to the dry cleaners on Saturdays with their money carefully wrapped in handkerchiefs to get their clothes for church the next day. Grantham's best friends were also connected to downtown businesses catering to African American and white consumers. Sylvia Klumok Goodman's family owned a clothing store, and Martha Andrews Mitchell's family owned the Western Auto. Indianola had two or three clothing stores where African Americans could buy clothing. Grantham remembers that the town's Jewish owners did allow African Americans to use the dressing rooms to encourage their business. Other stores did not. She also recalls a segregated section of town populated with some African American and Italian businesses. White consumers in Indianola did not often go into this section, except perhaps to fetch their maids.

Grantham noted that her family always had domestic help who were considered part of the family, but, like Welty, she knew few African Americans in her town. As an adult, she met an African American man who grew up in her town of four to five thousand at the same time she did. She had never crossed paths with him at all.

African Americans in Indianola who paid hard-earned cash to wear nice clothes to church represented a growing middle class that threatened the status quo of white society with its desire for, and growing access to, better education, jobs, and new consumer goods. In her photographs, Welty captures many of these well-dressed African American men and women strolling in downtown Jackson and small towns nearby. Two particular photos, taken in Jackson, portray the emerging African American middle class. One image shows a woman outside her home wearing a sparkling white nurse's outfit and a fashionable-looking coat with fur around the collar and sleeves.[18] A sign behind her reads, "Clara Humes Obstetric Nurse and Nursing." This woman obviously cares about how she is represented by the photographer, proudly displaying her status as part of the rising middle class. Another photo entitled *Schoolteacher on Friday Afternoon/Jackson/1930s* shows a fashionably dressed woman on a street corner with a valise, presumably waiting for a ride away for the weekend.[19] The woman stands proudly, with authority, hand on hip. These middle-class professional, educated women were important consumers. They very likely walked into department stores and demanded respectful treatment by salespeople as they made their purchases.

As both races responded to pervasive advertising, white and black women began to buy the same brands of hats or dresses, drink the same kind of soda, and drive the same model of car. Hale notes that "middle-class southern whites meeting middle-class African Americans experienced the shock of sameness" (195). Welty strikingly displays this phenomenon in a photograph of two pairs of women, one white and one black, walking toward each other on a narrow railroad train trestle, all dressed in very similar summer hats and dresses.[20] We long for the next frame. Who will give way on the narrow track?

In 1955 a small general store in Money, Mississippi, became the epicenter of a tragic drama played out for all Americans. A fourteen-year-old boy named Emmett Till entered Bryant's Grocery and Meat Market, a store that sold basic supplies to African American sharecroppers, and somehow offended the store-owner's wife, Carolyn Bryant. He was subsequently kidnapped from his uncle's home and found a few days later, dead, in the Tallahatchie River.[21] Mamie Till insisted on seeing her son after his body was returned to Chicago and demanded that the world see his battered corpse. While thousands of Chicagoans saw his body firsthand, photographers captured images that would haunt a national audience after they were published.[22] Till's mother allowed the public viewing of her son's body to become a spectacle in order to force the narrative to become public. Bryant's Grocery and Meat Market was probably similar to Welty's "Little Store," except that its customers were African American sharecroppers.[23] Violence resulted from Emmett Till's ignorance of the "muddled middle spaces" where he could shop but not violate white-imposed codes of behavior.

By the early 1960s, consumer culture in the South was changing even more rapidly, and these changes elicited fear and anger. During the civil rights movement, African Americans who bought goods in southern stores realized that their cash could be a weapon against segregation. They began to boycott stores, demanding more employment and better wages but also respectful treatment as customers (Ownby 152–53). African American customers insisted that they be addressed as Mr., Mrs., and Miss. They wished to try on clothes, and they wanted quality merchandise for their money. Myrlie Evers wrote in her 1967 book *For Us, the Living* that advertising was a kind of "torture" for African Americans because they understood that they were excluded from the American dream as represented by advertising. She explains, "American advertising is responsible for much of the Negro's current demand that he, too, be allowed to participate in the fulfillment of the American dream."[24] Their participation in the market for goods became a mark of freedom. Chain stores were the first to change their policies. They began to hire African American employees and impose policies about courtesy to customers. By the time she was a teenager, the little girl in Parks's photo could likely walk into the department store that had once relegated her to the "Colored Entrance" and have a very different shopping experience.

African Americans' growing participation in consumer culture is reflected in a grotesque "joke" recounted in a *Jackson Clarion-Ledger* column written just six days before Medgar Evers was killed: "It seems that a Negro woman singer of the [Lena] Horne variety, ambled into a New York department store. Espying a large mirror she sashayed up to the looking glass with: 'Mirror, mirror on the wall, who's the fairest of them all?' Answered the mirror: 'Snow White, Negro . . . and don't you forget it!'"[25] In spite of being met with continued racism, African Americans continued to shop in department stores in New York *and* Mississippi and to demand their time in front of the mirror. When they were dissatisfied with their treatment, they took action. Medgar Evers led an NAACP boycott of Jackson stores in December 1962 as part of a larger demand for desegregation (Ownby 152). College students in Jackson wore sweatshirts with individual letters spelling out "DON'T BUY ON CAPITOL STREET."[26]

In her memoir *Coming of Age in Mississippi*, Anne Moody recounts the story of her own involvement in the protests of the stores on Capitol Street while a student at Tougaloo College. Because of her involvement with the NAACP, Moody was chosen to participate as one of three students in a sit-in at the segregated lunch counter at Woolworth's. At first, the waitresses ignored the protestors but soon realized that the three students were asking for service. The employees quickly turned off the lights and headed for the back of the store. Soon, the newsmen arrived and watched as the students were assaulted by an angry white mob. The sit-in and assault went on for three hours before the manager closed the store to prevent looting by the mob.[27]

Welty depicts a deeply segregated Mississippi society in her 1941 story "A Worn Path." Her 1960s stories show a still-segregated world in which African Americans have, like Anne Moody, begun to resist. "Where Is the Voice Coming From?" (1963), written quickly in the wake of Medgar Evers's murder in Jackson and published in the *New Yorker* on July 6, not incidentally reflects changes in the consumer culture of 1960s Jackson.[28] Roland Summers, an educated, middle-class African American, contributes to the urban society of Thermopylae/Jackson and demands the right to equal participation in it. The uneducated white narrator, on the other hand, has to borrow his brother-in-law's truck to drive to Summers's house and notes that in contrast to the dirt road he lives on, "[Summers's] street's been paved" (727). As Suzan Harrison points out, "Summers's neighborhood and home are marked by the signifiers of middle-class America."[29] He drives a "new white car" onto his paved driveway and lives in a well-kept house adorned by nice green grass (728). After killing Roland, the narrator states, "I was on top of the world myself. For once" (729). While the Summers family demanded equal access to the consumer culture in Thermopylae and had money to contribute to the economy, the narrator and his wife are excluded by poverty and ignorance. The narrator's frustration with his own failure to achieve the "American dream" of consumer success leads to Roland's death. Standing over Roland's body, the narrator tells him, "Roland? There was one way left, for me to be ahead of you and stay ahead of you, by Dad, and I just taken it. Now I'm alive and you ain't. We ain't never now, never going to be equals and you know why? One of us is dead" (729). The narrator has created a lynch mob of one, determined to destroy the African American who challenges whites' position "on top of the world."

Through her childhood experiences recounted in "The Little Store," her 1930s photography, and her fiction spanning the 1930s through the 1960s,

Eudora Welty traces a history of consumerism and segregation, a separateness that allowed one race to deny the humanity of another. "The Little Store" portrays the segregation of shopping, with whites surrounded by racist advertising but separated from African Americans. In "A Worn Path," Phoenix successfully negotiates a "white" consumer culture far removed from her own experiences. "Livvie" depicts a hierarchical economy, an increasing desire for goods in the rural black community, and the impact of those desires on a marriage between a successful black landowner and a "purchased" younger wife. The setting on the Natchez Trace emphasizes the entire consumer history of America as new land was traded and "purchased" among different international governments, slaves were bought and sold to work the land, and the new settlers became important consumers of all kinds of goods. Finally, in "Where Is the Voice Coming From?," Welty portrays attempts by whites during the 1960s in Mississippi to stop African Americans who wished to participate in consumer culture as equals, thus keeping white positions secure "on top of the world."

In her photography, Welty uses consumer culture to display discrimination between whites and African Americans in segregated Mississippi. Welty's photo of the woman gazing thoughtfully into the store window emphasizes her removal from the contents of the store window. On the other hand, Welty's dignified portraits of professional African American women suggest new roles for an emerging black middle class. Finally, she shows white and black women occupying both sameness and the same space as they walk toward each other on the railroad track wearing similar clothes and hats.

In her photographs, stories, and essays, whether she photographs a department store window or holds up a mirror displaying a culture of ignorance in her writing, Welty directly confronts issues of race and a culture of segregation. She calls her camera an "eye" and claims, "It was what I used, at any rate, and like any tool, it used me."[30] As an African American photographer in the 1950s and 1960s, Gordon Parks faced similar issues. What could he do to change society? Like Welty, Parks decided to use artistic framing as a kind of weapon: "I picked up a camera because it was my choice of weapons against what I hated most about the universe: racism, intolerance, poverty. I could have just as easily picked up a knife or a gun, like many of my childhood friends did . . . but I chose not to go that way. I felt that I could somehow subdue these evils by doing something beautiful that people recognize me by, and thus make a whole different life for myself, which has proved to be so."[31] In the end, Welty chose words and images as her tools to record and critique the Jim Crow South. In her photograph of the window shopper, the plate glass of the store window might suggest the kinds of barriers commonplace in segregation: economic, social, educational, or even the separation between artist and subject. But Welty's art is not just about seeing the barriers. Hortense Powdermaker writes, "Nothing the White offers to the Negro is more significant in shaping the relations of the two races, than the respect he withholds" (42). Through her words and her images, Welty teaches respect, a respect that might possibly have led to a different interaction between a married woman and a fourteen-year-old boy in a store in Money, Mississippi, or between a white man and an African American man in a suburb of Jackson in 1963.

Notes

1. See Ownby's *American Dreams in Mississippi: Consumers, Poverty, and Culture, 1830–1998* and Hale's *Making Whiteness: The Culture of Segregation in the South, 1890–1940.*

2. Ownby, *American Dreams in Mississippi*, 1–2. Further references are given parenthetically in the text.

3. PDN Online, "Gordon Parks," *Legends Online*, last modified 2000, http://pdngallery.com/legends/parks/intro_set.shtml.

4. Welty, *Photographs*, 16.

5. Hale, *Making Whiteness*, 169. Further references are given parenthetically in the text.

6. Welty, *Stories, Essays, and Memoir*, 822. Further references are given parenthetically in the text.

7. "This Little Piggie Went to Market: The Advertising of N. K. Fairbanks & Co," *The Chicago History Journal*, last modified May 28, 2008, http://www.chicagohistoryjournal.com/2008_05_01_archive.html.

8. Waldron, *Eudora: A Writer's Life*, 15, 16.

9. Rowley, *Richard Wright*, 36.

10. Nostrandt, "Fiction as Event," 14.

11. Welty, *Photographs*, 69.

12. Powdermaker, *After Freedom*, 8. Further references are given parenthetically in the text.

13. Polk, *Eudora Welty*, 367.

14. Polk, *Eudora Welty*, 370.

15. Barnett and Burkett, "The Forks of the Road Slave Market at Natchez," *Mississippi History Now*, accessed September 23, 2011, http://mshistory.k12.ms.us/articles/47/the-forks-of-the-road-slave-market-at-natchez.

16. "An Interview with Eudora Welty," *Comment Magazine*, 24.

17. Barnett and Burkett, "Forks," *Mississippi History Now*.

18. Welty, *Photographs*, 7.

19. Welty, *Photographs*, 4.

20. Welty, *Photographs*, 63.

21. "The Murder of Emmett Till," *American Experience*, accessed September 25, 2011, http://www.pbs.org/wgbh/amex/till/peopleevents/p_defendants.html.

22. Pollack and Metress, "Emmett Till," 4.

23. "The Murder of Emmett Till," *American Experience*.

24. Evers, *For Us, the Living*, 32.

25. Marrs, *One Writer's Imagination*, 182–83.

26. Evers, *For Us, the Living*, 281.

27. Moody, *Coming of Age in Mississippi*, 264–67.

28. Polk, *Eudora Welty*, 375.

29. Harrison, "It's Still a Free Country," 642.

30. Welty, *One Time, One Place*, 11.

31. PDN Online, "Gordon Parks," *Legends Online*.

Bibliography

Barnett, Jim, and H. Clark Burkett. "The Forks of the Road Slave Market at Natchez." *Mississippi History Now*. Accessed September 23, 2011. http://mshistory.k12.ms.us/articles/47/the-forks-of-the-road-slave-market-at-natchez.

Evers, Mrs. Medgar, and William Peters. *For Us, the Living*. Garden City, N.Y.: Doubleday, 1967.

Grantham, Dee Cole. Interview by Mae Miller Claxton. August 22, 2011.

Hale, Grace Elizabeth. *Making Whiteness: The Culture of Segregation in the South, 1890–1940*. New York: Pantheon, 1998.

Harrison, Suzan. "'It's Still a Free Country': Constructing Race, Identity, and History in Eudora Welty's 'Where Is the Voice Coming From?'" *Mississippi Quarterly* 50, no. 4 (1997): 631–46.

"An Interview with Eudora Welty." In *Conversations with Eudora Welty*, ed. Peggy Whitman Prenshaw, 18–25. Jackson: University Press of Mississippi, 1984.

Marrs, Suzanne. *One Writer's Imagination: The Fiction of Eudora Welty*. Baton Rouge: Louisiana State University Press, 2002.

Moody, Anne. *Coming of Age in Mississippi*. New York: Dell, 1968.

"The Murder of Emmett Till." *American Experience*. Accessed September 25, 2011. http://www.pbs.org/wgbh/amex/till/peopleevents/p_defendants.html.

Nostrandt, Jeanne Rolfe. "Fiction as Event: An Interview with Eudora Welty." In *More Conversations with Eudora Welty*, ed. Peggy Whitman Prenshaw, 14–30. Jackson: University Press of Mississippi, 1996.

Ownby, Ted. *American Dreams in Mississippi: Consumers, Poverty, and Culture, 1830–1998*. Chapel Hill: University of North Carolina Press, 1999.

PDN Online. "Gordon Parks." *Legends Online*. Last modified 2000. http://pdngallery.com/legends/parks/intro_set.shtml.

Polk, Noel. *Eudora Welty: A Bibliography of Her Work*. Jackson: University Press of Mississippi, 1994.

Pollack, Harriet, and Christopher Metress. "The Emmett Till Case and Narrative[s]: An Introduction and Overview." In *Emmett Till in Literary Memory and Imagination*, ed. Harriet Pollack and Christopher Metress, 1–15. Baton Rouge: Louisiana State University Press, 2008.

Powdermaker, Hortense. *After Freedom: A Cultural Study in the Deep South*. New York: Atheneum, 1969.

Rowley, Hazel. *Richard Wright: The Life and Times*. New York: Holt, 2001.

"This Little Piggie Went to Market: The Advertising of N. K. Fairbanks & Co." *The Chicago History Journal*. Last modified May 28, 2008. http://www.chicagohistoryjournal .com/2008_05_01_archive.html.

Waldron, Ann. *Eudora: A Writer's Life*. New York: Doubleday, 1998.

Welty, Eudora. *One Time, One Place: Mississippi in the Depression*. Jackson: University Press of Mississippi, 1996.

———. *Photographs*. Jackson: University Press of Mississippi, 1989.

———. *Stories, Essays, and Memoir*. New York: The Library of America, 1998.

DAVID MCWHIRTER

Secret Agents

Welty's African Americans

Eudora Welty's oeuvre includes a handful of stories—I'm thinking of "Power-house," "A Worn Path," and "Livvie"—that focus squarely on African American characters. And as these stories—not to mention the extraordinary photographs of African American subjects she produced in the 1930s—testify, Welty was neither afraid nor incapable of directly representing what she once described as the "differences in background, persuasion of mind, and resources of character there were among Mississippians," including that "half of us" who lived on the other side of the color line under an apartheid regime.[1] "Power-house," which begins by focalizing its titular character, based on the black musician Fats Waller, through the eyes of his white audience at a segregated dance, but which also follows that character to a black café where he can be served during his show's intermission, is especially suggestive of the issues at stake in any white author's efforts to represent African Americans, as it self-reflexively examines the implications of perspective and audience in telling raced lives. Welty's awareness of those implications finds further testimony in biographer Suzanne Marrs's account of the writer's risky decision to read "Powerhouse" to a racially mixed audience—mixed in large part due to Welty's own insistence that the event be integrated—at the 1963 Southern Literary Festival at Millsaps College in Jackson.[2]

If "Powerhouse" is in one sense the exception to Welty's rule—her work, I argue here, more typically locates African Americans as significant but largely inscrutable presences at the margins of her narratives—it also calls attention to a characteristic reticence in her representations of African Americans. In what remains one of the best readings of "Powerhouse," Harriet Pollack explores Welty's strategies of "obstruction" in the story, her deliberately "opaque" representation of the titular character's "loneliness, disappointment, anger, and defiance."[3] For Pollack, Welty's refusal to tell, or tell directly, about Powerhouse is ultimately "a measure of her apprehension for successful interaction with her audience."[4] The story is thus a parable of the writer's encounter with the reader; and "the function of [Welty's] sometimes obstructing style is to transform" that reader—"the willing stranger"—into something like a family member. "Her obstruction of her reader's expectations" for access to the truth about Powerhouse "more than reflects, it enacts her characteristic theme of love and separateness; it leads the reader to experience isolation and to discover communion."[5] Yet if Pollack is surely right in identifying "Powerhouse" as "one of [Welty's] more 'obstructed' short stories,"[6] and nothing short of brilliant in tracing the implications of that obstruction for our understanding of Welty's conceptualization of the artist-audience relation, her reading may nonetheless run the risk of eliding or diverting our attention from another kind of separateness very much at stake in this story: the separateness of the African American in a rigidly segregated world ruled by whites, of the black man who, at the end of his long, improvised story about his suicide wife, Gypsy, and the villain Uranus Knockwood, and despite the demands of his white audience ("don't people always come out and hover near, leaning inward about them, to learn what it is? What is it? . . . Watch them carefully . . .—don't let them escape you" [*SEM* 159]), will only tell us in the end that he *hasn't* in fact told: "His hand stays in his pocket. 'Truth is something worse, I ain't said what, yet. It's something hasn't come to me, but I ain't saying it won't. And when it does, then want me to tell you?'" (*SEM* 168).

Pollack reads "Welty's narrative obstacles" as "leading one to read for the sake of encounter rather than appropriation."[7] But what I'd like to suggest here is that the obstructed quality of Welty's representations *of African Americans* is also a sign of her acute awareness that the structure of black-white relations in the early- to mid-twentieth-century South rendered *any* such encounter, in fact or in language, an all-too-likely scene of appropriation. Indeed, long before we academics began to talk about "subject positions" or to worry about "who can speak" for whom, Welty recognized—and, I would argue, resisted—the problematic patterns of literary representation identified by Toni Morrison in *Playing in the Dark*: the ways, that is, in which "the imaginative encounter with Africanism" so easily becomes merely a vehicle for "white writers to think about themselves"; "the process by which it is made possible to explore and penetrate one's own body in the guise of the sexuality, vulnerability, and anarchy of the other"; the habitual and "strategic use of black characters to define the goals and enhance the qualities of white characters";[8] thus the tendency, in a character like Quentin Compson but also sometimes in the writer who created him, to assume (and this is Quentin) that "a nigger is not so much a person as a form of behavior; a sort of obverse reflection of the white people he lives among"[9]— the tendency, that is, to "encounter" black lives only (Quentin once again) as "sudden sharp black trickles that isolate white facts for an instant in unarguable truth like under a microscope; the rest of the time just voices that laugh when you see nothing to laugh at, tears when no reason for tears."[10]

In a recent reading of *Delta Wedding*, Betina Entzminger applies Morrison's template to Welty, arguing that Welty's African American characters appear predictably as symbols rather than as "fully developed personalit[ies]" in the novel. Welty, Entzminger says, "casts her black characters in stereotypical roles . . . without revealing their internal motivations": the African American, in this case Pinchy, "provides a stage on which at least parts of the white drama unfold"; blackness itself becomes "a metaphor" through which, as Entzminger says quoting Morrison, "the [white] American self knows itself as not enslaved, but free, not repulsive, but desirable; not helpless, but licensed and powerful; not history-less, but historical; . . . not a blind accident of evolution, but a progressive fulfillment of destiny."[11] At best, in this account, Welty appropriates her black characters as symbols "of her own 'personal rebellion' and the repressed guilt associated with it."[12] Intriguingly, however, Morrison herself identifies Welty as an exception to her own analytical template in a 1977 interview in which she called Welty "fearless" on the topic of apartheid. "Nadine Gordimer and Eudora Welty," Morrison remarked, "write about black people in a way that few white men have ever been able to write. It's not patronizing, not romanticizing—it's the way they should be written about."[13] What, exactly, is Welty's difference here? How does she manage to "write about black people" in nonappropriative ways?

First and foremost: writing mostly about the lives of white Mississippians, Welty, I want to insist, knows—as when she acknowledges in *One Writer's Beginnings* that "the body of us" represented at the Mississippi State College for Women was really "only half of us, for we were all white" (*SEM* 921)—just how obstructed her own view of black lives is. If black Mississippians are largely invisible in her stories, that invisibility is itself often represented and called to our attention, nowhere more clearly than in her late story "The Demonstrators," a story which, as Suzan Harrison has convincingly shown, is more than anything else "about reading and writing race and about resisting and obstructing racial readings."[14] Dr. Strickland, who prides himself on his town-fatherly liberal benevolence, claims to know and care for the African Americans he encounters when called to the scene of a double stabbing on the other side of the tracks in his hometown of Holden, Mississippi: "I know Ruby, I know Dove, and if the lights would come back on I can tell you the names of the rest of you and you know it" (*SEM* 737). But Strickland in fact repeatedly fails to recognize black people—the maid who cleans his office; the laundress who informs him she "was washing for your mother when you was born" (*SEM* 739)—who have been part of the fabric of his everyday life for years. Indeed, the story increasingly stresses what he *doesn't* know and, perhaps more importantly, what he doesn't *know* he doesn't know, the things that "he hadn't seen in time" because "it wouldn't have occurred to him to look for" (*SEM* 744). "Don't you know her?" the story's black chorus cries as the doctor examines the female stabbing victim—"as if he never was going to hit on the right question" (*SEM* 736). At the end of the story, Strickland's African American cook "refill[s] his [coffee] cup without his noticing" (*SEM* 749). One incident in particular, based on a memory related in *One Writer's Beginnings*, shows Strickland suddenly recognizing "the old woman in the boiled white apron" as a figure from his earlier life, "the sole factotum at the Holden depot" in the days when he traveled east to medical school. Calling the stations with "just the power of her lungs," "walking slowly in front of the passengers, she saw to it that they left . . . As a boy, he had never even wondered what her name was—this tyrant? He didn't know it now" (*SEM* 740–41). In her memoir, Welty asserts not only that this "Angel of Departure," a formidable "black lady" attendant she frequently encountered at the Meridian, Mississippi, train station, "appears as herself in one story I wrote, 'The Demonstrators,'" but also that "she's there in spirit in many more . . . I thought how often, parked over there insensible in the sleeping car waiting for the same connection, in those earlier times, I'd slept through her" (*SEM* 937–38).

Welty, in other words, knows what she doesn't know about this "ancient and familiar figure," yet nonetheless acknowledges her power and agency as she appears and reappears with metamorphic insistence in a variety of roles, "changing herself" finally "one more time—now into the porter," to "start loading her arms and shoulders with all our suitcases, as many as she could carry at one time, and herd us down the platform to our day-coach, getting rid of us herself to make sure *we* were gone" (*SEM* 937–38). If Welty's representations of black characters in some senses inevitably marginalize or silence

African Americans—"how often I'd slept through her"—the reticent or deliberately withheld or obstructed quality of those representations, I believe, also works as a kind of vigilance *against* representation, against appropriating the (black) Other to shore up the (white) self or to ensure the self (as in the case of Dr. Strickland) of its own benevolence, and as a means to acknowledge the invisible agency of those others: *their* power, as it were, to see to it that *we* leave, and their capacity for resisting appropriation and/or mediation by white authors and readers, however well-intentioned. In this sense, Welty might be understood as anticipating Rey Chow's caution, in *Writing Diaspora*, that "our fascination with the native, the oppressed, the savage and all such figures is . . . a desire" (think *Powerhouse*) "to hold on to an unchanging certainty somewhere outside our own 'fake' experience"—"a not too innocent desire to seize control."[15] Welty, whose lifelong liberal and antisegregationist politics are a matter of record, nonetheless also recognized the double-binds inherent in *any* attempt by a white Mississippian to represent southern African Americans.[16] Vigilant against the forms of appropriation and, as Chow puts it, "defiled images" that would reduce them, *pace* Morrison, to the status of "white man's symptom," she also resists the equally disempowering impulse "to revere them as silent objects." "Defilement and sanctification," notes Chow, "belong to the same symbolic order": "is there any alternative for these 'natives?'"[17]

Like Chow, or like Gayatri Spivak, whose notorious question, "Can the subaltern speak?" has spawned two decades of intense and still-unresolved if productive debate around this "catch-22" of representation and silencing, Welty is committed to exploring non-appropriative representational, narrative, and linguistic "alternatives" in the encounter between raced strangers enacted in her own writing.[18] The strategies of reticence that inform her representations of African Americans, and the acts of obstruction or withholding performed by those characters in her texts, are analogous to the quality Spivak attributes to J. M. Coetzee (like Gordimer and Welty a writer profoundly affected by apartheid) in her reading of Coetzee's *Foe*. Unlike Defoe's *Robinson Crusoe*, Spivak argues, in which the "savage" Friday is converted into the obedient native informant, the Friday of *Foe* is "the unemphatic agent of withholding in the text. For every territorial space that is value coded by colonialism *and* every command of metropolitan anticolonialism to yield his 'voice,' there is a space of withholding, marked by a secret that may not be a secret but cannot be unlocked. The 'native,' whatever that might mean, is not only a victim but an agent. The curious guardian at the margin will not inform."[19] Welty's work, from Powerhouse to Pinchy to the Angel of Departure and beyond, is replete with such secret agents, black figures "at the margin who will not inform," guardians of an unassimilable—Spivak uses the term "non-narrativisable"[20]—margin, who in their stubborn refusal to inform signal their resistance to the aesthetic and epistemological systems that seek to understand them, even those that try to do so benevolently and responsibly, and whose presence signals in her stories a larger world of knowledge and purpose and motivation that is deliberately withheld. Welty's fictions thus share the qualities Spivak admires in narratives like *Foe* and Jean Rhys's *Wide Sargasso Sea*, the latter of which she praises for its ability to "mark, with uncanny clarity, the limits of its own discourse; in Christophine, Antoinette's black nurse."[21] Rhys's novel, in Spivak's formulation, "stages the non-containment of Christophine," a "powerfully suggestive figure" who is nevertheless, "in the end and textually, . . . let go" through an act of "textual . . . abdication" that is simultaneously "a move to guard the margin."[22] As in Rhys's treatment of Christophine, Welty's fictions "will not attempt to contain" the African Americans they must inevitably represent in rendering the lives of white Mississippians; like Christophine, Welty's black characters are "let go" (and let go *of*), "quietly placed out of the story" in a manner that calls attention to all that she doesn't know, and doesn't claim to know, about them.[23]

In one sense, to be sure, this pattern of obstructed or withheld representation points to Welty's career-long attraction to figures who can't and/or don't want to be known, don't want their stories told, and won't be made to tell them if they don't want to. I'm thinking here of the orphans in "Moon Lake," who, as Nina Carmichael enviously recognizes, "were not answerable . . . not answerable to a soul on earth" (*SEM* 425); of Eugene MacLain, who, as Virgie Rainey, sensing a kindred soul, thinks at the end of "The Wanderers," "had lived in another part of the world, learning while he was away that people don't have to be answered to just because they want to know" (*SEM* 552–53); of those instinctive Renfro rebels in *Losing Battles*—Vaughn and Gloria—who aren't so sure they want their stories to be told into the endless tale of a family in which telling and what can be told are the sum and end of life itself. Welty is always attuned to the "non-narrativisable" in her characters' lives, to their desire not to be known or tell or be told.[24] In an extraordinary moment in *One Writer's Beginnings*, Welty describes "one of those inexplicable stops" of a train in the middle of nowhere Tennessee. "It was sunset. Presently, without a word, a soldier sitting opposite me rose and stepped off the halted train. He hadn't spoken to anybody for the whole day and now, taking nothing with him and not stopping to put on his cap, he just left us. We saw him walking right away from the track, into the green valley, making a long shadow and never looking back. The train in time proceeded, and as we left him back there in the landscape, I felt *us* going out of sight for *him*, diminishing and soon to be forgotten" (*SEM* 941).

But something more, I think—something that signals Welty's specific and keen attention to the black lives at the margins of her text and her culture, and that amply justifies Morrison's praise of her writing about African Americans ("the way they should be written about")—is going on in Welty's persistently withheld portrayals of withholding African Americans.[25] *Delta Wedding* is probably the most obvious example here: think of Partheny and Aunt Studney and Man-Son, as well as Pinchy, figures Barbara Ladd long ago recognized, *contra* Entzminger, as "never simply a 'sign' for the white characters."[26] As Ladd puts it, "*[s]omething* happens" to the black characters in this novel "behind the veil" that separates them from the white characters, but "we never know exactly what does happen"—a not knowing, I would argue, that Welty paradoxically understands and practices as a necessary way of approaching and representing African American lives and histories. Indeed, as Ladd suggests, it is in some sense precisely Welty's refusal to reveal the secret—of Pinchy's "coming through," of Root's knife fight with Big Baby, of Partheny's "mindlessness"— that allows her to "claim for her black characters" the same agency, "the same impulse to love and separateness . . . that she claims for her white characters."[27] Aunt Studney, her name an audible echo of the *only* response she ever provides to the demand that *she* inform, tell, reveal ("Ain't studyin' you"), becomes—to lean on Spivak once more—emblematic of all the stubbornly uninformative guardians of the heterogeneous space of subalternity that was the space occupied by African Americans in the South Welty knew. "That's what she says to everybody—even Papa," Roy tells Laura. "Nobody knows what she's got in the sack."[28] Aunt Studney's obstructing response to the demand that she reveal what's in her bag, or in her life, is also a measure of her refusal to *be* studied. Watching her holding the mouth of her sack, "it occurred to Laura that Aunt Studney was not on the lookout for things to put in, but was watching to keep things from getting out" (*CN* 266). At Dabney's wedding, when all of the novel's black characters appear at the margins of the Fairchild world, the servants "in a ring inside the parlor walls," the windows "full of black faces," Aunt Studney, "wherever she was, was keeping out of sight" (*CN* 300).

The subject of *Delta Wedding*, a historical novel about plantation life set at a very specific historical moment in 1920s Mississippi, dictated what was for

Welty an unusually large cast of African American characters. But the novel's persistent attention to its black characters' obstructive strategies, their refusals to tell or inform, as well as Welty's repetition of that obstruction in the occlusions and withholdings that mark her own narrative, can, I believe, provide a useful template for thinking about the importance of African Americans in her fictions where, to put it somewhat paradoxically, their marginality is less obviously central. By way of example, I want to consider the case of *The Golden Apples*, a text in which black characters only rarely come into direct focus, even, I argue, as their marginal presences repeatedly project hints of their power and agency in the history of Morgana, Mississippi, from the 1910s to the 1940s that is traced in Welty's story sequence. On its surface, that history is exclusively white and largely middle class. In "June Recital," the housebound Loch Morrison, with the aid of his father's telescope, watches the dairyman, "Mr. Fate Rainey and his song" ("Milk, milk, / Buttermilk, Fresh dewberries and— / Buttermilk"), as "he would go past the Starks' and circle the cemetery and niggertown, and come back again" (*SEM* 336–27)—the only occasion in *The Golden Apples* when the existence of Morgana's African American neighborhood is even mentioned. From Katie Rainey's casual observation about the young MacLain twins in "Shower of Gold" ("We heard them charge out, but we thought it was just a nigger that was going by for them to scare, if we thought anything" [*SEM* 14]), to the more ominous moment when the campers and counselors at Moon Lake begin to talk themselves into believing that "the nigger deliberately poked her off in the water, meant her to drown" (*SEM* 444), to Virgie's characterization of the "old wrapped-up negro woman" sitting beside her on the MacLain courthouse stile at the end of "The Wanderers" as "the old black thief" (*SEM* 277), Welty represents southern white racism straightforwardly and without comment. We are made aware throughout this text of white Morgana's dependence on black labor: the work of domestics, cooks, chauffeurs, messengers, and nurses; of yard maintenance and milking and beating snakes and alligators out of the lake; "the sweat of negro diggers" Virgie smells in the Morgana cemetery (*SEM* 543). But such labor does not, in Morrison's terms, remedy the "history-less-ness" of black subjects in the text. Old Plez, however "trustworthy," is only "one of Mrs. Stark's mother's niggers" (*SEM* 327). Juba is "Mrs. Stark's Juba" (*SEM* 548): the "only thing I can do for people any more, in joy or sorrow," remarks Mrs. Stark to Juba as she packs her off to prepare the Rainey household for Katie's funeral, "is send 'em you" (*SEM* 515). In Morgana, it is white people who do things, black people who are used to doing them: African American men and women are everywhere in this text, but their labor, lives, and agency almost disappear, subsumed into Welty's narrative focus on white lives, as they are into the totality of "Southern History."

Almost. Paradoxically, however, the marginalization of African Americans in *The Golden Apples* often works, as it does elsewhere in Welty's oeuvre, to call our attention to the lives and histories this narrative isn't, in any direct way, telling. A reflection in part of her white characters' unwillingness or inability to *see* black lives ("it was just a nigger"), the marginal status of African Americans in *The Golden Apples* is also a function of Welty's own narrative and representational choices, her conscious refusals, as it were, to *see into* those lives, force them to tell. What doesn't happen in *The Golden Apples* is the sort of appropriative idealization of black subjectivity and experience we get in Faulkner's portrayal of Dilsey in *The Sound and the Fury*. What we get instead are rare but crucial moments when African Americans *do* come into focus, not to "isolate white facts" or "reflect" white lives, but to identify, in however fragmentary and opaque a fashion, what Ladd describes as their capacity "to create change"—to point to "their separateness, their dignity, and their power."[29]

In *One Writer's Beginnings*, Welty remarks that, as a child, "long before I wrote stories, I listened for stories. Listening *for* them is something more acute than listening *to* them" (*SEM* 854). And such "listening for"—rather than listening to, let alone presuming to tell—is the hallmark of her portrayals of African Americans in *The Golden Apples*. Welty repeatedly stages instances of obstructed insight that provoke us to ask "What's his story?" or "What's her story?" even as she withholds, and allows her black characters to withhold, the stories in question.[30] In "The Wanderers," Juba, in response to Mrs. Stark's peremptory demand, "How come you weren't here yesterday?" explains, with an opacity that in fact *explains* nothing, that she was at her sister's in the country: "I was comin' back. Sister's place a place once you get to it—hard time gettin' out" (*SEM* 515). At the end of "Sir Rabbit," Mattie Will Holifield looks down on "Morgana all in rays, like a giant sunflower," taking in "the Stark place . . . and the fields, and their farm, everybody's house above trees, the MacLains'—the white floating peak—and even Blackstone's granny's cabin, where there had been a murder one time" (*SEM* 411). In "Music from Spain," Eugene MacLain, wandering San Francisco with his chance companion, the Spanish guitarist, overhears music emanating from a basement club and remembers "away back: there was an old Negro and everybody in Morgana knew when he was in trouble at home; he walked into the store and asked them to play him a record—'Rocks in My Bed Number Two,' by Blind Boy Fuller. Through a basement window he saw an upright piano and a big colored woman playing the keys. She looked like a long way from home. He could not hear her, and realized that there was much noise outside here, in the streets" (*SEM* 498). Such instances of blocked, fragmented access to the African American lives at the margins of Welty's narrative—moments that, like the black figures they momentarily focalize, or like *Foe*'s Friday or Rhys's Christophine, refuse to inform—may themselves be said to listen *for* stories while refusing to know or possess them, a strategy reiterated in a striking scene from "Moon Lake" where Easter, Nina, and Jinny Love, walking back to camp, hear a bird cry from the lake's opposite shore:

> "Hear him?" one of the niggers said, fishing on the bank; it was Elberta's sister Twosie, who spoke as if a long, long conversation had been going on, into which she would intrude only the mildest words. "Know why? Know why, in de sky, he say 'Spirit? Spirit?' And den he dive *boom* and say 'GHOST'?"
>
> "Why does he?" said Jinny Love, in a voice of objection.
>
> "Yawl knows. *I* don't know," said Twosie, in her little high, helpless voice, and she shut her eyes. They couldn't seem to get on by her. On fine days there is danger of some sad meeting, the positive danger of it. "*I* don't know what he say dat for." Twosie spoke pitifully, as though accused. She sighed. "Yawl sho ain't got yo' eyes opem good, yawl. Yawl don't know what's out here in woods wid you."

Twosie, who is described elsewhere in this story as "a tiny daub of black cotton . . . stationed . . . at the edge of things" (*SEM* 421), reminds the girls of what they can't or don't or won't know ("Yawl sho ain't got yo' eyes opem") even as she refuses *their* demand that *she* tell ("Yawl knows. *I* don't know") by putting on the obstructing mask of Butterfly McQueen's Prissy. Her occluded presence—as the girls depart, "she seemed to be fishing in her night's sleep" (*SEM* 420)—hints not only at untold and unheard stories but at alternative languages and epistemologies, at other, potentially powerful ways of knowing and being. But Welty, to echo Spivak's phrase, lets Twosie go. Later, at night, lying "dreamily" in bed and contemplating "the other way to live" she glimpses in the orphan Easter, Nina thinks that "There were secret ways . . . I've only been thinking like the others. It's only interesting, only worthy, to try for the fiercest secrets. To slip into them all—to change. To change for a moment into Gertrude, into Mrs. Gruenwald, into Twosie—into a boy. To *have been* an orphan" (*SEM* 435). Nina here in one sense exemplifies the appropriative "fascination with the native, the oppressed, the savage, and all such figures" Chow finds so problematic: the desire to change into Easter or Twosie is a demand for something "outside [her] own 'fake' experience," the form taken by her "dream that her self might get away from her" (*SEM* 427). And Nina may also be said to figure the artist's—which is to say, Welty's own—assumed metamorphic power to experience and explore otherness, to "slip" into lives as other as Easter's, Miss Eckhart's, Eugene MacLain's, or Virgie Rainey. "I never doubted," Welty once remarked, "that imagining yourself into other people's lives is exactly what writing fiction is."[31] But she nonetheless resolutely resists the desire to "slip into" Twosie, the urge to grasp her secret. In African American figures like Twosie, Welty's text, as Spivak puts it, "mark[s] . . . the limits of its own discourse."[32] It's worth noting, too, that Welty decidedly does not put lower- or working-class whites "off limits"—a clear contrast to her narrative reticence regarding African Americans. Race, not class or gender, marks the self-imposed limits of her discourse.[33]

Part of what we glimpse but can't grasp or know or contain in these "un-narrativised" moments of obstructed actual and textual encounter with African Americans is the degree to which their untold stories are bound up with, and agents of change in, the lives of Morgana's whites. I'm thinking of withheld figures like "the nigger in the hedge" who rapes Miss Eckhart (*SEM* 365)—what, we might do well to ask, was *his* story?—and Exum, doubly mysterious and "apart" to the "Moon Lake" campers as "boy and nigger to boot," "moving along an even further fringe of the landscape" (*SEM* 436), who, giving "Easter's heel the tenderest, obscurest little brush, with something of nigger persuasion about it," causes her plunge into the mysteries of the lake (*SEM* 437). But I also have in mind here characters, secret agents all, such as Plez, that "real trustworthy nigger" whose refusals to tell what he knows about King's Halloween appearance and disappearance in Morgana not only inform Snowdie MacLain's experience of the event—"no'm, Mistis, I don't recollect one soul pass me, whole way from town"—but also shape Katie Rainey's narrative of it (King was "going like the wind, Plez swore to Miss Lizzie Stark," who thinks "she got the truth out of him"; "though he couldn't swear to the direction—so he changed and said") (*SEM* 327, 331–32); or Blackstone, who despite Mattie Will's command—"Turn *your* self around and start picking plums!" (*SEM* 408)—is witness, "in the ecstasy of knowing the end of it ahead of time," to her mythic encounter with King, the empowering moment when "she had to put on what he knew with what he did" (*SEM* 404, 409); or "the old black thief"—an avatar, no doubt, of

Welty's tyrannical Angel of Departure—who sits "alone and together" on the stile with Virgie at the end of *The Golden Apples*, to ensure, it may be, the latter's departure from Morgana, just as her original in the Meridian train depot "ma[d]e sure *we* were gone," but also to hear with Virgie "the magical percussion, the world beating in *their* ears. *They* heard through falling rain the running of the horse and bear, the stroke of the leopard, the dragon's crusty slither, and the glimmer and trumpet of the swan" (*SEM* 556; my emphasis).

As these examples suggest, Welty's African Americans, their uncanny, withholding presences, are persistently mixed up with white lives, nowhere more so than at moments when those lives undergo metamorphic transformation. Indeed, if black agency is habitually evacuated from Morgana's sanctioned narratives and histories, that agency returns powerfully in the fragments of that alternative discourse of history—its "undoing" or "unwrit[ing]," Ladd calls it[34]—embodied in the myths that at any juncture in this text might turn the prosaic residents of Morgana, Mississippi, into potent archetypal wanderers, "something [they] had always heard of" (*SEM* 409). When Jinny Love, responding to Twosie's assertion that "[y]awl don't know what's out here in woods wid you," demands, "Well, what?" Twosie tells her that "Yawl walk right by mans wid great big gun, could jump out at yawl. Yawl don' even smellim" (*SEM* 419–20). "Fishing in her night's sleep," Twosie is linked to the Aengus of Yeats's poem, the figure who, "because a fire was in [his] head," "cut and peeled a hazel wand / And hooked a berry to a thread," and "dropped the berry in a stream / And caught a little silver trout,"[35] and who haunts Cassie Morrison's meditations on untold otherness in "June Recital." (Elsewhere, Nina thinks of "the niggers, fishing" on Moon Lake: "But their boat must be full of silver fish!" [*SEM* 433].) The suggestion, moreover, that Twosie has encountered King MacLain—famously, as we know, a frequenter of Morgan's Woods, and a "mans wid great big gun" who "could jump out at yawl"—implicates her life in the mythography through which Morgana's white women and girls articulate their desires and tell their histories.

The list of the "Main Families in Morgana, Mississippi," with which Welty opens *The Golden Apples*—MacLains and Starks and Morrisons, Carmichaels and Moodys and Mayos and Raineys—concludes with: "*Also* Plez, Louella, and Tellie MORGAN, Elberta, Twosie, *and* Exum MCLANE; Blackstone *and* Juba, *colored*" (*SEM* 317). And if this gesture is in one sense clearly an echo of the end of Faulkner's Compson genealogy ("And that was all. These others were not Compsons. They were black"[36]), it also adumbrates the strategies Welty employs throughout *The Golden Apples* to write about black people, about *their* lives and histories. Relegated to the margins of Morgana's "main families," Welty's African Americans are nonetheless acknowledged as members of and agents in those families. Plez and Louella and Tellie are, like Mrs. Stark, Morgans, the family for whom Morgana itself is named; Twosie, like Elberta and Exum, is a McLane, even, perhaps, as that name might suggest, a "daughter of the swan" like Easter and Virgie, one of King's legendary brood of "children, known and unknown, scattered-like," "growing up in the 'County Orphan's,'" but also in the middle-class households of Morgana (*SEM* 320).[37] Welty here is of course reminding us of a racial—and interracial—history in the South that, like so much about race in her own fiction, is more often than not veiled or blocked from view. But she is also pointing us toward "the positive danger" of such obstructed representational encounters, not only the risks but the possibilities for glimpsing another kind of history in and through the acts of withholding modeled by her black characters and practiced textually in her own narrative occlusions of their powerful presences.

Writing of Welty's "obstruction of the patriarchal plot" and her "displacement of the father," Ladd argues persuasively that *The Golden Apples* "lays a foundation for a different aesthetic of History, an aesthetic of subtly broken silences, strategically dropped stitches, and powerfully authorizing undertows—analogous to those private documents, indirect, tangential, or extraneous references . . . wherein the stories of women are archived."[38] But this description of Welty's aesthetic seems even more compelling in connection with her obstructed and obstructing portrayals of African Americans, those mostly "silent," "tangential," seemingly "extraneous" "guardian[s] at the margin [who] will not inform." Ladd's formulation resonates as well with Dipesh Chakrabarty's effort, in *Habitations of Modernity*, to imagine "another moment of subaltern history, one in which we stay . . . with that which is fragmentary and episodic, not in the sense of fragments that refer to an implicit whole, but in the sense of fragments that challenge, not only the idea of wholeness, but the very idea of the fragment itself (for, if there were not any wholes, what would fragments be fragments of?). Here, we conceptualize the fragmentary and the episodic as those which do not, cannot, dream the whole called *the state* and must, therefore, be suggestive of knowledge forms that are not tied to the will that produces the state."[39] Like Chakrabarty, Welty models a way of writing about subaltern lives that acknowledges the "parts of society," and of history, "that remain opaque to the theoretical gaze of the modern analyst" or author, however liberal or benevolent: "It seems . . . that cultural practices have a dark side. We cannot see into them, not everywhere."[40] Practitioner of the "fragmentary" and the "episodic," of "broken silences" and "dropped stitches," of reticences and withholdings and secrets that will not be unlocked, Welty refuses to represent what she does not know, even as she reaches for the "positive danger" of encounter, for the possibility of other "knowledge forms" that might resist the totalizations of a racist society and history. I point in closing to that other formidable black figure in *One Writer's Beginnings*, bookend to the Angel of Departure, the "black sewing woman" Fannie, whose "tantalizing," gossipy tales, silenced by Eudora's overprotective mother, nonetheless reminded Welty that "listening children know stories are *there*," and taught her "to listen for the unspoken as well as the spoken" (*SEM* 854).

Notes

1. *One Writer's Beginnings*, in Welty, *Stories, Essays, & Memoir*, 921; hereafter cited in the text as *SEM*.

2. Marrs, "'Huge Fateful Stage,'" 78. For Marrs's full account of the episode, see 74–80.

3. Pollack, "Words Between Strangers," 481, 489.

4. Pollack, "Words Between Strangers," 496.

5. Pollack, "Words Between Strangers," 505.

6. Pollack, "Words Between Strangers," 487.

7. Pollack, "Words Between Strangers," 505.

8. Morrison, *Playing in the Dark*, 51–53.

9. Faulkner, *The Sound and the Fury*, 53.

10. Faulkner, *The Sound and the Fury*, 104.

11. Entzminger, "Playing in the Dark with Welty," 65, 53, 59, 60; Morrison, *Playing in the Dark*, 52.

12. Entzminger, "Playing," 64.

13. Toni Morrison, interview with Mel Watkins, 50. For a reading of Morrison's efforts to restore agency to the "ghostly" Native Americans who frequent the margins of her primarily Afro-American–centered texts—a reading that suggestively parallels my own analysis of Welty's oblique strategies for representing African Americans—see Virginia Kennedy's insightful essay, "Indian Presence in the Fiction of Toni Morrison."

14. Harrison, "'Racial Content Espied,'" 94.

15. Chow, *Writing Diaspora*, 53.

16. For an account of Welty's political liberalism, see Marrs, "'Huge Fateful Stage,'" 69–87 *passim*, as well as her *Eudora Welty: A Biography*.

17. Chow, *Writing Diaspora*, 30, 33, 54.

18. Spivak's essay, which famously concludes with the assertion, "The subaltern cannot speak" (308), was originally published in 1988. A recent collection of essays, *Can the*

Subaltern Speak? Reflections on the History of an Idea, edited by Rosalind Morris, suggests the range of the debates to which Spivak's provocation has given rise.

19. Spivak, *Critique of Postcolonial Reason*, 190.

20. In an interview, Spivak attributes the strength of subaltern resistance in the face of modern capitalism to the fact that subalterns are "non-narrativisable"; see *The Post-Colonial Critic*, 144.

21. Spivak, *Critique*, 129.

22. Spivak, *Critique*, 125 n.23, 129, 131, 132.

23. Spivak, *Critique*, 130. For a recent critique of Spivak's reading of Christophine that might suggest the limits and contradictions potentially inherent in Welty's liberalism on race issues, see Shakti Jaising's "Who Is Christophine?" Jaising argues that Spivak's (and subsequent critics') postcolonial critique, while providing "a powerful intervention within Anglo-American criticism of *Wide Sargasso Sea*, . . . has also overlooked how depictions of agency by the formerly enslaved acknowledge innate individuality while simultaneously masking the encumbered nature of this individuality. Rhys's novel . . . sets limits to the agency of the black Creole woman in the very act of depicting her as autonomous and individualistic." Thus a character often read "as emblematic of resistant subalternity" is simultaneously "the product of a longstanding racial and colonial typology" (831).

24. Virgie herself "had often felt herself at some moment callous over, go opaque; she had known it to happen to others." She had, Welty writes, "felt a moment in her life after which nobody could see through her, into her—felt it young" (*SEM* 545).

25. It hardly needs to be stressed that strategies of reticence, silence, and withholding were often a matter of survival for African Americans in the South, where, as Richard Wright observes in *Black Boy*, "the penalty of death awaited me if I made a false move" (172). The fraught nature of the black-white "encounter" in pre–World War II Mississippi, and its implications for assessing Welty's own *textual* encounters with African Americans, are highlighted by Richard Brodhead's sketch, drawn from a scene in *Black Boy*, of an imaginary meeting between Welty and Wright in the Jackson they both inhabited:

> A scene dear to me because it comes as close as we get to encountering Eudora Welty in the pages of *Black Boy* shows the workings of Wright's psychic life as a racially terrorized subject. When young Richard tries to raise money by selling his dog in a "white neighborhood [of] wide clean streets and big white houses," a pleasant young woman comes to the door . . . But when this girl disappears into the house to look for her money, Wright cannot *not* attach this pleasant individual white person to the omnipresent, disembodied force of white terror that his world has instilled in him as the primary connotation of whiteness. In mounting anxiety he believes the girl must have gone to summon the force he expects and fears whites to bring to bear on blacks: a lynch mob.

See Brodhead, "Two Writers' Beginnings," 11; Wright, 69–71.

26. Ladd, "'Coming Through,'" 550.

27. Ladd, "'Coming Through,'" 551.

28. *Delta Wedding*, in Welty, *Complete Novels*, 262; hereafter cited in the text as *CN*.

29. Ladd, "'Coming Through,'" 550–51.

30. I'm echoing here a moment in "The Wanderers" when Virgie, passing the grave of King MacLain's grandfather, thinks, "Who remembered his name and what he did? . . . Didn't he kill a man, or have to, and what would be the long story behind it, the vaunting and the wandering from it?" (*SEM* 553).

31. Welty, "Looking Back at the First Story," in *Occasions*, 304.

32. Spivak, *Critique*, 129.

33. Virgie and Easter, in particular, function for the more privileged middle-class girls of Morgana in ways that resonate with Chow's analysis of the idealized "native."

34. Ladd, *Resisting History*, 53, 52.

35. Yeats, "The Song of the Wandering Aengus," in *Collected Poems*, 57.

36. Faulkner, "Appendix: Compson, 1699–1945," in *The Sound and the Fury*, 236.

37. "Daughters of the swan" is Yeats's phrase from "Among School Children" (*Collected Poems* 213), an echo of his own account of the Zeus/Leda myth in "Leda and the Swan," a poem itself alluded to in "Sir Rabbit." In that story, Junior Holifield tries to ward off King's advances toward his wife, Mattie Will, by telling King that "There's something else ain't what you think . . . Ain't e'er young lady folling after me, that you can catch a holt of—white or black" (*SEM* 405)—a further suggestion that King's legendarily numerous offspring are a racially mixed lot.

38. Ladd, *Resisting History*, 60.

39. Chakrabarty, *Habitations of Modernity*, 34–35.

40. Chakrabarty, *Habitations of Modernity*, 45.

Bibliography

Brodhead, Richard H. "Two Writers' Beginnings: Eudora Welty in the Neighborhood of Richard Wright." *Yale Review* 84 (1996): 1–21.

Chakrabarty, Dipesh. *Habitations of Modernity: Essays in the Wake of Subaltern Studies.* Chicago: University of Chicago Press, 2002.

Chow, Rey. *Writing Diaspora: Tactics of Intervention in Contemporary Cultural Studies.* Bloomington: Indiana University Press, 1993.

Entzminger, Betina. "Playing in the Dark with Welty: The Symbolic Role of African Americans in *Delta Wedding*." *College Literature* 30, no. 3 (2003): 52–67.

Faulkner, William. *The Sound and the Fury.* Ed. David Minter. New York: W. W. Norton, 1987.

Harrison, Suzan. "'Racial Content Espied': Modernist Politics, Textuality, and Race in Eudora Welty's 'The Demonstrators.'" In *Eudora Welty and Politics: Did the Writer Crusade?*, ed. Harriet Pollack and Suzanne Marrs, 89–108. Baton Rouge: Louisiana State University Press, 2001.

Jaising, Shakti. "Who Is Christophine? The Good Black Servant and the Contradictions of (Racial) Liberalism." *Modern Fiction Studies* 56, no. 4 (2010): 815–36.

Kennedy, Virginia. "Native Americans, African Americans, and the Space That Is America: Indian Presence in the Fiction of Toni Morrison." In *Crossing Waters, Crossing*

Worlds: The African Diaspora in Indian Country, ed. Tiya Miles and Sharon P. Holland, 196–217. Durham: Duke University Press, 2006.

Ladd, Barbara. "'Coming Through': The Black Initiate in *Delta Wedding*." *Mississippi Quarterly* 41, no. 4 (1988): 541–51.

———. *Resisting History: Gender, Modernity, and Authorship in William Faulkner, Zora Neale Hurston, and Eudora Welty*. Baton Rouge: Louisiana State University Press, 2007.

Marrs, Suzanne. *Eudora Welty: A Biography*. New York: Harcourt, 2005.

———. "'The Huge Fateful Stage of the Outside World': Eudora Welty's Life in Politics." In *Eudora Welty and Politics: Did the Writer Crusade?*, ed. Harriet Pollack and Suzanne Marrs, 69–87. Baton Rouge: Louisiana State University Press, 2001.

Morris, Rosalind, ed. *Can the Subaltern Speak? Reflections on the History of an Idea*. New York: Columbia University Press, 2010.

Morrison, Toni. Interview with Mel Watkins, *New York Times Book Review*, September 11, 1977: 50.

———. *Playing in the Dark: Whiteness and the Literary Imagination*. Cambridge: Harvard University Press, 1992.

Pollack, Harriet. "Words Between Strangers: On Welty, Her Style, and Her Audience." *Mississippi Quarterly* 39, no. 3 (1986): 481–505.

Spivak, Gayatri. "Can the Subaltern Speak?" In *Marxism and the Interpretation of Culture*, ed. Cary Nelson and Lawrence Grossberg, 217–313. Urbana, Ill.: University of Illinois Press, 1988).

———. *A Critique of Postcolonial Reason: Toward a History of the Vanishing Present*. Cambridge: Harvard University Press, 1999.

———. *The Post-Colonial Critic: Interviews, Strategies, Dialogues*. Ed. Sarah Harasym. New York: Routledge, 1990.

Welty, Eudora. *Complete Novels*. New York: Library of America, 1988.

———. "Looking Back at the First Story." In *Occasions: Selected Writings*, ed. Pearl Amelia McHaney, 299–305. Jackson: University Press of Mississippi, 2009.

———. *Stories, Essays, and Memoir*. New York: Library of America, 1998.

Wright, Richard. *Black Boy [American Hunger]: A Record of Childhood and Youth*. New York: Harper, 1998.

Yeats, William Butler. *The Collected Poems*. New York: Macmillan, 1956.

SARAH FORD

Laughing in the Dark

Race and Humor in Delta Wedding

When Eudora Welty worked for the WPA, she traveled all over Mississippi taking photographs of people whose lives were marked by the hardships of the economic depression. Many of her subjects were African Americans, as evidenced by several published books of her photographs. Her most anthologized short story, "A Worn Path," details the courageous journey of an elderly African American woman seeking medication for her sick grandson. Welty even wrote a story responding to the murder of Medgar Evers, giving a voice to the raw, racist mind-set that would lash out at a civil rights worker; she makes this voice condemn itself by its utter evil. Yet despite the many ways Welty's work is intersected with ideas and depictions of race, scholars do not seem to have a clear and consistent message about what Welty's work means to the issue of race. *Delta Wedding* is a case in point.

When first published in 1946, critics found the novel technically interesting but protested its seemingly nostalgic portrayal of a highly segregated South. Diana Trilling wrote, "I find it difficult to determine how much of my distaste for Eudora Welty's new book, 'Delta Wedding' . . . is dislike of its literary manner and how much is resistance to the culture out of which it grows and which it describes so fondly."[1] Scholars have since argued that its nostalgia comes from the characters themselves and that although Welty confines point of view in the novel to the white female characters, she also shows us that this view is biased and limited. Patricia Yaeger, for example, finds that the white characters ignore the African American characters around them to the point that the African Americans are simply part of the atmosphere of Shellmound and are part of a story that is "*omnipresent but not heard.*"[2] Betina Entzminger takes a slightly different path in arguing that the African American characters play a symbolic role; they reflect the anxieties of the white female characters when, for example,

Pinchy "reifies Robbie's rebellion."[3] And Barbara Ladd traces the association between the African American characters and danger or violence.[4] Although these critics differ on the specific role of African American characters, they each acknowledge that the role is portrayed as subordinate and argue that the text highlights the limitations of the white characters' views. These contemporary readings certainly challenge the contention that the book is nostalgic, but the novel actually offers us more information about race than these readings suggest. We can see glimpses of the African American characters' actual response to the world that subjugates them if we look in the right places.

One place to look is the kitchen of the Fairchild family. Kitchens in southern literature are often a key space for white and African American characters to interact. In one scene Ellen Fairchild puts her coconut cake made from Mashula's famous recipe into the oven as her daughter Dabney sweeps into the kitchen and asks her mother if she is beautiful. Roxie, sitting on the back porch, "could be heard laughing, two high gentle notes out in the dark."[5] The reader does not know exactly what makes Roxie laugh, but certainly the overwrought sentimentality of the scene in the kitchen deserves laughter. The reader also does not know if Roxie was actually heard by the other characters, just that she "could be heard," if, that is, anyone should happen to be listening. It is in the African American characters' use of humor that we can see indications of their responses to the Fairchild family's behavior. In order to hear this telling laughter, we will have to take on the tricky business of reading through or even around the perspective of the white characters.

We must first, however, see laughter as a tool of subversion, as a way of speaking back to those in power. Critics and readers often dismiss the humor in Welty's writing, but it can be a credible weapon.[6] When the family in *Losing Battles*, for example, enacts the forgiving ceremony where they absolve Judge Moody for wrecking his car, for bringing his wife to the reunion, for living, and finally for sending Jack to the penitentiary, they use their laughter to turn the powerful judge into a penitent in need of forgiving. Their humor reverses the power structure. If this rural family trying to survive the Depression is without power, the African American workers in *Delta Wedding*, still living in pseudoslavery conditions, are even more so. The lack of power renders both groups apt to use humor because it is not an overt weapon. Because the humor is subtle and under the radar, it does not pose the kind of threat that could get workers in trouble. It can be, nonetheless, a tool used by African Americans to respond to the system. In his introduction to *Invisible Man*, for example,

Ralph Ellison discusses his decision to use humor in his novel. Ellison actually wanted to write a more serious work of fiction on the "complex human emotions and philosophical decisions faced by a unique individual," but he kept being taunted by a disembodied, ironic, irreverent voice.[7] Although he was annoyed at first by the interruption of his serious narrative, he began to realize the potential force of this voice: "Given the persistence of racial violence and the unavailability of legal protection, I asked myself, what else *was* there to sustain our will to persevere but laughter? And could it be that there was a subtle triumph hidden in such laughter that I had missed, but one which still was more affirmative than raw anger?"[8] Ellison connects laughter to a triumph over oppression. The African American characters in *Delta Wedding* seem to accept their oppression. They do not stage a protest against their labor conditions, and with Troy as overseer, a man who is able to marry into the wealthy family in part because he learns the key is in "knowing how to handle your Negroes," these workers are not going to revolt (125). They do, however, as Roxie shows, punctuate the book with laughter.

Although Roxie is portrayed as laughing out on the back porch in the dark, for most of the novel she takes her place inside the Fairchild home as a faithful domestic servant who seemingly mirrors the family's opinions. When Ellen frets that the shepherdess crooks, certainly the silliest aspect of Dabney's wedding, will not arrive on time, Roxie is the one to reassure her: "'Dey come,' Roxie prophesied. 'Ain't nothin' goin' to defeat Miss Dab, Miss Ellen'" (126). Roxie shares Ellen's concern that the house look just right for Dabney's wedding; she has to mop the hall floor repeatedly as the family members track in dirt. She is also just as aghast as the family members at Robbie's unexpected arrival during their noonday meal and announces Robbie with, "Miss Ellen, surprise. Miss Robbie cryin' at de do'" (202). Ellen's pronouncement on Robbie's gift of all her nasturtiums for Dabney's wedding, "But it was every nasturtium Roxie had—she *loves Dabney*," seems apt (269). We have every indication that Roxie is devoted to the Fairchild family, but her relationship to them may be a bit more complicated than simple devotion.

We can see the complication by examining the scene in the kitchen that sparks Roxie's laughter. When Ellen tries to shoo Roxie out of the kitchen so she can make a cake for George's arrival, Roxie refuses to leave. This is not an act of disobedience. Instead, she anticipates Ellen's needs: "You loves *them* . . . You're fixin' to ask me to grate you a coconut, not get out" (29). Roxie is the one to suggest that Ellen make the famous four-layer cake, anticipating Ellen's desire to make George's arrival a special occasion. Ellen wants to celebrate the unorthodox marriage of George and Robbie because she hopes their success will bode well for Dabney's success in marrying the family's overseer.[9] That she is proud of her creation is evident when she greets Dabney's entrance into the kitchen with, "Smell my cake?" Although Ellen "was always nervous about her cakes," she takes such great care in its preparation because George would be "so appreciative" (33). Dabney, however, has other things on her mind, and her actions turn the scene to melodrama. "Radiant" in a pink dress and "spreading [it] to let her mother see," Dabney asks Ellen, "urgently, almost painfully, . . . 'Oh, Mother, am I beautiful—tonight?'" and then "rushed across the kitchen and threw her arms tightly around her mother and clung to her" (33). The scene ends with India's voice chanting, "Star light, Star bright," as "they all held still," while India wishes. The bride's grand entrance, the mother's offering of a cake, and the young girl's wish all contribute to a romantic fantasy about love and marriage. Cue the beautiful music, as we seem to be in a fairytale. The only element that seems strange is Roxie's laughter out "in the dark." Roxie's ability to guess that Ellen would want to prepare the special cake shows her understanding of the white family members' perspectives on their lives. Her laughter could also be her answer to Dabney's petty need to be reassured that she is the fairytale bride, when her supposedly fairytale marriage has her marrying the family's overseer and when her family's income, allowing the purchase of radiant pink dresses, depends on the exploitation of African American laborers.

The scene becomes more complicated when we consider who tells us that Roxie laughs. Welty employs free indirect discourse in *Delta Wedding* to give us the point of view of various white female characters.[10] Dorrit Cohn explains that free indirect discourse is "the rendering of a character's thoughts in his own idiom, while maintaining the third-person form of narration."[11] The narrator tells the story but takes on the character's opinions, thoughts, and language. In this novel, Welty's narrator moves from one character to another, so that we witness the viewpoints of several white female characters. Free indirect discourse can be a powerful way for an author to share the point of view of characters who would not otherwise speak their opinions or even think through their ideas about events, and in the case of *Delta Wedding* the narrative strategy works to privilege a set of voices that might otherwise go unheard. Suzan Harrison argues that "Welty's narrative strategies in *Delta Wedding* subvert Shellmound's silencing of women by allowing them to speak those things they 'have to keep to themselves.'"[12] Danielle Fuller goes a bit further in arguing that "the women's differing perspectives on the function and behaviour of the Fairchild men, marriage, and family represent an ongoing critique of the social codes and structures within which they live."[13] This critique may, however, only exist in the discourse of thought; Margaret Bolsterli points out that "ideologically speaking, most of these women are still making bricks in Egypt."[14] However radically we might read the white women's perspective, we at least hear their thoughts. The thoughts of the African American female characters, with two brief exceptions I will address later, are left out of the experiment in free indirect discourse. We do not, then, have Roxie's point of view on the kitchen scene except for that laughter, and it must come through Ellen's point of view.[15]

We do not know if Ellen hears Roxie or if the narrator pulls back from Ellen's perspective here to note to the reader that Roxie "could be heard laughing." Critics of free indirect discourse are split on the subject of whether the discourse contains two "selves," a narrator and a character or simply one. Ann Banfield, in her influential study *Unspeakable Sentences*, argues that only one "self" can be present in an utterance at a time and the narrator is completely silenced in free indirect discourse.[16] In her view the narrator cannot be distanced from the character, so that it would indeed be Ellen who notes that Roxie is laughing. Ellen either understands that Roxie finds the kitchen scene humorous but does not consider this important or realizes the laughter could be heard but chooses not to listen, which is perhaps the stronger reading since Ellen throughout the novel tends to ignore ideas that do not correspond with her worldview. When Howard, for example, wishes that roses did not exist because of their thorns, Ellen tells him twice to "just hush" (298).

Other theorists of free indirect discourse, however, argue that the fusion that Banfield sees of narrator and character is not always present; the narrator can report the character's thoughts but present them with either sympathy or irony. Brian McHale explains, "It is indicative of the complexity of FID that it is routinely naturalized both as a mode of ironic distancing from characters and as a mode of emphatic identification with characters."[17] In our example, if the narrator is the one noting that Roxie is laughing, and the narrator is doing so against or around Ellen's perspective, the laughter could take on a subversive element that questions Ellen's constructed reality of the kitchen scene. Although the fusion reading provides a unity to the free indirect discourse that makes the utterances cleaner in terms of discourse analysis, a reading that considers the possibility of irony makes more sense in *Delta Wedding* because although the white characters show little interest in the activities and opinions of the African

American characters, these latter characters still manage to remain, to borrow Yaeger's word, "omnipresent." Their presence signals the narrator's presence, and the narrator shows us their laughter. This is not to say, however, that the narrator is clearly inserting only irony here or that the narrator is always ironic. McHale notes that the free indirect discourse in a text may be "equivocal" between sympathy and irony; I would argue that *Delta Wedding* shifts between the two in an incredibly complex dance between narrator and characters. At times the narrator appears sympathetic and shares the character's viewpoint; at other times the possibility of irony is hard to dismiss. Although I will argue in the scenes I discuss for the presence of enough distance between narrator and character for irony to slip through, Welty's use of free indirect discourse allows the possibility of overlooking this distance and reading the narrator as sympathetic to the character. Kathy Mezei describes free indirect discourse as "an expression of the character's bid for freedom from the controlling narrator rather like the gingerbread man gleefully escaping from his creator. Unfortunately, both the character and the gingerbread man are inevitably gobbled up, if not by their creator, then by the wily fox, another character, or the waiting reader."[18]

Mezei's image points out the crucial piece of the puzzle, the reader. When early reviewers of *Delta Wedding* such as Trilling read the novel as nostalgic for the aristocratic lifestyle of the Fairchild family, they assumed that the narrator sympathizes with the white characters and that the narrator represents the author, Welty. Although critics have complicated and contested this reading in the years since the publication of *Delta Wedding*, the reading is at least plausible because of the ambiguity inherent in free indirect discourse. I would argue, however, that the case for recognizing an ironic element is stronger because the humor is too pervasive in the novel to be simply dismissed. Understanding the humor, however, requires that the reader understand the free indirect discourse as having more than one voice present in the narrative. As Monika Fludernik explains, "Free indirect discourse will always have to rely on a reader's active interpretative strategy."[19]

A text can, however, help the reader along. McHale suggests that the reader "must be gradually 'schooled' by the novel itself to organize its semantic continuum into the appropriate voices."[20] Welty includes a scene early in the novel that helps point the reader to the narrative technique. Tempe arrives at Shellmound to help Ellen prepare the house and family for the wedding that she considers inappropriate. Although she is appalled at the idea of her brother's daughter marrying the overseer, this marriage at least makes her feel better about her daughter's marriage to a Yankee. As Tempe surveys the current state of Ellen and Battle's house, India watches her aunt, and, we are told, "India could read her mind" (128). She knows that "the table lamp provoked Aunt Tempe" and that Tempe thinks Shellmound was "*outdated*—it didn't do for marrying girls off in" (128, 129). India follows Tempe's gaze around the room: "on the table before her now a Tinker-Toy windmill was sitting up and *running*—with the wedding two days off—right next to the exquisite tumbler with the Young Pretender engraved on it, that was her wedding present to Battle and Ellen— cracked now" (129). When Tempe's gaze lands on the guns standing in the corner of the very room where the ceremony will take place, India actually even "sighed with Aunt Tempe" (130). Here, India takes on the role of the narrator in free indirect discourse; she is the speaking voice, but what she voices are Tempe's opinions and even words; "*outdated*" and "exquisite" sound more like an adult's view than a child's. By having India as the narrator, though, we see what Tempe's views would mean to a resident of the house. India obviously admires Tempe, so Tempe's critique of Ellen's ability to manage the household has a direct bearing on India. The voices of both Tempe and India are present and important. Having India read Tempe's mind "schools" the reader on how to read the free indirect discourse in the rest of the novel. We have two voices, which are at times in sympathy but at other times a little distant.

Once we understand the dual voice, the reader is prepared to see the humor used by the African American characters. At times the reader has physical clues of humor: laughing, smiling, giggling. At other times the humor is in the form of performances where the African American characters mock the actions of the white characters. Both types of humor are subversive; the African American characters are using humor to question the white family's supposed superiority, although the white characters cannot see the subversion. In writing on how minority writers make fun of the majority culture, Sarah Blacher Cohen explains, "Since humor often depends on outsiders making fun of insiders, it is very difficult for insiders to discover what is laughable about themselves."[21] The Fairchilds as insiders do not acknowledge either the physical signs of humor or the performances, so the reader, now trained in free indirect discourse, must be able to see around the point of view to get the humor. Michael Mulkay analyzes humor from a sociological view and argues that to "get the joke" the audience must accept an "interpretative duality."[22] Humor is necessarily allusive and couched in language or behavior that has more than one meaning.

Vi'let's behavior toward Tempe reflects this ambiguity and need for interpretative duality. Tempe asserts her authority in the family by giving orders
the second she enters the house. She calls Vi'let and asks her "what dead zin-
nias were doing in front of the [painting of the] original Mr. George Fairchild"
(128). Vi'let then brings Tempe a pitcher of lemonade "so strong it would bring
tears to the eyes" (130). The narrator shifts from India's perspective to Ellen's, as
Ellen asks Tempe how her daughter, who had just had her first child, was doing.
When Tempe answers by complaining about her Yankee son-in-law, "Oh, the
mortification of *life*," Ellen's response points out that Tempe is too dramatic:
"Now, Tempe, you're always further beside your self than you need to be" (138).
But Tempe keeps complaining, drinks her lemonade, and asks "pitifully for a
little tiny bit of sugar" (138). Vi'let here seems to read Tempe's character, anticipating Tempe's need for attention and validation by bringing the "sugar on an
unnecessarily big silver tray" (140). We are then told that "Ellen watched her
treat Tempe very specially and tell her how young and pretty she looked, not
like no grandma, and she was going to bring her some of that cake" (140).

If we read the narrator as sharing Ellen's point of view sympathetically here,
this scene could show us how Ellen looks down on her servants. Vi'let does
not know which tray to use, and telling a grown woman she looks "young and
pretty" seems silly. Vi'let's compliments are overdone. If, however, we decide to
read some distance between the narrator and Ellen, we can see the possibility
of irony. Vi'let's actions are exaggerated to the point of mocking Tempe, and
her compliments go a bit too far to remain innocent. Tempe's request for sugar
is preceded by her self-indulgent whining, so Vi'let matches the tone by bringing the sugar on an overly fancy dish. In all of her complaining Tempe has not
voiced any concerns about being thought old as a grandmother, but Vi'let slips
this thought into the conversation under the disguise of a compliment about
how pretty Tempe looks. Vi'let's attempts to humor this difficult character demonstrate the humor in her serving performance to expose Tempe's melodra-
matic lunacy.

The free indirect discourse allows the ambiguity in the scene as we know
that "Ellen watched," but we do not know if Ellen sees Vi'let's actions as silly
or actually registers the potential humor and its subversive quality. Ellen does
not outwardly protest the use of the silver tray or make any response to Vi'let's
comments to Tempe, but perhaps Ellen is just not capable of registering Vi'let's
comic performance, so the narrator pulls back to signal to the reader that the
tray was not just big, but "unnecessarily" so. By pulling back a bit from Ellen,

Vi'let's voice also comes through, with the use of the idiomatic, "not like no grandma." This phrase exemplifies that duality in meaning Mulkay finds in humor, because when the double negative is treated literally, Vi'let's compliment dissolves into the positive, "like a grandma."

Partheny gets her turn to humor the Fairchilds when Shelley, India, and Laura come to her house to bring her some food since she has recently been "mindless," and to ask if she might know where Ellen's garnet brooch might be. Partheny was cooking dinner on the last night Ellen remembers wearing it, so Ellen thinks Partheny may have seen it. The scene is told through Laura's point of view, who describes Partheny as currently in her right mind because "she had put a tight little white cap on her head, sharp-peaked with a frilly top and points around like a crown" (168). Shelley begins by calling her "Parthenia" and invites her to Dabney's wedding in a polite but condescending voice. Shelley then asks her if she had seen the pin, "floating around somewhere." Partheny is expressing her regret that Ellen has lost such a treasure when India compliments her hat. Partheny exclaims, "It's a drawer-leg" while she is "giggling up very high" (169). Shelley continues her patronizing by assuring her, "Yes, it's real pretty." Although the young girls attempt to humor this supposedly "mindless" domestic with their wedding invitation (Ellen actually wants her to help in the kitchen) and their silly compliments, she laughs right back at them. She humors their mother's absurd request to think about where her pin might be by looking around her own home, saying, "Don't suppose that pin could have flown down *here* anywhere, do you?" (169). Laura then observes, "Partheny looked, patting the bed quilt and tapping the fireplace, and then disappearing into the other room where they could hear her making little sympathetic, sorrowful noises, and a noise like looking under the dishpan." Even the outsider Laura understands that Partheny was "playing-like looking for it." Partheny's performance makes their request look ridiculous; the humor does its job of subverting the power structure the girls assumed with their patronizing compliments.

When we shift to Shelley's point of view, the tone becomes darker. Shelley thinks, "This was a lowly kind of errand, a dark place to visit, old Partheny was tricky as the devil" (170). She is closer to the truth than even she realizes. The girls' call to Partheny's house is seemingly made with goodwill, but Ellen's question, whether Partheny knows where her brooch is, seems strange. While it might suggest the possibility of the poor domestic stealing from the rich employers, Ellen does not appear to be making an accusation. The reason that Ellen gives for seeking Partheny's help, however, does not make sense because Ellen would not have taken her jewelry off until long after the dinner party Partheny helped with was over. Another possibility hinted at in the text is that Ellen wants to tap into Partheny's undefined power. Early in the novel, Partheny calls for Ellen's help because of her spell of being "mindless." She then tells Ellen a story (or maybe a dream or vision) of almost jumping in the Yazoo River, which is associated throughout the novel with mystery and death, and of being rescued by Troy. During the girls' visit, Partheny gives them a cake with "a look of malignity, pride, authority" made with ingredients, "a little white dove blood in it, dove heart, blood of a snake—things," that point to voodoo (171–72). She tells them to give it to George so "his love won't have no res' till her come back to him" (172). When Shelley asks her, "How did you know *she'd* ever gone, Partheny?" Partheny only answers, "Ways, ways" (172). Later, just before Dabney's wedding, she orders everyone else out of Dabney's room; Dabney thinks, "the way a big spider can shake a web to get a little straw out, seeming to summon up all the anger in the world to keep the lure of the web intact" (281). We do not know exactly what "ways" Partheny has, but only that she seems to care about the white family's affairs and that she is powerful like a big spider. Certainly she is not someone to placate with silly compliments.

When the girls leave the house, the reader is told: "As they put up the umbrella she considered them gone, for she nodded over to a hidden neighbor and drawled out, 'Got a compliment on my drawer-leg'" (172–73). If we read the narrator as continuing to share Shelley's point of view, the comment circles back to the beginning of the visit when Laura thought Partheny was wearing a hat. Deflecting Partheny's dark power, Shelley could hear the comment about the drawer-leg as reifying the mindlessness of Partheny. There may, however, be some distance here between the narrator and Shelley. Under the umbrella, the girls certainly cannot see her, so the narrator has to separate from Shelley's view to show the reader Partheny nodding to the pretend neighbor. The reader can again play the role of audience for the humor that the insiders, here the young girls, cannot or will not recognize. If we read the separation between narrator and character, Partheny's humor answers their inappropriate behavior by mocking their mock politeness, but if the girls can hear her, they do not respond.

Even Pinchy, who spends most of the novel "seeking" in her religious initiation of "coming through," can find humor in the Fairchilds. Although Pinchy is present during much of the novel, the white characters pay her so little attention that her "seeking" is never actually even explained or defined for the reader. That it has import to the other African American characters is clear when all the servants abandon their various duties on the night Pinchy finally comes through, crying, "Hallelujah! Hallelujah!" (238). It also just happens to be the very night when Dabney's rehearsal dinner is supposed to take place. Ellen seems to take their absence in stride, serving everyone wine and cake with the explanation, "with that excitement in the kitchen, there's no telling how or when or in what state our supper will get to us" (240). Disdain, though, is evident as Tempe mocks their celebration: "Well, hallelujah" (239). At the wedding the other African American characters accord Pinchy special status, letting her stand in the front, but Dabney puts her in charge of swatting flies.

When Ellen sees Pinchy the morning after the wedding, she concludes that Pinchy looks at her "stupidly" (300). As she was coming through Pinchy "had not looked at [Ellen] at all, but simply turned up her face, dark-purple like a pansy, that no more saw her nor knew her than a pansy." Pinchy goes from not acknowledging Ellen at all to looking at her "stupidly," according to Ellen. Ellen then notices that Pinchy is dressed up "in her glittering white," and asks her where she is going. Pinchy replies, "To *church*, Miss Ellen." With a "soft, lush smile," she says, "*This* is *Sunday!*" It is certainly possible for a reader to equate the narrator and Ellen's viewpoints and to read Pinchy's look and smile as "stupid." But since Ellen is the one confused about the day, Pinchy's smile could also suggest the humor in Ellen's misguided question, a detail the narrator must pull back to tell, because Ellen would surely never use the word "lush." Now Ellen is the one who feels stupid having just seen Aunt Mac off to the bank to get the payroll on a Sunday. Ellen thinks, "We have every one lost track of the day of the week" (301). Her "we" here, of course, does not include Pinchy even if Pinchy is wearing "glittering white." Pinchy can smile at Ellen's mistake even if Ellen does not notice, and with that "lushness" the narrator questions Ellen's construction of Pinchy's look as stupid.

With Roxie, Vi'let, Partheny, and Pinchy, the laughs, smiles, and performances reveal that they use humor as a tool to undermine the authority of the white family, even if the family members cannot recognize or acknowledge the humor and its subversive import. The one African American character who does not use humor, Aunt Studney, becomes the proverbial exception that proves the rule. Aunt Studney does not smile or laugh, but she also does not respond to the family at all. Her stance is complete disengagement. When any family member asks her a question, her reply is always, "Ain't studyin' you" (229). Despite the refrain, she does show a bit of interest in their affairs. When Laura and Roy visit Marmion, Dabney's future house, they find Aunt Studney with her mysterious sack. As with Partheny's cake and Pinchy's seeking, we are not told what is in the mysterious sack or what Aunt Studney's behavior in the house means. At one point, she cries out "a cry high and threatening like the first note of a song at a ceremony, a wedding or a funeral, and like the bark of a dog too, somehow" (232). Laura then notices bees everywhere and surmises they originate from Aunt Studney's sack. Aunt Studney could be performing some voodoo ritual to curse the house of the family she disdains (Dabney is marrying the overseer after all), but it is also possible the bees represent fertility. Roy earlier tells Laura he thinks her sack is "where Mama gets all her babies" (228). We do not find out whether Aunt Studney's cry indicates a funeral with a curse or a wedding with fertility because Laura, who is viewing the scene, does not find out. The narrator does not pull back enough to resolve the mystery. Aunt Studney's cry counters, though, the humor of the other characters. She hovers around Shellmound but can remain aloof at the same time. The other characters, who because of their employment must remain engaged with the family, have to choose humor as a more subtle response.

The depictions of their responses, however, rely on a reader who can see around or through the white characters' points of view to understand the humor. As Fludernik argues, free indirect discourse relies on the reader to actively interpret the text; the reader of *Delta Wedding* must perceive that the portrayal of the African American characters comes mostly through the limited and biased view of the white characters. The reader must also be able to put aside the white characters' view to see the humor subverting it. This is tricky business, indeed, for it makes the activity of reading itself subversive. If a reader laughs, for example, with Pinchy at Shelley's attempt to feel superior by placating the supposedly "mindless" servant, the reader works against the dominant discourse of the text to align with the outsider. In his influential 1900 essay on laughter, Henri Bergson discusses the communal nature of humor: "Laughter always implies a kind of secret freemasonry, or even complicity, with other laughers, real or imaginary."[23]

This potentially radical complicity is reflected in the two very brief passages narrated from Roxie's point of view. When George, the designated family hero and the center of attention, rides up to Shellmound on a horse, the description comes through Roxie's point of view: "Then coming over the grass in the yard rode Mr. George Fairchild—in his white clothes and all—on a horse they had never seen before. It was a sorrel filly with flax mane and tail and pretty stockings" (63). At first the passage seems so nondescript that we might wonder why Welty chose this moment out of all the novel (and not, for example, Pinchy's coming through or Aunt Studney's digging in her sack) to enter the mind of an African American character. The passage confirms for the reader that Roxie indeed mirrors the family's opinions. She sees George as the hero dressed all in white, riding in on a beautiful horse. The second passage from Roxie's viewpoint suggests that she also has moments of subversion. After Robbie arrives during the Fairchild's lunch in order to surprise her husband who is not even there, Vi'let interrupts the conversation by appearing in the doorway and shouting, "Bird in de house! Miss Rob' come in lettin' bird in de house!" (209). Although Robbie has now been in the house for a while, Vi'let knows enough about the family to blame Robbie, since the family is currently miffed at her for leaving their beloved George. Roxie then adds, "Bird in de house mean death!" and the family members scatter throughout the house trying to catch the bird. Added to all of the commotion of the bird is Robbie's declaration to Ellen that George had begged her to love him. Ellen gives the newly arrived George an "imploring look" and "fell to the floor" (219). A tenth pregnancy, a daughter about to marry, and the uproar of family are simply too much for Ellen, and she faints. Roxie thinks, "Poor Miss Ellen just wasn't strong enough *any longer* for such a trial. She wasn't strong enough for Miss Dabney and Miss Robbie and everything *right now*" (220). Roxie's sympathy here seems sincere; she feels for "poor" Ellen. But then Roxie remembers another time when Ellen fainted, when she lost a baby, and thinks, "Wasn't it pitiful to see her so white?" Roxie here pities Ellen, an emotion that is caring but also superior. Her use of humor comes with the irony of the word "white." While Ellen may appear white from fainting, she is "so white" and pitiful because she is weak and constrained by her role as white southern lady. Roxie can pity Ellen because white equals weak. The other characters cannot perceive Roxie's view because it is all internal and only expressed for that reader who is part of the "freemasonry" and gets the joke in the duality of the word "white."

Roxie's final laugh confirms the potential power of a complicit audience and hints that the next generation of Fairchilds might be different. After Howard is bold enough to tell Ellen he does not like roses, causing her to tremble, Ellen walks through the garden and "could hear India and Roxie laughing in a wild duet" (298). This time Ellen is the one outside and Roxie is in the house with India, but the more important difference is that we know that Ellen registers the sound of the laughter; instead of knowing that Roxie's laughter "could be heard," we know this time "[Ellen] could hear" (298). The difference is admittedly subtle, but the shift may happen because Roxie is not laughing at the family but with a family member, India. We might wonder, however, why the laughter was "wild." Is it because Roxie is laughing in a "duet" with India? In their laughter we have a brief image of humor shared across the color line, distinct from the humor of the rest of the novel. This humor shared between a black woman and a white child may be even more subversive then the bits and traces of humor showing the African American characters reacting to the antics of the white family; it in fact may be wild.

In *Delta Wedding*, we are left with possibilities and traces. In deciding how to think about the intersection of Welty's work and race, we must decide what to do with these traces. Welty may not be guilty of being too nostalgic but perhaps of being too subtle. The traces are few, and much is left undetermined by the text. We do not know if the white characters recognize the humor used by the African American characters, we do not know the reactions and thoughts of the African American characters other than the glimpses of humor, and we do not know how much the narrator sympathizes with the characters and how much the narrator finds their views ironic. Free indirect discourse, as Kathy Mezei explains, puts "the onus on the reader, who has to decide where in all this the author stands. The author, of course, may wish to leave the threads of ambiguity dangling."[24] Welty certainly leaves us with ambiguity. Harriet Pollack, in analyzing Welty's style in "Powerhouse," finds that Welty's "fiction repeatedly elicits expectations that it promptly defies. Yet the mistaken expectations that a reader develops as he follows the experience provided by her language are a part of her directions to the text's meaning. The effect is to invite the reader to return to the story again and again, to urge him to read it closely and attentively."[25] Reading *Delta Wedding* can likewise potentially educate a reader in how to fill in the gaps in the narrative. The process of filling those gaps can become a powerful performative act if we find ourselves laughing with the African American characters, establishing that "complicity" Bergson finds in laughter. The most interesting dimension of the way the novel intersects with the issue of race may not be in the words on the page but in the performance required by the reader of those words. We can stay in the kitchen where Ellen is baking the coconut cake or move outside to see what makes Roxie laugh in the dark.

Notes

1. Trilling, "Fiction in Review," 578.
2. Yaeger, *Dirt and Desire*, 98.
3. Entzminger, "Playing in the Dark," 58.
4. Ladd, "'Coming Through.'"
5. Welty, *Delta Wedding*, 33. Hereafter cited parenthetically.
6. Sharon Baris, for example, argues that although Welty's novel *The Ponder Heart* "has typically been seen as a colorful depiction of the delightful habits and folkways of a sleepy southern town," the novel "as Welty's fictional case study of American beliefs about truth, evidence, and justice . . . makes consensus itself a major talking point—or laughing question—for serious discussion" (180, 181).
7. Ellison, "Introduction," xv.
8. Ellison, "Introduction," xv–xvi.
9. Louise Westling and Ann Romines both emphasize the importance of the cakes in the novel and the symbolism of the white cake in this scene. Westling discusses the contrast of the white cake Ellen makes with the black cake Partheny makes ("Food" 35). Romines discusses the importance of cake baking to the feminine world of the novel ("Reading the Cakes"). Laura Sloan Patterson argues that Ellen's thoughts are a "stronger" matter in the scene when Ellen thinks about George and Robbie's escapade in the river resulting in a "metaphorical rape-within-a-recipe-within-a-narrative" ("Sexing the Domestic" 38).
10. See Suzan Harrison for the possible influence of Virginia Woolf on Welty's narrative strategy.
11. Cohn, *Transparent Minds*, 100.
12. Harrison, "The Other Way," 52.
13. Fuller, "'Making a Scene,'" 298.
14. Bolsterli, "Women's Vision," 154.
15. Anne Romines argues that "Welty now switches to a wider lens and an outsider's vision, as if some act of enlarging transmission is completed with the cake" and sees Roxie's laughter as "an ironic note to the chorale that ends the cake-baking scene" (*The Home Plot* 224, 225).
16. Banfield, *Unspeakable Sentences*.
17. McHale, "Free Indirect Discourse," 275.
18. Mezei, "Who Is Speaking Here?" 68.
19. Fludernik, *Fictions of Language*, 81.
20. McHale, "Free Indirect Discourse," 273.

21. Cohen, "Introduction," 10.

22. Mulkay, *On Humour*, 31.

23. Bergson, "Laughter," 64.

24. Mezei, "Who Is Speaking?" 72.

25. Pollack, "Words Between Strangers," 59.

Bibliography

Banfield, Ann. *Unspeakable Sentences: Narration and Representation in the Language of Fiction*. Boston: Routledge and Kegan Paul, 1982.

Baris, Sharon. "Judgments of *The Ponder Heart*: Welty's Trials of the 1950s." In *Eudora Welty and Politics: Did the Writer Crusade?*, ed. Harriet Pollack and Suzanne Marrs, 179–201. Baton Rouge: Louisiana State University Press, 2001.

Bergson, Henri. "Laughter." In *Comedy*, ed. Wylie Sypher. New York: Doubleday Anchor Books, 1956.

Bolsterli, Margaret Jones. "Women's Vision: The Worlds of Women in *Delta Wedding*, *Losing Battles*, and *The Optimist's Daughter*." In *Eudora Welty: Critical Essays*, ed. Peggy Whitman Prenshaw, 149–56. Jackson: University Press of Mississippi, 1979.

Cohen, Sarah Blacher. "Introduction: The Variety of Humors." In *Comic Relief: Humor in Contemporary American Literature*, ed. Sarah Blacher Cohen. Urbana: University of Illinois Press, 1978.

Cohn, Dorrit. *Transparent Minds: Narrative Modes for Presenting Consciousness in Fiction*. Princeton, N.J.: Princeton University Press, 1978.

Ellison, Ralph. Introduction to *Invisible Man*. New York: Vintage International, 1947.

Entzminger, Betina. "Playing in the Dark with Welty: The Symbolic Role of African Americans in *Delta Wedding*." *College Literature* 30, no. 3 (2003): 52–67.

Fludernik, Monika. *The Fictions of Language and the Languages of Fiction: The Linguistic Representation of Speech and Consciousness*. New York: Routledge, 1993.

Fuller, Danielle. "'Making a Scene': Some Thoughts on Female Sexuality and Marriage in Eudora Welty's *Delta Wedding* and *The Optimist's Daughter*." *Mississippi Quarterly* 48, no. 2 (1995): 291–318.

Harrison, Suzan. "'The Other Way to Live': Gender and Selfhood in *Delta Wedding* and *The Golden Apples*." *Mississippi Quarterly* 44, no. 1 (1990–91): 49–67.

Ladd, Barbara. "'Coming Through': The Black Initiate in *Delta Wedding*." *Mississippi Quarterly* 41, no. 4 (1988): 541–51.

McHale, Brian. "Free Indirect Discourse: A Survey of Recent Accounts." *PTL* 3 (1978): 249–87.

Mezei, Kathy. "Who Is Speaking Here? Free Indirect Discourse, Gender, and Narrative Authority in *Emma*, *Howard's End*, and *Mrs. Dalloway*." In *Ambiguous Discourse: Feminist Narratology and British Women Writers*, ed. Kathy Mezei, 66–92. Chapel Hill: University of North Carolina Press, 1996.

Mulkay, Michael. *On Humour: Its Nature and Its Place in Modern Society*. Cambridge: Polity Press, 1988.

Patterson, Laura Sloan. "Sexing the Domestic: Eudora Welty's *Delta Wedding* and the Sexology Movement." *Southern Quarterly* 42, no. 2 (2004): 37–59.

Pollack, Harriet. "Words Between Strangers: On Welty, Her Style, and Her Audience." In *Welty: A Life in Literature*, ed. Albert J. Devlin. Jackson: University Press of Mississippi, 1987.

Romines, Ann. *The Home Plot: Women, Writing, and Domestic Ritual.* Amherst: University of Massachusetts Press, 1992.

———. "Reading the Cakes: *Delta Wedding* and the Texts of Southern Women's Culture." *Mississippi Quarterly* 50, no. 4 (1997): 601–16.

Trilling, Diana. "Fiction in Review." *The Nation* 162, May 11, 1946, 578.

Welty, Eudora. *Delta Wedding.* New York: Harcourt, 1946.

Westling, Louise. "Food, Landscape, and the Feminine in *Delta Wedding*." *Southern Quarterly* 30, nos. 2–3 (1992): 29–40.

Yaeger, Patricia. *Dirt and Desire: Reconstructing Southern Women's Writing, 1930–1990.* Chicago: University of Chicago Press, 2000.

JEAN C. GRIFFITH

"I Knowed Him Then Like I Know Me Now"

Whiteness, Violence, and Interracial Male Intimacy in Delta Wedding and "Where Is the Voice Coming From?"

Looking back on her career in the preface to her *Collected Stories*, Eudora Welty tells us that all her works have "reflected their own present time," and that the two uncollected stories in the volume, "Where Is the Voice Coming From?" (1963) and "The Demonstrators" (1968), are no exceptions.[1] As Welty suggests, the depictions in these stories of what she called "the changing sixties" and of 1963, in particular, in "Where Is the Voice Coming From?" do seem to reflect their present moment, dovetailing with other commentaries made on that time. Like Martin Luther King Jr.'s *Why We Can't Wait* (1964), Eleanor Roosevelt's *Tomorrow Is Now* (1963), and even George Wallace's "segregation now, segregation tomorrow, segregation forever," Welty's texts demonstrate a keen awareness of living in a watershed moment, one in which possibilities long suppressed and conflicts thought by many to be settled were shaping black-white race relations to an unprecedented degree.[2] Although both stories capture this heightened awareness of impending change, "Where Is the Voice Coming From?," Welty tells us, is "unique . . . in how it came about" (x). As an immediate response to the assassination of Jackson NAACP leader Medgar Evers, the story is distinctive, she tells us, in its close relationship to its context: "Whoever the murderer is," she recalls thinking as she began to write, "I know him: not his identity, but his coming about, in this time and place," a knowledge she claims to have felt "with overwhelming directness" (xi). Welty's comments here make plain that, although she titled her story with a question, it is one to which she thought she already had an answer: she knew (or thought she knew) exactly where the voice was coming from. And the murderer she thought she knew gave voice to what she characterizes as "the unease, the ambiguities, the sickness and desperation of those days in Mississippi" (x). Yet she goes on to say, in a comment that ends the preface, that "what I do in writing of any character is to try to enter into the mind, heart, and skin of a human being who is not me." On the one hand, then, she tells us that "Where Is the Voice Coming From?" is unique because she felt she knew the real killer on whom she based her narrator "with overwhelming directness"; on the other, she says that she tries to know all of her characters in that way.

Such remarks indicate that Welty thought her story of Evers's murder was both distinctive to *and* typical of her work: distinctive in the sense of it being a keenly felt response to the murder of a real person and typical in the sense of it being an attempt to understand her character. Welty's comments prompt readers to wonder what, if anything, might make the text of the story itself distinctive from and, at the same time, comparable to other works. In particular, we might wonder, given the racially charged nature of the Evers murder, how Welty thought she knew his killer "with overwhelming directness" and how that knowledge might have influenced the ways in which she depicted race relations in her work. Given, too, that her knowledge is imagined not to be of Evers but of his killer, whose race she shared but whose gender and class status in the story differed from Welty's own, we also might wonder how the Evers assassination in particular and "those days in Mississippi" more generally altered how she portrayed boundaries between whites. How is this story "unique" in the sense of its being a response to a time of great crisis and change?

In order to explore such questions, I will examine Welty's first novel, *Delta Wedding* (1946), alongside her story of Evers's murder, focusing specifically on the ways both works prominently feature black and white men in violent yet oddly intimate encounters. In *Delta Wedding*, one of these encounters is described by Shelley Fairchild as she happens upon the family's plantation overseer and her future brother-in-law, Troy Flavin, pointing a gun at a farmworker, Root M'Hook, who threatens him and other field hands with an ice pick. Intervening in an altercation already in progress, Troy shoots Root's finger off and then offers to place another young man, Big Baby, across his knee to remove buckshot from his backside. Earlier in the novel, Shelley's sister and Troy's fiancée, Dabney, recalls a similar scene in which her naked Uncle George, having gone swimming in the river, came upon two brothers—future Fairchild workers, like Root and Big Baby—engaged in a bloody knife fight. As Troy does, George broke up the violence and went on to engage in intimate encounters with the combatants: while Troy removes buckshot from a private part of Big Baby's body, George, as Dabney recollects, held the injured and crying boys to his chest in a close embrace. Although the killer in "Where Is the Voice Coming

From?" is not personally acquainted with his victim and shares no physical intimacy with him, he repeatedly rehearses how well he knows Roland Summers, who, as Medgar Evers was in reality, is something of a Jackson celebrity, and he predicts mundane aspects of Summers's domestic routine even as he takes aim and shoots him.

In many ways, his criminal act is an odd inversion of the acts of George and Troy in *Delta Wedding*, both of which are meant to end violence between black men already in progress. But the killer's crime as well as his efforts to predict Summers's movements in the scene are attempts to achieve the same sense of *noblesse oblige* Troy and George both display toward their workers. Thus in all three cases, the responsibility to physically control black men, whether it is socially sanctioned (as in the cases of Troy and George) or outside the law (as in the killer's) defines a white man's status relative to other white men. As a member of a prominent plantation family, George is expected to exert such control; Troy and the killer attempt—successfully in Troy's case, unsuccessfully in the killer's—to use such control to prove their worth as white men despite their non-elite status. In using black men to pair Troy, the overseer, and George, the plantation owner, Welty crosses lines of class in her novel, collapsing the distinctions between the working class and the aristocracy that make the marriage between Troy and Dabney so problematic to her family. Although the killer's act in "Where Is the Voice Coming From?" is an attempt to collapse those very same distinctions, it is a failed one: his feelings of inadequacy and his resentment for those above him seem unaffected by the violence he perpetrates against an African American.

Related to this contrast between the ways characters in the early novel and the late story use black men to negotiate class boundaries is the fact that all three encounters are seen through the point of view of white women. Shelley Fairchild's perspective filters our view of the dispute in Troy's cabin, and the scene involving George is recalled in the memory of Dabney as she contemplates her impending marriage and her family's response to it. The assassination in "Where Is the Voice Coming From?" is told from the perspective of the killer himself, but that telling is shaped by his wife's response to his crime as well as by Welty's sense that she "knew" the man upon whom her narrator is based. The knowledge Welty assumed she possessed of Evers's killer is loaded with presuppositions about his working-class status, even though, as it would turn out, the real assassin, Byron de la Beckwith, fit the stereotype of the "poor but proud" son of fallen plantation aristocracy more than he did the chronically "poor white," urban type from which Welty draws. Both Shelley's and Dabney's responses to the encounters they witness between white and black men are informed by class-based assumptions similar to Welty's as she tried to imagine Evers's killer: that working-class white men are more prone to violence against African Americans than are genteel men, who are responsible instead for ending violence. But, as I will argue, the novel provides us with various ways to counter Shelley's notion that Troy is inferior to a "real Deltan," while in many ways Welty herself maintains the class boundaries in the later story that she had blurred earlier in her novel.[3] What about Evers's murder and "those days in Mississippi" might account for such a reassertion of stereotypes that, decades earlier, she had questioned in her novel?

Although written in 1946, less than two decades before "Where Is the Voice Coming From?," *Delta Wedding* is set in 1923, and the temporal gap between 1923 and 1946 is just as important to Welty's construction of whiteness as the one between 1946 and 1963. In her 1923 setting, Welty references a time when whites of different classes and what we now call ethnicities would likely be distinguished from one another, not just culturally, but biologically as well. As Matthew Frye Jacobson claims, the dominant conception of "difference" in the first decades of the century posited that "one might be both white *and* racially distinct from other whites."[4] By 1946, though, the idea that essential differences existed among whites had lost much of its influence, largely because such a position, which was at the heart of the "science" of eugenics, informed the fascist movement against which the United States was at war. *Delta Wedding*'s wartime composition might also explain why much of its female characters' attention is directed at contemplating white masculinity. While some of the characters in the novel distinguish between the Fairchild men and Troy Flavin, who is not only working class but also vaguely Irish, the narrative point of view works to break down those distinctions. Such a discrepancy between the characters' and the narrative points of view could account for the paradoxes in the novel's depiction of the Fairchild men. As Laura puts it, "it was the boys and the men that defined that family always. When she looked at the boys and the men Laura was without words but she knew that company like a dream that comes back again and again, each aspect familiar and longing not to be forgotten" (102). What Laura describes as the ephemeral quality of the Fairchild men, Ellen terms "a paradoxical thing," a "fineness and tenderness" that "called to mind their unwieldiness, and the other way round" (110, 111). This lack of clarity around a set of characters meant to be definitive of the family (and of Deltan society in general) speaks to uncertainties about what does and does not separate redheads from "real Deltans."

In particular, parallels between Troy and George are repeatedly drawn that contradict the family's belief that immutable differences between Troy and Dabney make their marriage problematic, for as Dabney herself observes, "sometimes Troy was really ever so much like a Fairchild" (121). Although there is considerable anxiety expressed about the union, the family's complaints about Troy are idle ones because, as various characters reluctantly point out, another "mixed" marriage between George and Robbie Reid has already set the precedent. Dabney and Troy are engaged on the same day George and Robbie have their falling out about his rescuing Maureen from the *Yellow Dog*. George, rather than one of Dabney's brothers, serves as Troy's best man. And if Troy is in some senses like a Fairchild, the Fairchilds are in some senses not like one another, despite the claims to family resemblance made by a number of women. Indeed, while the Fairchilds think they are all alike and that they are different from others, many of the family members (Dabney, Shelley, George) also believe that other family members stick out or that they themselves do. As Susan Donaldson has written, "however much the Fairchilds protest that nothing really changes at Shellmound, however much they might insist upon their persistent sameness, the portent of cataclysmic change and of difference is all too imminent."[5] I would add to Donaldson's point that the portent of sameness between the family and those some of its members wish to keep at arm's length is also imminent. Although subtly drawn, Troy's Irishness is signaled in a number of ways, most of which have to do with his red hair, about which I will have more to say later. The Fairchilds' Anglo roots are symbolized in the heirloom Aunts Primrose and Jim Allen give to Dabney when she makes her pre-wedding visit: a nightlight that memorializes the Great Fire of London. Upon returning to Shellmound that evening, Dabney breaks this symbol of the family's English descent, uttering "no cry at all" as it shatters and Uncle George tells her that Troy awaits her in the house (141).

The fact that Troy is an overseer is important in this respect, for the very structures that had once divided white southerners from one another—including those that distinguished between planters and overseers—had begun, in the new, more mobile South, to highlight sameness among whites. This was achieved, of course, largely through segregation, which is to say, through legal measures buttressed by assumptions of difference between blacks and whites. As Suzanne Marrs has written, these assumptions of difference provide the

Fairchilds opportunities "to assert family solidarity," opportunities that are much more effective, I would argue, than their attempts to use Troy in the same manner.[6] Indeed, nothing in the novel makes George and Troy more alike than their encounters with their African American farmhands. The scene in Troy's cabin quickly moves from the aggressive male competition we might expect in scenes depicting overseers and slaves to paternalistic, almost homoerotic intimacy, with a white man, older and higher in status, treating an injured black man in a private area of the body and thereby making clear that he controls that body.[7] Having shot Root in the finger in a symbolic act of emasculation, Troy responds to Big Baby's groans with a mixture of pity and laughter, just as George had both chided and comforted Man-Son and his brother, holding them in a moment of homoerotic (he is naked, after all) yet patriarchal intimacy (124). The similarities between the two scenes are reinforced by the fact that it is precisely when Dabney remarks that Troy is "ever so much like a Fairchild" that she notices Man-Son, who prompts her to recall George's intervention in the farmhand's dispute with his brother. As Shelley does later in the text, Dabney focuses on the blood spilled in this encounter, and she thinks that the knife George took away from the boys "was as big as the one Troy could pull out now" (123).

Despite the shock with which both women respond to these encounters, such scenes are apparently not rare in the Deltan society of the novel, nor are they indicative of Troy's origins. Both George and Battle, like Troy, take responsibility for intervening in African Americans' disputes. Describing to Ellen how he adjusted to life in the Delta, Troy tells her, "by now, I can't tell a bit of difference between me and any Delta people you name . . . it's just a matter of knowing how to handle your Negroes" (183). Ellen's response—"well, Troy, you know, if it was that at first, I believe there's more to it"—suggests that Troy's characterization of what it takes to become a Deltan is not so much incorrect as it is reductive (183–84).[8] His paternalistic attitude toward his underlings is apparently one with which he is increasingly comfortable, for Troy treats the odd chain of events between himself, Root, and Big Baby matter-of-factly, or as Marrs notes, expeditiously and dispassionately.[9] Asking Shelley if she came to watch him remove the buckshot from Big Baby's buttocks, Troy even treats her presence nonchalantly, replying to her comment about Root's blood being on the floor with "then you'll have to jump over it, my darlin'" in what is described as a "sing-song" voice (285). In his analysis of class and paternalism in the novel, Brannon Costello argues that the links between these encounters display the "Fairchild revulsion" toward "active engagement with their work-ers"; I would say that the revulsion Shelley and Dabney feel has to do with the violence that seems to reinforce rather than preclude the intimacy in these scenes.[10]

That is why it is significant that both encounters are described by Fair-child women, whose perspectives dominate the novel and who therefore most often articulate notions of Fairchild family distinctiveness. Both Shel-ley's and Dabney's responses to the interactions they witness between white and black men are informed by the assumption that some white men—red-headed overseers—are more fitting participants in such scenes than "real Del-tans" are, despite evidence to the contrary. As she watches the scene between her future brother-in-law and her family's workers, Shelley realizes, "as if the sky had opened and shown her," "the reason why Dabney's wedding should be prevented. Nobody could marry a man with blood on his door" (285). Shelley's shock at the blood she sees, though, morphs into a focus on Troy's red hair, which she thinks of throughout the novel. As she watches Troy work on Big Baby, she sees not the ice pick prying the black youth's skin but the white man's "hand bright with red hairs." Thinking that, too, "red hairs sprang even from his ears," Shelley is more concerned with Troy's identity than she is, it would seem, with his actions or the blood they spill.

What concerns Shelley is that a man who would engage in such encounters could also be engaged to a member of the family. What concerns her sister, Dabney, as she remembers witnessing a similar scene is that such encounters already take place within the family and that, in particular, George's response to Man-Son and his brother is not what she considers to be an appropriate one. For it is this memory that makes Dabney aware that "there were surprising things in the world which did not surprise him. Wonderfully, he had reached up and caught the knife in the air. Disgracefully, he had taken two little black devils against his side. When he had not even laughed with them all about it afterwards, or told it like a story after supper, she was astonished, and sure then of a curious division between George and the rest" (124). Dabney's disappoint-ment that George did not tell of his experience "like a story after supper" sug-gests that contact between white men and their black employees is all part of being a Deltan, whether one is born one, as Battle and George are, or becoming one, as Troy is. George's uncharacteristic response to his masculine role implies the ubiquitous nature of encounters like the ones he, Troy, and Battle have with African Americans, encounters that, apparently, are made digestible to women through talk. Dabney is astonished that George takes no credit for his act of paternalism, just as Shelley is shocked by the offhanded way Troy assumes the same kind of control.

Attributing Troy's nonchalance to a "convincing performance," Shelley begins to worry that all men are equally inauthentic performers of genteel white masculinity: "Suppose a real Deltan only imitated another Deltan. Suppose the behavior of all *men* were actually no more than this—imitation of other men. But it had previously occurred to her that Troy was trying to imitate her father. (Suppose her *father* imitated . . . oh, not he!)" (285–86). Bank characterizes Shelley's response as recognition that Troy is "part of a system of oppression that extends beyond him as an individual."[11] But Shelley's dawning awareness of the intertwined nature of patriarchy and racism only goes so far, for her realization is followed by the remark that "Women, she was glad to think, did know a *little* better—though everything they knew they would have to keep to themselves . . oh, forever!" (286). As Ann Romines has written, Shelley preserves gender as the one distinction that is really real.[12] Shelley's observations suggest that white women have greater awareness of the interworkings of racial patriarchy, but that they can do nothing to change them. In fact, as Betina Entzminger argues, rather than seeing the marginalization of African Americans, white women see blacks as symbols of their own oppression.[13]

Perhaps that explains why the scenes Shelley and Dabney witness disturb them, for, ultimately, the intimacies they observe symbolize not a breaking down of boundaries between blacks and whites, but rather a breaking down of boundaries between whites of different classes and ethnicities, a symbol that becomes literal through another institution key to the maintenance of racial patriarchy: marriage. In the novel and in all of Welty's works, the very same institutions designed to reinforce boundaries can also break them down. Once Shelley is faced with Troy's nonchalance, she realizes that her sister's marriage cannot be prevented, for "what was going to happen was going to happen" and, in fact, already has happened in the union of George to Robbie Reid (285). The contradictory characteristics George possesses as a Fairchild man pave the way, it would seem, for a Fairchild woman to break with tradition and align herself with more inclusive notions of whiteness. In fact, the only differences between the scenes in Troy's cabin and on the banks of the Yazoo are that Troy needs a knife to subdue Root, whereas George was able to restrain Man-Son and his brother even without clothing. George may be more adept than the overseer at exhibiting the *noblesse oblige* required of a planter, but Shelley's evolving response to her sister's marriage and the marriage itself stress an apparently inevitable process whereby redheads can, finally, become real Deltans.

If *Delta Wedding* depicts a genteel, rural society that assumes its own insularity despite evidence to the contrary, "Where Is the Voice Coming From?" portrays a tumultuous urban environment that, as I point out above, effectively captures what Welty called "the unease, the ambiguities, the sickness and desperation of those days in Mississippi" (x).[14] And as I also note above, this description likewise sums up her narrator, who experiences in the course of this very short work all of the things Welty attributes to Mississippi in the early 1960s. However important interactions between the races are in *Delta Wedding* in determining whites' places in the social order of rural Mississippi in the 1920s, those interactions elicit little emotion from the white characters themselves, who take the presence of African American servants and field hands largely for granted. Quite the opposite is the case in "Where Is the Voice Coming From?" Naming the Jackson-like setting of the story Thermopylae, Welty alludes to a battle that occurs in the killer's consciousness as he vacillates between an array of keenly felt emotions toward his victim that, ultimately, tell us more about himself.[15] Here Welty echoes the assumption made by generations of southerners before her that the genteel classes (like that to which the Fairchilds belong) shared an affinity with African Americans that was lacking in African Americans' interactions with working-class whites. As we saw above, Troy's effort to become a "real Deltan" is partly a matter of "knowing how to handle your Negroes" (183). In "Where Is the Voice Coming From?," the killer, despite his intense emotional response to Summers, does not appear to have any "Negroes" at his command to handle, and we are led to believe that his act is a desperate and ultimately futile effort to exert the same control over black men that makes Troy like a "real Deltan."

Thus the narrator tries to impress upon his listeners how well he knows Summers: where he lives, what time he will arrive at home that night ("I *thought* I'd beat him home"), and what he looks like from behind ("I knowed him then like I know me now. I knowed him even by his still, listening back").[16] He tells us of the aftermath of the killing—"I stood a minute, just to see would somebody inside come out long enough to pick him up. And there she comes, the woman"—as if the scene before him is so familiar that he can predict events as well as orchestrate them (604–5). Yet at the same time, the killer displays the hostility toward African Americans believed to be characteristic of his class, denying any association with Summers and contradicting himself about the extent to which he can identify his victim: "Never seen him before, never seen him since, never seen anything of his black face but his picture, never seen his face alive, any time at all, or anywheres, and didn't want to, need to, never hope to see that face and never will. As long as there was no question in my mind" (604). The narrator's conflicted response to Summers indicates that his knowledge of his victim comes from his being his neighbor, not his employer. He can give directions to Summers's house—"so you leave Four Corners and head west on Nathan B. Forrest Road . . . turn before you hit the city limits"—because, living nearby, he makes much the same journey to his own house (603).[17] Welty imagined the assassin to be a man who feared being equal to African Americans, not one who could take his white privilege for granted.

Indeed, some of what the narrator tells us indicates that he fears not only not being superior to, but also being less than Summers, who, as he begrudgingly notes, owns his own car and can afford to leave his lights on all night. His attempt to fall back on racist stereotypes (specifically, that African Americans are naturally violent) is, given the circumstances, an obviously absurd one not meant to be convincing. Just before firing at Summers, he again brags about recognizing him—"he had to be the one"—but then unwittingly places his victim in a position to judge him: "his back was fixed, fixed on me like a preacher's eyeballs when he's yelling 'Are you saved?'" (604). Despite the success of his crime, the narrator cannot realize the kind of mastery over black men that seems effortless to George Fairchild and becomes increasingly so to Troy Flavin. The fraught nature of his attempt at control perhaps explains why the sexually intimate elements of the interracial encounter are more blatant here than they are in Troy's confrontation with Root and his treatment of Big Baby. After he shoots Summers, Welty's narrator experiences a kind of sexual release, claiming "I turned loose of my load" in reference to throwing aside his weapon (604). Contrary to the usual association of the gun and the phallus, though, the gun here gives the man who wields it only momentary power: as he later tells his wife, he dropped the gun involuntarily because it was "scorching" (605). And, as it turns out, his feelings of being emasculated by Summers remain after he has taken his life. After shooting his victim, he confesses to him that his crime is an attempt to protect a social position that he feels has become increasingly precarious: "Roland? There was one way left, for me to be ahead of you and stay ahead of you, by Dad, and I just taken it" (604).[18] His attempt to reassure himself that his crime will safeguard his privilege ("we ain't never now, never going to be equals") is belied by his fear that the murder will, in fact, make Summers even more prominent. "On TV and in the paper," he tells us of the public response to his crime, "they don't know but half of it. They know who Roland Summers was without knowing who I am. His face was in front of the public before I got rid of him, and after I got rid of him there it is again—the same picture. And none of me. I ain't ever had one made. Not ever!" (606).

Along with a nagging sense that he is not, in fact, better than Summers are two even more traumatic realizations: that, in defining himself against Summers, he is dependent upon him and, because of that, his slaying of Summers will turn out to threaten his position rather than bolster it. His claims that Summers's death will keep him ahead of the African American man are contradicted by everything else he tells us, including his description of the very moment of his crime: "He was down . . . And it wasn't till the minute before, that the mockingbird had quit singing. He'd been singing up my sassafras tree. Either he was up early, or he hadn't never gone to bed, he was like me. And the mocker he'd stayed right with me, filling the air till come the crack, till I turned loose of my load. I was like him. I was on top of the world myself. For once" (604). Here, the killer alters his earlier metaphor of how he sees Summers (his blood spreads upon his back "like the wings of a bird") to how he is trying to see himself, on top of the world. But the comparison of Summers's blood to the wings of a bird suggests, in addition to death, rebirth, which, of course, undermines the killer's intensions and reinforces the notion that in the reprinting of his photograph, Summers's legacy will live on. The text's use of the pronoun "he" in the passage above obscures the metaphor in a way that foreshadows a quick return of the insecurities and paranoia the narrator feels before killing Summers. All three—the two men and the mockingbird—have been up all night, which raises the possibility that the mockingbird—which, after all, flies away just as the killer takes Summers's life—symbolizes not the killer elevated in social status but Summers himself (or perhaps his spirit). As Suzan Harrison asserts, there is an odd similarity between his description of the dead Summers, "He was down," and the song the murderer sings at the end of the story ("sing-a-down, down"), a similarity that suggests he is satisfied with the outcome of his crime.[19] But perhaps satisfaction is something he wishes for rather than something he has achieved, for the song is a blues lullaby of sorts, something sung in an effort to provide rather than express comfort.

Harrison further argues that, in the killer's references to degrading images of African Americans, Welty illustrates "white America's dependence on a particular construction of black racial identity." It also shows the inaccuracy of that construction and operates as an act wherein "whites are touched by the blacks they would lampoon and are in the process told on, revealed."[20] The story reveals much about Welty's construction of white male identity—or at least the identity of a particular class of whites—while telling us next to nothing about African Americans. In *Delta Wedding*, as Betina Entzminger has written, Welty "casts her black characters in stereotypical roles of servant or underling without revealing their internal motivations."[21] From Partheny's patty cake and Studney's bag to Pinchy's "coming through" and its connection to Root's behavior in Troy's cabin ("Pinchy cause *trouble* comin' through," Juju announces after Troy has shot Root [285]), African Americans are exotic and unknowable in *Delta Wedding*, as they are in many of Welty's pre–civil rights era works. In "Where Is the Voice Coming From?," what little we know about Summers—that he has an income sufficient to possesses a new car and a well-groomed lawn, for example—suggests that, except for his race, he could be considered quite typical of middle-class American manhood. By making Summers so "normal," Welty's story makes the killer and the kind of white man he represents look all the more abnormal.

Thus violence and intimacy between white and black men in *Delta Wedding* signal a version of paternalism, unique to the Jim Crow era, that has the potential to level ethnic and class differences between whites, while the urban, civil rights–era violence and intimacy in "Where Is the Voice Coming From?" is imagined to be grounded in a racial hatred spawned by whites who exist just above (if not alongside) blacks in the region's pecking order. In such a configuration, class, not gender, becomes the salient factor dividing whites. While in the novel Welty takes pains to link Troy to the aristocratic Fairchild men, the narrator in the story resents members of his own racial community (Goat Dykeman, the would-be assassin of James Meredith, and especially the governor) and eschews affiliation with other white men who share his racist views. Instead of uniting whites across class lines, as segregation and white-supremacist ideology often do, the civil rights movement seems to be fracturing white solidarity even as white men of various class groups struggle to maintain existing racial hierarchies.

Another critical difference between the novel and the story lies in the position of white women in the texts. As we saw above, the responses Shelley and Dabney have to the interactions they witness between Troy, George, and the African Americans in their employ are kept to themselves, and Shelley does not attempt to prevent Troy's marriage to her sister because of what she sees. By contrast, the killer's wife—the only person, besides readers and the dead victim himself, to whom he admits his crime—has much to say about her husband's actions, and all of it is critical. She speaks to him almost as if he is a child ("didn't the skeeters bite you?" she asks when he arrives home from the killing), disparaging her husband for leaving the gun, for choosing the wrong victim, and for drawing more attention to Summers (605). Warning him that "you're the one they'll catch," the narrator's wife then delivers the following prophesy: "I say it's so hot that even if you get to sleep you wake up feeling like you cried all night!" (606). Recall that in *Delta Wedding*, Shelley comments that all men are like "little children," but it is the black men in the novel (Big Baby, Man-Son) who are most obviously so, whereas here, Summer seems the adult and the killer the child, an idea his wife reinforces. If his working-class status emasculates him, she makes him feel even less self-mastery, playing on the very insecurities that inspire him to attack Summers. Her final words to her husband, which recount the young Caroline Kennedy's remark that when she grew up, she wanted to marry James Meredith, insinuate that black men are more attractive to white women than white men are. Shelley's realization that there might be little difference between Troy and "real Deltans" is valid and insightful, but her remarks that accompany it—that women, in knowing "a little better," do not participate in the "convincing" performances with African Americans that men do—absolve her of responsibility and suggest that white women do not enjoy (or exploit) white privilege to the extent that white men of all classes do. In "Where Is the Voice Coming From?," the unnamed wife's jabs at her husband, however humorous and well-deserved, exploit rather than critique the social structures at work in his actions, only managing to make the killer look like more of a buffoon than he already appears to be. Her taunts seem motivated more by an apolitical "war between the sexes" than by a meaningful evaluation of social boundaries. In thus not placing the white woman in a position of moral authority, the story scrutinizes in a way that the novel does not the limitations of white-centered feminist critiques like Shelley's to adequately address racial injustice in the South.

Thus one of the things that the Evers killing and the "changing sixties" seems to have affected is Welty's stance on the place of genteel white women in the South's racial and class hierarchies. But just as Shelley maintains a sense of class superiority over Troy, so, too, in the writing of "Where Is the Voice Coming From?," did Welty appear to maintain a sense of her own class superiority to the man she imagined "with overwhelming directness" to be the killer. Although Welty tells us in the preface to the *Collected Stories* that she had to change some of the details of the text so as not to influence the trial of Byron de la Beckwith, her portrait of the killer and the one Beckwith presented of himself are incongruent in many respects. In his dapper appearance and his hob-knobbing with the governor, who dramatically interrupted the trial during Myrlie Evers's testimony to shake Beckwith's hand, "Delay" presented himself as a poor-but-proud southern gentleman of good family if limited means, one whose patriarchal prerogative—recognized by the governor himself—was intact.[22] The question Welty thus asks in her title is not merely rhetorical, for the origin of the voice in the story ultimately is not just the killer's, but Welty's own voice as she tries to understand and, simultaneously, to locate racist violence in the white working class.

So when Beckwith's identity was made known, Welty was forced to acknowledge the validity of her friend's observation that "you thought it was a Snopes and it was a Compson."[23] Such an acknowledgment suggests that the man she thought she knew was less unlike her than she thought he was. As Welty later stated, "I felt that anybody who read that story would recognize things they had seen or heard or might even have said, in some version, or imagined or feared themselves."[24] His voice, as disdainful as it is, would be familiar to the arguably more benign, paternalistic voice of the Fairchilds in *Delta Wedding* (and to Welty, as she herself claims). Noel Polk points out that in Welty's works, "the enemy is not . . . easily recognizable," but perhaps, in another way, the enemy here is all too recognizable, for Welty seems to have come to understand her own social position better in her attempt to imagine the killer's.[25] This is certainly one of the most important effects the death of Medgar Evers had on Welty, and perhaps her story of that death can, and should, have a similar effect on readers, especially white ones. In an essay on teaching the story or, rather, on why she cannot teach it, Ruth Vande Kieft has written that "Where Is the Voice Coming From?" lacks credibility for her because she does not "believe that a man cowardly enough to shoot his helpless victim in the back would be capable of thinking of that victim humanely," and thus that, worse still, she does not "feel free to hate" the killer "along with his deed."[26] But it is the existence of such contradictions in whites' attitudes toward African Americans that the story so brilliantly documents. Welty's story can and should make us feel uncomfortable both because the narrator is repulsive *and* because, for many readers, he remains hauntingly, if only partially, familiar. In a lecture on the assassination's literary legacy, Minrose Gwin has recently asserted that in Welty's works and others, "we find Medgar . . . only to lose him," but we also find an opportunity to discover how America's racial past has shaped those who have benefited most from it. Just as the killer's conflicted responses to Summers reflect upon himself, our conflicted responses to the killer—shaped by Welty's own conflicted response—can reflect upon ourselves, inviting us to see those whom we scapegoat and what part each of us plays in maintaining social boundaries between ourselves and others.

Notes

1. Preface to *The Collected Stories of Eudora Welty*, x. Subsequent references will be cited parenthetically in the text.

2. These references suggest that Welty was not alone in viewing 1963, the year she wrote "Where Is the Voice Coming From?," as a defining moment in race relations: Roosevelt's work was published that year, and much of King's, the first chapter of which is titled "The Negro Revolution—Why 1963," was also completed in 1963, the year King led his march on Washington. Wallace's remarks, part of his inaugural speech as governor of Alabama, were also given that year.

3. Welty, *Delta Wedding*, 285. Subsequent references will be cited parenthetically in the text.

4. Jacobson, *Whiteness of a Different Color*, 6.

5. Donaldson, "Gender and History," 7.

6. Marrs, "The Metaphor of Race," 699.

7. Romines, "Reading the Cakes," 616.

8. As Brannon Costello notes, "Ellen's inability to formulate a specific rejoinder to Troy's characteristically forward remark reveals a fracture in the Fairchilds' sense of their lofty place in Delta society" (*Plantation Airs* 38).

9. Marrs, "The Metaphor of Race," 698.

10. Costello, *Plantation Airs*, 49.

11. Bank, "Dark-Purple Faces," 72.

12. Romines, "Reading the Cakes," 616.

13. Entzminger, "Playing in the Dark with Welty," 63. The term "racial patriarchy" is taken from Laura Doyle's excellent book, *Bordering on the Body*. The interactions between blacks and white women in the novel further reinforce this gender distinction, for while white women share the paternalism of white men's attitudes, they lack the violence framing white men's dealings with African Americans. As Ann Romines and Susan Donaldson have both asserted, the female world that dominates *Delta Wedding* is grounded in women's domestic rituals rather than the traditionally masculine world of physical conflict. See Romines's "Reading the Cakes" and Donaldson's "Gender and History."

14. Ladd points out that *Delta Wedding*, written about a time Welty thought was uneventful, nonetheless registers that "change is coming," a fact that would have been evident to Welty as she wrote the novel in the 1940s. See Ladd, "'Coming Through,'" 541.

15. Thermopylae is an important site in the ancient world where a small troop of Greeks fought against a more powerful Persian force.

16. Welty, "Where Is the Voice Coming From?" in *Collected Stories*, 603, 604. Subsequent references will be cited parenthetically in the text.

17. The name for this road—which memorializes one of the earliest and most prominent leaders of the KKK—is an ironic reminder that the violent nature of the killer's attempt at suppressing African Americans has a long history in the American South. Often associated with the white working class, the KKK nonetheless had its share of businessmen, politicians, and other men of the elite.

18. In "Portrait of an Assassin," Hargrove points out that the killer's defensiveness, insecurity, and bitterness are all responses to his own marginalization that he directs toward Summers because, as a black man, Summers provides a likely scapegoat for him (83).

19. Harrison, "'It's Still a Free Country,'" 645.

20. Harrison, "'It's Still a Free Country,'" 640; Lott, *Love and Theft*, 4. Building on the obsession with "white male–dark male dyads" first identified by Leslie Fielder, Lott's analysis of the minstrel show, like my own analysis of Welty's works here, notes the ways interracial male intimacy helps to structure manifestations of whiteness.

21. Entzminger, "Playing in the Dark with Welty," 53.

22. In much the same way, Bob Dylan's song about the Evers killing, "Only a Pawn in Their Game," attributes working-class status to the assassin, making him a hapless actor in a system that ultimately benefits only the white elite. Other media sources on Beckwith, such as a 1963 article appearing in *Time*, noted that Beckwith was both the grandson of Delta aristocracy and the son of a degenerate Californian who died of alcoholism. The article goes on to draw a parallel between the maternal uncle who raised Beckwith after his parents' deaths, a man who liked to catch catfish and stuff them "into a dresser drawer at home" to rot, and the rotting family home in Greenwood, Mississippi. Quoting a Greenwood merchant who told *Time* that Beckwith was reared in "the sort of place white people ought not to live in," the article notes that, nonetheless, "the premises were cluttered with mementos of the family's better days: a letter to Beckwith's grandmother from Jeff Davis: pieces of china from Beauvoir, the Davis mansion near Biloxi. To Beckwith, these must have suggested lush plantations, colonnaded mansions—and white supremacy." See "Civil Rights: A Little Abnormal."

23. Quoted in Linda Kuehl, "The Art of Fiction," in Whitman Prenshaw, *Conversations with Eudora Welty*, 83–84. Gwin, too, notes that Welty was troubled by her mistake after she published the story.

24. Quoted in Tom Royals and John Little, "A Conversation with Eudora Welty," in Prenshaw, *Conversations with Eudora Welty*, 259.

25. Polk, *Faulkner and Welty*, 9.

26. Vande Kieft, "'Where Is the Voice Coming From?': Teaching Eudora Welty," in Trouard, *Eudora Welty: Eye of the Storyteller*, 200.

Bibliography

Bank, Tenley Gwen. "Dark-Purple Faces and Pitiful Whiteness: Maternity and Coming Through in *Delta Wedding*." *Mississippi Quarterly,* Supplement (2009): 59–79.

"Civil Rights: A Little Abnormal." *Time*. July 5, 1963. http://www.time.com.

Costello, Brannon. *Plantation Airs: Racial Paternalism and the Transformation of Class in Southern Fiction, 1945–1971*. Baton Rouge: Louisiana State University Press, 2007.

Donaldson, Susan. "Gender and History in Eudora Welty's *Delta Wedding*." *South Central Review* 14, no. 2 (1997): 3–14.

Doyle, Laura. *Bordering on the Body: The Racial Matrix of Modern Fiction and Culture*. New York: Oxford University Press, 1994.

Entzminger, Betina. "Playing in the Dark with Welty: The Symbolic Role of African Americans in *Delta Wedding*." *College Literature* 30, no. 3 (2003): 52–67.

Gwin, Minrose. "Remembering Medgar Evers: Writing the Long Civil Rights Movement." Center for the Study of the American South, University of North Carolina Chapel Hill. February 8, 2011. http://vimeo.com/19758543.

Hargrove, Nancy. "Portrait of an Assassin: Eudora Welty's 'Where Is the Voice Coming From?'" *Southern Literary Journal* 20, no. 1 (1987): 74–88.

Harrison, Suzan. "'It's Still a Free Country': Constructing Race, Identity, and History in Eudora Welty's 'Where Is the Voice Coming From?'" *Mississippi Quarterly* 50, no. 4 (1997): 631–47.

Jacobson, Matthew Frye. *Whiteness of a Different Color: European Immigrants and the Alchemy of Race*. Cambridge, Mass.: Harvard University Press, 1998.

Ladd, Barbara. "'Coming Through': The Black Initiate in *Delta Wedding*." *Mississippi Quarterly* 41, no. 4 (1988): 541–51.

Lott, Eric. *Love and Theft: Blackface Minstrelsy and the American Working Class*. New York: Oxford University Press, 1995.

Marrs, Suzanne. "The Metaphor of Race in Eudora Welty's Fiction." *Southern Review* 22, no. 4 (1986): 697–707.

Polk, Noel. *Faulkner and Welty and the Southern Literary Tradition*. Jackson: University Press of Mississippi, 2008.

Prenshaw, Peggy Whitman, ed. *Conversations with Eudora Welty*. Jackson: University Press of Mississippi, 1984.

Romines, Ann. "Reading the Cakes: *Delta Wedding* and the Texts of Southern Women's Culture." *Mississippi Quarterly* 50, no. 4 (1997): 601–17.

Vande Kieft, Ruth M. "'Where Is the Voice Coming From?': Teaching Eudora Welty." In *Eudora Welty: Eye of the Storyteller*, ed. Dawn Trouard, 190–204. Kent, Ohio: Kent State University Press, 1989.

Welty, Eudora. *Delta Wedding*. In *Complete Novels*. New York: Library of America, 1998. 89–336.

———. Preface to *The Collected Stories of Eudora Welty*. San Diego: Harvest/Harcourt Brace, 1980. ix–xi.

———. "Where Is the Voice Coming From?" In *The Collected Stories of Eudora Welty*. San Diego: Harvest/Harcourt Brace, 1980.

DONNIE MCMAHAND

Bodies on the Brink

Vision, Violence, and Self-Destruction in Delta Wedding

Nowhere does Eudora Welty disparage agitprop more than in her essay "Must the Novelist Crusade?" (1965), in which she compares such fiction writing to a rabble, adding, "Nothing was ever learned in a crowd, from a crowd, or by addressing a crowd."[1] In the same piece, Welty promotes quiet authorial voices that balance subtle calls for justice with incisive observations of persons, places, and events. Commenting on the historic killings of Michael Schwerner, Andrew Goodman, and James Cheney, Welty writes, "To deplore a thing as hideous as the murder of the three civil rights workers demands the quiet in which to absorb it. Enormities can be lessened, cheapened, just as good and delicate things can be."[2] Since the original publication of "Must the Novelist Crusade?" at the height of the civil rights movement, critics have regarded the essay as a guidepost in recognizing the thorny position of white southern writers who face inherent limitations to their cross-racial literary imagination. To this end, François Pitavy, in his reading of Welty's story "Keela, the Outcast Indian Maiden" remarks on the writer's reluctance "to explore the black consciousness . . . a territory she does not consider hers. A white woman, she will not tread there."[3] The accuracy of Pitavy's judgment resonates throughout David McWhirter's contention that "Welty's black characters are 'let go' (and let go *of*) . . . in a manner that calls attention to all that she doesn't know, and doesn't claim to know, about them."[4] McWhirter takes his claim further, asserting that "Welty is always attuned to . . . [her characters'] desire not to be known or tell or be told."[5] For Pitavy and McWhirter, the black presence in Welty's writings is almost entirely obstructed, if not inscrutable. Their claims stem from the fact that Welty's black characters routinely lack backstory, their inner thoughts rarely expressed.

Not that McWhirter's argument lacks persuasion, but in my reading of *Delta*

Wedding (1946), I would call attention to the fallibility of reading the novel's black characters as inscrutable. I am not ready to let them go, not without inquiry into the part of their presence Welty seldom obstructs—their bodies. When Welty *does* obscure the black body, the effect stresses the narrow perspective of the novel's operative white gaze. What the black characters say and do, how they appear and disappear in the text, communicates not so much the specifics of their daily lives but the specified reality of their existence in the segregated South. To see and know these figures more fully, if not completely, the reader must be willing to decipher the signs of their bodies, a challenge that almost every white character in the novel fails even to attempt. Their failure to investigate casts the black body into a state of strange, unknowable disruptiveness, an ontic force to fear, control, or dismiss but not understand. Despite the white characters' failure to see and know their black counterparts, readers retain an opportunity to situate them in the larger context of segregation and to examine their evocations of play, rebellion, distress, and (self-) destruction. Even as Welty's black characters refuse, as McWhirter claims, to tell their stories, their bodies prove less reticent.

Deciphering these signs requires seeing around the obstructive view of the white gaze. In her essay "Place in Fiction," Welty describes viewpoint "as a sort of burning-glass, a product of personal experience and time . . . It is an instrument—one of intensification; it acts, it behaves, it is temperamental."[6] Here, Welty describes her active, prismatic sense of perspective, one where I detect a shrewd, subtle separation of narrator and character and, in the case of the novel, a preliminary closeness between protagonist and author. Welty's *One Writer's Beginnings* relates an intimacy between her younger self, excited by her family's summertime travels, and Laura McRaven, who, arriving on a train, has come to Shellmound to witness her cousin Dabney Fairchild marry overseer Troy Flavin. In the memoir, Welty writes, "The trips were wholes unto themselves. They were stories . . . When I did begin to write, the short story was a shape that had already formed itself and stood waiting in the back of my mind. Nor is it surprising to me that when I made my first attempt at a novel, I entered its world—that of the mysterious Yazoo-Mississippi Delta—as a child riding there on a train."[7] Dispatched in Laura's character, the voice of the young Welty contends with that of the more reflective, authorial Welty. A motherless, poor relation, Laura senses her status as an outsider and throughout her visit to Shellmound presents a double vision, relaying her reality as set apart from that of her rich, tight-knit relatives. Even the colorful contrast of their last names, Fairchild and McRaven, indicates with racialized overtones their fundamental difference. As this name-play illustrates, any critique Welty levels at Shellmound must abide by the demands of her quiet, nonpolemical voice and by her writerly conviction that the storyteller "is always seeing double, two pictures at once . . . his and the world's, a fact that he constantly comprehends; and he works best in a state of constant and subtle and unfooled reference between the two."[8] Occupying the space between narrator and various viewpoints, the black body exposes and agitates the writer's double vision, dilating the difference between how the novelist perceives and judges the world and how her characters make such assessments.

This agitation quite possibly led Welty to reimagine the southern pastoral, a genre that in its original form began appearing in print as early as the nineteenth century. Published in 1832, John P. Kennedy's *Swallow Barn* set the standard for much of the pastoral plot, populated with gallant white planters, dutiful wives and offspring, and contented black slaves, the old, familiar feudal system with every participant put in his rightful place. Evidently dissatisfied with this model, Welty quietly but radically altered it. Harriet Pollack's essay "On Welty's Use of Allusion" uncovers the complex ways Welty "has freely appropriated legend, history, folklore, myth, ballad, and poetry" and in the process "has reworked the Southern gothic, romantic, and pastoral formulas."[9] In her study of the southern pastoral, Elizabeth J. Harrison explores how Willa Cather, Zora Neale Hurston, and other female pastoralists moved the focus away from male-centered spaces of political and economic power in order to illuminate shifts in women's relationships with men, other women, and the land itself.[10]

Welty ultimately devises the pastoral as a narrative in transition, in which the precepts of the past give way, slowly, inexorably, to the future while African Americans hover between subject and object, between Welty's personal vision and the more restrictive outlook of her white characters. Like *Delta Wedding*, Toni Morrison's *Song of Solomon* (1977) probes the dislocation of black subjectivity in pastoral settings, but where Welty has to negotiate the restrictedness of her subject position, Morrison has only to embrace the advantage of her African American perspective. However, Morrison rejects the notion that subject position alone limits a writer's capacity to penetrate social boundaries. In an interview in 1980 she compares her ability to capture black male subjectivity in *Song of Solomon* with the cross-racial imaginations of Nadine Gordimer, Lillian Hellman, and Eudora Welty. These authors, Morrison argues, depict blacks "with . . . astounding sensibilities and sensitivity," their representations "not patronizing, not romantic, just real."[11] Affirming her admiration for Welty's writing, Morrison explains that Welty lived in a "totally racist" location, and in striving to take a leap away from its perceptions, she had to "make it totally."[12] Given Welty's dispassionate use of the white gaze, readers might regard her opposition to it as somewhat less apparent than Morrison does; however, I would argue that Welty reveals her objection to the racialist lens by working within its purview to interrogate and undermine its presence. Before publishing *Delta Wedding*, Welty had unveiled in "Powerhouse" and "A Worn Path" a keen awareness of black southern life, an awareness she extended throughout her career. In the novel, Welty's astuteness comes across at an angle, the black characters no less complex for their placement in the white gaze, which in some instances further complicates their figuration.

Their presentation in the novel changes dramatically, marking Welty's manipulation of the fixed, white lens imprinted in the novel's shifting viewpoints. To explore these changes, my discussion focuses first on those black figures who all but vanish in the text as well as those who become mesmerizing and ghostlike. These disembodied figures differ spectacularly from their subversive counterparts. Though filtered through the white gaze, these rebels act of their own accord, their actions evoking the futility of their defiance and the damage such futility places on their individual psyches. The same hegemonic view that transforms active, breathing bodies into nonentities shapes the lives of the rebels. However much they confront and challenge the view, they also abide counterintuitively by its devastating forces. Refusing to portray African Americans as uniformly agential or heroic, Welty depicts the psychic damage black subjects incur when they unwittingly accept and absorb the white gaze. That depictions of psychic damage in *Delta Wedding* (and, as I discuss briefly, in *Song of Solomon*) develop from mutable displays of black self-assertion, defiance, and rage all the more verifies the historic pairing of white supremacy and black self-destruction.

In the opening scene of Welty's novel, Laura's arrival at Shellmound aboard the *Yellow Dog* illustrates the tendency of the white gaze to blot out the black presence even to where it dematerializes on the page. Welty describes the formation of the *Dog* as an engine fronting "four cars, freight, white, colored, and caboose" (309). That Laura sees but does not see black passengers is a matter of no small consequence. Despite racially designated cars, she would observe these travelers at the station, on the platform, and possibly passing through the train's aisles. Onboard, she notices the engineer, the conductor, and a drummer wearing a straw hat. Debarking, she sees only Fairchilds: "Each mane of light hair waved like a holiday banner, so that you could see the Fairchilds everywhere" (4). Can the black travelers be standing so far away? Possibly *felt* but not acknowledged or imaged, they become spectral entities amid Laura's excitement in returning to Shellmound, where the Fairchilds practice a willful blindness and disregard toward their black servants and fieldworkers.

In *Constructing the Black Masculine*, Maurice Wallace refers to this act of seeing and not seeing as *spectragraphia*, a phenomenon whereby African Americans, imaged in photographs, advertisements, and literature, figure as little more than spectacles of the body. This process of selective vision contains an inverse scale in which the subject's humanity (or *humanness*) diminishes proportionately with a hyperconcentration on surface features—skin, hair, clothes, build, and voice. Whatever the medium or format for looking, the spectragraphic viewpoint sustains a stereoscopic disposition, swooping the individual into the generic and delimiting the black body to a frame that exposes the exterior but denies the existence of—or access to—the interior. Wallace thus defines spectragraphia as "a chronic syndrome of inscripted misrepresentation" that enfolds an "iconic simultaneity of the spectral and the spectacular."[13] By this estimation, the spectragraphic subject materializes in the eyes of the seer mainly as a specimen, a suspect, a body without thought, principle, or sensitivity.

Aligning indistinct or distorted images of the black body with depictions of temporary blindness in her white characters, Welty signals spectragraphia as a central element of the Delta mind-set. Traveling with her cousins to the farm in a car that Welty pointedly describes as encased in a "cloud of dust like a blind being" (5), Laura makes only a fleeting observation of black life in the Delta. In a catalog of geographic markings, including a railroad track, cemetery, cotton gin, and compress, the Negroes of Brunswicktown enter Laura's thoughts only marginally and generally, "smoking now on every doorstep" (5). At the farm, in a crush of memories from a previous summer, Laura recalls "the Negroes, Bitsy, Roxie, Little Uncle, and Vi'let" (8), servants, who all but for a moan that Vi'let makes, remain disembodied in the passage. From the train station at Brunswicktown to the plantation, the black presence at the onset of the novel lies mostly in the disclosure of names and in brief descriptions of action. Later, when Ellen Fairchild happens upon a runaway girl in the woods, Welty reveals how the spectragraphic view confounds the color line, further complicating reality. Not seeing the child fully in the daylight but assuming her to be black, Ellen is surprised to learn otherwise: "So she was white. A whole mystery of life opened up" (90). The revelation of the girl's whiteness forces an immediate shift in Ellen's attitude about the child, suddenly piquing Ellen's interests—where did the runaway come from, and where is she going, and how did she come to wander about in the woods? Departing, Ellen tells her, "I reckon I was the scared one, not you . . . In the beginning I did think I was seeing something in the woods—a spirit . . . —then I thought it was Pinchy, an ignorant little Negro girl on our place" (93). Ellen collapses her fear of spirits with her disregard of the black Other, a collapse that fixes her concept of blackness with that of an otherworldly, ghostly threat. This wild child may be a runaway, penniless and unaffiliated with any of the respected families in the bayou (a conclusion Ellen herself comes to), but the girl's whiteness alone makes her a person of relevance, worthy of Ellen's time, thought, and feeling.

When Pinchy does show up in the text, she indeed evokes a spectral presence, a figure detached from any discernible narrative. What is told, what does penetrate the white gaze, is her uncanny ability to unsettle the perceptions of those around her. Upset with her husband, George, Robbie forces Pinchy to stand outside a cotton shack while she takes refuge inside. From a window she intently watches Pinchy "dangle as if suspended in the light" (194). The text's description of Robbie's eyes as "fastened hypnotically" (194) builds tension between her and the narrator's view and demonstrates Robbie's dazed perception of Pinchy as a nebulous entity, as not quite there. Riding up on his horse, Troy reinforces Robbie's narrow view, telling Pinchy, "I get tired of seeing you everywhere" (196). To be seen "everywhere" occasions offense—black bodies must be continually positioned. In truth, Troy and Robbie only partially see Pinchy, her body quickly dispersing in the day's light, as when she walks away, "out into the light, like a matchstick in the glare, . . . swallowed up in it" (197). The tendency of the black body to dissolve into earthly elements continues at novel's end, where Laura accompanies her cousins and their servants on a picnic in the bayou. Welty cloaks the scene in night, into which Little Uncle, driving the buggy that carries Laura, becomes "invisible" (315). A seemingly insignificant detail, the servant's disappearance underscores the absenting of nearly every black figure in the novel: no exception, Little Uncle's body signifies a cipher, a nonentity.

If Little Uncle, Roxie, Bitsy, Pinchy, Vi'let, and the train's black passengers personify absence, appearing more as shadows than as vital subjects, they also validate McWhirter's argument that Welty's refusal to present the black mindscape marks it as withheld. The inscrutable presence of these characters inscribes the extent to which their bodies are absented, put away, materializing mainly in acts of servitude to the Fairchilds. Pinchy's unspecified religious conversion provides a rather minor distraction to the family, while Little Uncle, Roxie, Bitsy, and Vi'let rarely, if ever, interrupt the flow of daily life on the plantation. However, other black characters in *Delta Wedding* openly oppose this shadow formation in that they do not consistently conform to the behavioral norms set forth at Shellmound. Consequently, they do not appear as ghosts; they are not disembodied, and, to be sure, they do not evaporate into daylight or dark of night, nor do they dematerialize on the page. These rebel figures enter the white gaze as spectacular beings, their menace distorted and electrified by an excessive sense of their presence. While some rebels subtly dispute the dictates of their oppression, others resort to violence as a way to smash against their confinement.

Emerging from the cotton fields, Man-Son models Wallace's notions of *specimen* and *suspect*, notions that instill fear and fascination in the seer. For Man-Son's encounter with Dabney, Welty turns again to the motif of blindness to emphasize the narrowness of Dabney's viewpoint and, more specifically, her inability to perceive Man-Son as anyone other than a field laborer or as a bloody, scrapping child. Welty suggests that Dabney's apprehension about the looming changes in her life triggers her temporary vision loss. On horseback, she and her younger sister India cross Troy's path, and Dabney "saw a blinding light, or else was it a dark cloud—that intensity under her flickering lids? She rode with her eyes shut" (38). On their way to visit their unmarried aunts, the sisters pass several black fieldworkers who "lift up and smile glaringly and pump their arms" (37) in honor of the coming nuptials. Man-Son's greeting, however, is unexpected and disconcerting, his manner unlike the customary addresses Dabney receives from the other black workers. That Dabney persists in riding "blindly and proudly" with "her eyes shut against what was too bright" (42) adds a telling frame to her unforeseen meeting with Man-Son, whose transgression is not simply that he tips his hat or that he wishes her and Troy well on their wedding day but that he does so standing directly in front of her. For Dabney, he has broken the frame for which he is made: "How strange—he should be picking cotton, thought Dabney" (43). In her eyes, Man-Son's existence, emanating entirely from his body's labor, prohibits the very possibility of his intellect and emotion, and his active disruption of his role as a cotton picker imparts his shift from spectral to spectacle.

Contrary to his gentle (gentlemanly) manner, Man-Son arouses Dabney's memory of him as a child fighting another black boy, his brother. In the flashback, Dabney recalls how "[t]wo of their little Negroes had flown at each other" (44) with knives and how Uncle George, intervening, gets blood on his hands and legs. All menace and violence, the black body envelops Dabney's temporary purview of the text. During the fracas, the two boys become a blur of "thrashing legs and arms" (44), first subdued then "hollering," one's face "crumpled" and the other bearing a wounded back and a "black pole" of a chest (45). These fleshly images, including the sight of spilled blood, clinch Dabney's memory of the brothers, distinguishing them from the other workers: "Dabney had never forgotten which two boys those were, and could tell them from the rest" (45). Except for his single bid to Dabney that "you'n and Mr. Troy find you happiness" (46), Man-Son has little else to say, so that his existence becomes for Dabney his imposing, bodily presence. "Nodding sternly" and admonishing him to "get to picking" (43, 46), Dabney can only dismiss the experience as an aberrant one, the "song of distant pickers" (47), adding a more familiar, acceptable element to the sisters' outing. The depiction of Negro voices "start[ing] up like the agitation of birds" (43–44) confirms for Dabney the proper place for black bodies—as atmosphere, as geographic marking, and not much else.

Although Dabney regards his gesture as an imposition and as potential mischief, Welty allows the reader a wider view. And while Dabney may not realize the existential entendre of her question "Man-Son, what do you mean?" (46), the nuances prevail, growing out of the break between Dabney's thoughts and the narrator's perspective. What *does* Man-Son mean? Judging even by this tiny box of time, what do his actions say about him? If nothing else, he would understand the hard and tacit rules controlling the proximity of black men's bodies to white women on the farm. That he does not stand back, staring and waving like the other cotton pickers, indicates his readiness to take a risk, to crack the boundary between his black male self and Dabney's white womanhood. Besides bestowing good wishes on Dabney's wedding day, Man-Son's greeting exposes his desire to be seen, to be acknowledged as an individual, not merely part of a collective. As a risk-taker, he has to balance his nonconformity with his obvious awareness of the possible consequences to his wayward behavior, which involves at the least losing his job—his own brother "had given trouble . . . and [Dabney's] father had let him go" (45). Designated "a good Negro" (45), meaning *obedient, inconspicuous*, Man-Son stays on at the plantation but flouts such perceptions of goodness. Whether he tips his hat out of earnestness or as evidence of a placating mask or as subversive play, the text does not make plain. Nor does the novel resolve the contradictory images of him as a garish brute and gallant youth, two polarizing categories of his physical presence. Remarkably, Welty combines her barrier to the black perspective with Man-Son's act of obstruction, particularly his attempt to redefine his body, the only part of his being available for review in the Fairchilds' eyes. To what end his efforts impact Dabney's outlook remains indeterminate. What becomes clear is his resistance to being contained, physically and conceptually—by Welty's readers, by his brother, and by his white employers at Shellmound. All the more evident is Man-Son's essential difference from the disembodied black characters in the novel. Even as Pinchy receives attention for her wanderings, for her knack of being seen "everywhere," her position in the white gaze shifts only slightly from geographic marker to phantom. Apart from her religious transformation, her character virtually lacks an outward show of self-assertion. Unlike Pinchy and Little Uncle, who mostly accept their roles, *staying in their places*, Man-Son slyly refuses to play his scripted part.

Yet, for all its strangeness, Man-Son's conduct pales in comparison to the outrage exhibited by Root M'Hook, who stabs his way into Troy's office and the text, tearing at the permanency of the Fairchilds' idyll. Bursting into Troy's office, Shelley acts as a spectator to the violence and finds the sudden and grisly appearance of black men so alarming she initially mistakes a key detail of what she sees: "Shelley walked into the point of a knife. Root M'Hook, a field Negro, held the knife drawn; it was not actually a knife, it was an ice pick; Juju and another Negro stood behind, with slashed cheeks, and open-mouthed; still another, talking to himself, stood his turn apart" (257). Shelley's correction stresses the instability of the scene, if not also her view of it. Although Welty never fully explains the origin of the commotion—which comes *in medias res*—one of the other fieldworkers, Juju, says that it traces back to Pinchy's "coming through," or religious conversion (257). The text relays few additional remarks from the men, but their actions and the state of their bodies provide telling glimpses into their experience, defining their individual connection to the violence. The attack on Troy implies his prior involvement in the conflict, possibly at its inception. Why does Juju blame Pinchy for instigating the fight? Has Root discovered a sexual indiscretion between Troy and Pinchy? Or does this dispute pertain to the payment of wages? As the aggressor, Root unleashes a murderous rage against white authority while the other men look on like bystanders. Obviously, the dynamics and focus of their fight have changed with Troy's inclusion; now the men "stood behind," awestruck by Root's auda-cious charge and Troy's reaction. "Open-mouthed," they are shocked to witness Root's refusal to surrender to this figure of white power. If Root's aggression has an unspecified beginning, his defeat is more definite, as the loss of his finger furthers the scene's display of injured bodies. One of the unnamed men, stand-ing apart from the others and "talking to himself," signifies a psychic injury, his distress intimated by his distance from the others, by his anonymity, and by the sheer desperation of his distracted speech.

Repulsed by the spill of black blood on the doorsill and determined to avoid touching it, Shelley, the novel's would-be visionary, fails to look past her own privileged disposition, showing little interest or insight into the field-workers' discontent. Adding absurdity to the disturbance, a man calling him-self Big Baby admits to having a backside filled with buckshot. If Shelley were to look more thoughtfully at the workers, she would realize that, like Dabney's inevitable subordination to a husband—"what was going to happen was going to happen" (258)—the men's lives bear as severe a *fait accompli*, their destiny broadcast by Root's rage and by the small tragicomedy of Big Baby's predica-ment. Between one man's hostility and the other's humiliation, the showdown in Troy's office conveys a range of responses to white dominance. Despite the men's individual demeanor, they dramatize in total a crisis of the black body, a body on the brink, confronting a political and economic advantage it cannot defeat. Preoccupied with Troy's marriage to her sister, Shelley does not grasp the parallel between her fear that Troy will suppress Dabney's independence and the impact of white paternalism on the affairs of the black workers. Her racial shortsightedness hinders the discernment that drives her feminist vision, and as a result, the black men, alternately violent and laughable, become spec-tacular objects, seen and unseen, relegated to the shadows. The scene in Troy's office ends as abruptly as it begins, the dénouement left unspecified. By de-nying a resolution, Welty does not suggest that none exists but that Shelley does not anticipate its occurrence and that the fury that fomented this outburst must linger on in the dark of the workers' unnarrated lives, in the same dark-ness where the racial discord and economic inequality of the segregated South would continue to grow.

Entering this darkness through little Roy's and Laura's fascinated eyes, Aunt Studney figures as the most complex projection of the white gaze. In almost all aspects of her spectragraphic figuration, Aunt Studney becomes a study of con-trasts, her spectral identity merging at times with her ardent, bodily opposition to white dominance. Going even further than Man-Son's boundary-crossing, Aunt Studney sets her own itinerary, irrespective of property lines and racialized restrictions, challenging the controlling intent of the white gaze—but with marginal success. Explaining that Aunt Studney hails from "Back of the Deadening," a location that clearly literalizes the old woman's ghostly presence, Roy tells his cousin, "You'll see her walking the railroad track anywhere between Greenwood and Clarksdale" (228). Retracing Aunt Studney's peripatetic steps, Roy intimates at once the panoptic lens the white community fixes on her movements as well as her self-determination in making the journey. The mere sight of her mesmerizes Laura. By virtue of her wanderings, color, and age, Aunt Studney engenders for Laura a spectacle of the black body: "coal-black, old as the hills, with her foot always in the road" (228). In the child's eyes, Aunt Studney's skin color becomes an object of exhibition, one more detail in a canvas already crowded with oddities.

Divided by the polarizing force of the children's fascination, Aunt Studney's ontological formation—as body and phantom—comes into sharp focus. A roving spirit, she rambles through the rooms of Marmion, the vacant house the newlyweds plan to inhabit after the ceremony. Exploring the extravagant foyer, the children do not see her but sense her presence through disembodied noises: "There was an accusing, panting breathing, and the thud of a big weight planted in the floor" (230). An imposing bodily presence, the woman lifts her arms "balefully" and hovers over her sack, guarding it "like an old bird over her one egg" (231). Like a conjurer, casting a spell over the house, Aunt Studney transforms Laura's perceptions of the place and her position in it: "'Is it still the Delta in here?' Laura cried, panting" (231). Clearly, Laura's re-vision of Marmion and the Delta as a physical and cultural space threatens to shatter the limits of the white gaze that cannot contain Aunt Studney's emergent self. To no avail, the children voice their desire to know the contents of the woman's bag. When the children are not looking, Aunt Studney opens the sack and releases a cloud of bees into the house. Setting the terms of Aunt Studney's otherness, the attack figures as the most fanciful act of black aggression in the novel. To be sure, the sudden swarm of bees leaves the children all the more confounded, with Roy laughing and asking, "Aunt Studney! Why have you let bees in my house?" (232). Sphinx-like, Aunt Studney has no response for him; her actions stand alone, her strangeness multiplied within the mechanism of her control.

The mystery deepens when after fleeing the house Roy pushes Laura into the Yazoo River: "As though Aunt Studney's sack had opened after all, like a whale's mouth, Laura opening her eyes head down saw its insides all around her—dark water and fearful fishes. A face flanked by receding arms looked at her under water—Roy's, a face strangely indignant and withdrawing" (234–35). Laura's imagination of the water as the interior of Aunt Studney's sack distinguishes her from her relatives, especially Dabney and Shelley, in that Laura, her eyes "opening," tries to see past her own limited view. However, her failure to see or truly know emphasizes her lack of experience. Laura is transitioning, no longer the distracted person arriving on the *Yellow Dog* but by no means the enlightened individual she may become. Harriet Pollack refers to river baptism in Welty's work as "an immersion in female nature,"[14] but how does race inform, if not thoroughly impede, the redemptive change implied by baptism? If Laura's interest in Aunt Studney resonates with her own sense as an outsider, she has yet to fulfill her potential of perceiving black bodies apart from the racist characterizations that saturate the Delta mind-set. Her general lack of compassion becomes clear when her cousin Maureen in an earlier incident pushes a woodpile onto her, an act that physically and psychically marks her. Looking down at the abrasions on her skin, "lick[ing] the blood away," and feeling excluded from the other children, Laura regards herself as "black and ugly as a little Negro" (97). Laura mitigates the pain of her alienation by comparing herself to a predicament and a body she considers worse than her own; consequently, her ability to envision life beyond the Fairchild perspective progresses only as far as her wavering desire to do so.

Whatever Laura fails to see, whatever lurks in the dark, the narrative implies she can hardly comprehend its contents, a failure that adds new depths of purpose to the novel's delicate interplay between strategic restriction and rich suggestion, between blindness and foresight. The blending of the river and the sack, the merging of a shadowy black existence and the water's undertow, marks the apogee of Welty's attempt to splinter her characters' myopic perspective with her own wider view. Unlike Ellen's and Dabney's, Laura's bout with blindness does not erase the reality of what eludes her sight but renders its mystery all the more vivid. More to the point, Welty's depiction of the black ghost reinvokes the half-hidden history of the Delta, specifically the Yazoo, or "River of Death" (256). This sobriquet is not Welty's invention, and its use by other Mississippians precludes definitive origins, although many historians attribute the name to the outcome of several Civil War battles that transformed the river into a warehouse of sunken ships. Newspaper reports from the turn of the twentieth century relate that the river burst its banks and filled its floodplain many times before the catastrophic flood of 1927 (four years after the time of *Delta Wedding*). However, true to Welty's aesthetic, the novel never traffics in the cold light of these facts, relying, instead, on atmosphere and historical trace, not least the practice of consigning black bodies to Mississippi's waterways. In *A Festival of Violence*, Stewart E. Tolnay and E. M. Beck comment on one case in which a black insurrection on a plantation in Yazoo County led to the killing of the three ringleaders, Minor Wilson, C. C. Reed, and Willis Boyd: "As so often happened, . . . the wheels of formal justice were not allowed to grind this case to its natural completion. While being transported to Silver City, Wilson, Reed, and Boyd were taken from law enforcers by a mob of determined whites. The three men were shot to death, then their bodies were weighted down and thrown into the Yazoo River."[15]

Prior to arriving at Troy's office, Shelley passes by this River of Death. Her unease in the bayou, "filled with its summer trance, its winter trance of sleep" (256), redoubles the deadly impression of the river that Partheny, the old Fairchild nurse, gives one evening while lying on her cot, confessing her suicidal thoughts to Ellen: "I were mindless . . . I were out of my house. I were looking in de river. I were standing on Yazoo bridge wid dis foot lifted. I were mindless, didn't know my name or name of my sons. Hand stop me. Mr. Troy Flavin, he were by my side, gallopin' on de bridge. He laugh at me good—Old Partheny. Don't you jump in dat river, make good white folks fish you out! No, sir, no, sir, I ain't goin' to do dat! Guides me home" (101). Partheny's suicide attempt furthers Welty's formulation of the self-destructive Negro. Not unlike Root and Big Baby, Partheny retains enough distinction from the novel's dominant viewpoint to evoke a separateness of being, one that bends inchoately between self-assertion and self-defeat. Drawing on various theories by Mikhail Bakhtin, Gloria Anzaldúa, and Homi Bhabha on the development of subaltern identities into formidable cultural forces, Evelyn Jaffe Schreiber asserts, "When those marginalized in a culture become subjects through articulation of identity difference, they begin to fashion an emergent culture."[16] The emergence of a minority subjectivity illustrates what Schreiber calls "the double process" of cultural shift, whereby the dominant "weakens from encounters with otherness" and the marginalized eventually "[reject] . . . their subordinate status."[17] However, as Welty's novel suggests, this process of emergence meets with countless social and psychological impediments. As social change triggers violent reprisals from the dominant culture, it also uncovers a tendency toward self-destruction in the subdominant. Here, then, Morrison's commendation of

Welty's black characters as "not patronizing, not romantic, just real"[18] seems particularly salient. Perhaps the "realness" Morrison appreciates lies in Welty's willingness to weigh the agency of her black characters against the absoluteness of their oppression, demonstrating that in the segregated South not every act of subversion is constructive or that subversion itself can camouflage a defeatist sensibility. This defeatism reifies a fundamental failure in the black subject to disconnect fully from the white gaze. Without this disconnection and without the mobilization of organized resistance, the black characters in *Delta Wedding* emerge partway, expelling the pernicious influences of the racialist lens nominally and with dubious effect.

Like the projected image of the black body metamorphosing from apparition to fleshly spectacle, self-destruction in the novel manifests both as a spiritual and physical phenomenon. Whereas Partheny's suicidal longings present the most forthright expression of self-destruction, the incident in Troy's office offers a more complex picture of the problem, staging an intricate interchange between insurrection and foregone defeat. Without narrating the origins of the fight, Welty places focus squarely on unanswered questions in the falling action. How positive, for instance, is Root's future after his confrontation with Troy? Even if he survives his gunshot wound, even if he achieves some sense of victory in challenging Troy, he now faces a greater risk of vigilante justice, imprisonment, or, at best, a fugitive status, *ramifications he would have known*. The cost to Big Baby's humanity is similarly steep. In name and action, Big Baby resorts to infantilism as his primary mode of survival. Even if he acts out of a deliberate strategy to inflate Troy's ego in order to spare the men from any retributory violence Troy might inflict, Big Baby still has to sacrifice his own ego. His presence in Troy's office summons three possible scenarios: a masked performance, an internalization of his supposed inferiority, or an active permutation of these two possibilities. In any case, his actions (performative or not) denote a stunted subjectivity. Either donning the mask of racial inferiority or, worse, embedding it, Big Baby obliterates any notion of self-worth he might have. Although spectacular, his appearance contrasts the reckless mode by which other black men in the novel come into view, their bodies embroiled in bursts of wasteful aggression, their masculinity fashioned out of fury, desperation, and brutish force. The two relevant scenes that Dabney and Shelley witness relay a pattern of black-on-black violence, first between Man-Son and his brother, then between Root and the other workers, and possibly between Big Baby and whoever has shot him in the buttocks. The spilling of black blood by other blacks refocuses (without entirely transforming) the historic paradigm of violence in the segregated South—from interracial to intraracial. Such violence emphasizes the absence of the workers' agency. Root's rage imparts a patina of power, a sideshow that in the end points up his ineffectualness in resisting Troy's dominance.

Although Aunt Studney's situation seems less immediately dire than Partheny's or Root's, her subversive doings amount to little more than derision for Shellmound's white residents. To be sure, her defiance hardly predisposes her destruction but by no means do her actions alter or improve her plight. That she opens and closes her bag as she chooses and controls her verbal exchange with the Fairchilds indeed confers agency to her character, but such agency is so diminished that it doesn't disrupt in any genuine way the habits and routines of the people she scorns. Nevertheless, her destruction seems certain, imminent, and interwoven with the strange obscurity that defines her life. Soon after Laura's plunge in the Yazoo, Roy shows her where Aunt Studney lives, pointing out "through a screen of trees a dot of cabin; it was exactly like the rest, away out in a field where there was a solitary sunflower against the sky, many-branched and taller than a chimney, all going to seed, like an old Christmas tree in the yard" (235). While this "seed," "sunflower," and "Christmas tree" imagery suggests regeneration, those images hardly mitigate the reality of her ruinous state, nor do these images communicate what may be regenerating, other than an ongoing existence in the margins. At the same time, any recognition of Aunt Studney's misery must remain speculative, given the children's insular view, a constraint accented by the phrase "screen of trees." Still, the ruinous state of her dwelling place—the "dot of cabin . . . going to seed"—stresses the reality that for all the fascination the old woman generates, her poverty and implied degradation override her uniqueness, consequently making her home and dual depiction as spectacle and specter "exactly like" like that of any other Delta Negro.

Tantalizing yet restrictive, the "screen of trees" highlights the narratological split between Welty's insight and her characters' shallower vision, typifying both the purchase and the problem of the novel's use of the myopic white gaze. How, then, does the reader consider these contradictory elements, and how useful can the novel's gaze be in a reading that tries to interrogate black interiority? Obviously, these questions demand an expansion of analysis. If Welty's "screen" precludes a wholly reliable interrogation of black self-destruction, Morrison's *Song of Solomon* adds a corroborative comment on the matter, taking Welty's use of the white gaze beyond its limits while retaining the ethos of its design. Just as *Delta Wedding* routinely probes the thoughts and feelings of its white characters and relegates the black psyche to the implications of speech and action, Morrison's novel plumbs the thoughts and actions of its black characters, all but to the exclusion of whites, who in reverse of Welty's text are cast as shadow and atmosphere. Imparting an insider's view of black life, Morrison's depiction of self-destruction bypasses the issue of authorial credibility.

In *Song of Solomon*, protagonist Milkman Dead squares off with his onetime friend Guitar Bains, who has recently joined an outfit called Seven Days. The radical group resorts to killing unsuspecting whites as restitution for the unjust killing of blacks. Extolling the effectiveness of this covert operation, Guitar tells Milkman, "It's about trying to make a world where one day white people will think before they lynch" (160). Ironically, Guitar poses more of a threat to Milkman than white vigilantes, now that lynch mobs have given way in their lives to a new violent focus, the brute force of enraged black men. Rewriting the paradigm of Welty's novel in which white men stand at the center of black male aggression and wield the ultimate stroke of power—George's intervention, for instance, in the knife fight between a young Man-Son and his little brother—Morrison suggests that black male violence contains significant connections to southern history. In the novel's final scene, Milkman finally inhabits the myth of the flying African that he traces along the path of his family's southern roots in Shalimar, Virginia. Reenacting the myth with Guitar, Milkman does not retrace the legendary return to Africa but soars into "the killing arms of his brother" (337). Staging the men's clash on such a grand scale and on southern soil—Solomon's Leap, where Milkman's great-grandfather Jake began his airborne journey back to Africa—the scene belies the agency to which the men aspire. Milkman's possible *flight* into death obviously undercuts his potential to develop and relish his newfound spiritual awareness and cultural connectedness. As in *Delta Wedding*, violent exertions against white power engender defeat, and in the cases of Root M'Hook and Guitar, such opposition leads to—or corresponds with—an immediate or impending destruction of the self.

Morrison's most direct and telling intertext with Welty's literary landscape involves Milkman's encounter with Circe, the former servant of the wealthy Butler clan, whose trickery and murder enable them to steal the Dead family's property. (Though set in Pennsylvania, the old Dead/Butler property eerily evokes the faded grandeur of Dixie homesteads.) Her bitterness as thick as Aunt Studney's, Circe centers her entire being around wreaking revenge on the Butlers. Intent on destroying even the remnants of white privilege, Circe lingers in the house after the death of the last Butler to ensure that "[e]verything in this world [the Butlers] lived for will crumble and rot" (247). Critics who accept Circe's stance tend to celebrate her life as a continuous act of self-assertion, will, and protest, "a mission" executed, as Margaret I. Jordan puts it, "in the service of honor and righteousness—a justice denied by law and society."[19] However, Jordan overlooks or minimizes the fact that Circe, notwithstanding her fortitude and dignity, lives a life so rooted in destruction, not least her own, that her commitment to justice demands her physical and psychic exposure to the literal waste and decadence of a bygone era. Milkman's accusatory remark to her, "you still loyal" (247), implies that her devotion to ruin has left her alienated and incomplete in herself. She herself expresses contempt for the county's black population: "I don't like those Negroes in town" (246). That she fixates so completely on the Butlers confirms Milkman's claim that even now she is committed to the white gaze. As with Root's and Guitar's narrative, the strands of retaliation and self-destruction intertwine, so that one reality scarcely threads apart from the other.

At their most powerful, Aunt Studney and Circe figure as paradoxes. Their autonomous feats distinguish them from other subjugated blacks but not so far as to liberate either woman from her oppressors' control. Certainly, the women's rebellion touches the threshold of their all but negated relationship with white dominance, though not beyond and not without destroying their prospects of creating more productive, fulfilling lives. Circe's occupation of the Butler house reinvokes Aunt Studney's preoccupation with the Fairchild residence at Marmion, her liminal presence within the white gaze there and elsewhere comparable to Circe's literal fixedness to the white imaginary of the old, crumbling property in which she readily expects to perish.

These images of black annihilation ultimately indict the insidious legacy of America's color line. Searching the murky, peculiar spaces where empowerment verges on self-defeat, Welty and Morrison deftly mark the psychic damages incurred by opposition. Morrison's signification lends focus and cogency to Welty's thematics of limitation, an aesthetic that commemorates the southern pastoral while critiquing the racialist ethos that frames it. Undoubtedly, the black presence in *Delta Wedding* casts more than a collective shadow over the Fairchild clan. The signs of vanishing, fighting, and wounding in the novel chart not only the crucible of the Jim Crow South but also an intriguing instance in Welty's imagination, in which the author counterbalances the absented black body with an emergent, rebellious black subject. Welty's characterization consequently exemplifies a new beginning in cross-racial representation, occupying a seminal break between object and subject, between shadow and character, and—most daring for Welty—between self-assertion and self-destruction. In a conversation with Mel Watkins in 1977, Morrison, evidently struck by Welty's sensitivity and boldness, declared her "fearless," adding, "Welty write[s] about black people in a way that few white men have ever been able to write."[20] Echoing Morrison's sentiments here, François Pitavy argues that, as women, both Welty and Morrison "could see through the male system of unseeing, could see what was in plain sight."[21] Possibly as women, with something to gain from unwriting the male vision of the pastoral South and rural North, Welty and Morrison could present African Americans without the distraction of romance or patronizing control, conceiving, instead, realistic black people who reflect the widest possible range of human behavior.

In contrast to the fieldworkers in *Delta Wedding*, Phoenix Jackson, the ancient protagonist of "A Worn Path" (1941), proves that not all of Welty's assertive black characters suffer for their defiance and that not every defiant act deteriorates into self-negation. In the story, Phoenix etches out an indelible impression of her life-force as she undertakes an arduous journey along the Old Natchez Trace to obtain medicine at a doctor's office for her ailing grandson. Unlike the halcyon fields of Shellmound, the path she follows winds through a wintry terrain that eerily reiterates the South's rhetoric of racialized violence: "Big dead trees, like black men with one arm, were standing in the purple stalks of the withered cotton field. There sat a buzzard."[22] Phoenix remains undaunted, even while staring down the gun of a white small-game hunter. Her lack of outward fear denies the hunter a satisfactory sign of her surrender. Persistent in her journey, she rebuffs his menacing gaze as well as his verbal threat (disguised as advice) to "stay home, and nothing will happen to you."[23] Nothing about Phoenix's response, "I bound to go on my way, mister,"[24] suggests a masked performance or self-sabotage. Yet she and Aunt Studney possess a similar trajectory: old peripatetic survivors of the southern landscape, both undeterred by white eyes and both beset by trying tasks, the full meaning of which only they can know. As racialized subjects, both women embody Welty's prismatic sense of perspective. With Aunt Studney appearing faintly tragic and Phoenix triumphant, the controlling vision alone—the seen subject and the process of seeing—illuminates for the reader a flickering significance, ever expanding and refracting.

Notes

1. Welty, "Must the Writer Crusade?" 153.
2. Welty, "Must the Writer Crusade?" 153.
3. François Pitavy, "From Middle Passage to Holocaust," 60.
4. McWhirter, "Secret Agents: Welty's African Americans," 119.
5. McWhirter, "Secret Agents: Welty's African Americans," 119.
6. Welty, "Place in Fiction," 124.
7. Welty, *One Writer's Beginnings*, 68.
8. Welty, "Place in Fiction," 125.
9. Pollack, "On Welty's Use of Allusion," 312.
10. Harrison, *Female Pastoral*, 3–9.
11. Morrison, "The Visits of the Writers Toni Morrison and Eudora Welty," interview with Kathy Neustadt, in *Conversations with Toni Morrison*, 91.
12. Morrison, "The Visits of the Writers Toni Morrison and Eudora Welty," 91.
13. Wallace, *Constructing the Black Masculine*, 30.
14. Pollack, "On Welty's Use of Allusion," 328.
15. Tolnay and Beck, *Festival of Violence*, 41.
16. Schreiber, *Subversive Voices*, 6.
17. Schreiber, *Subversive Voices*, 6.
18. Morrison, "The Visits of the Writers," interview with author. Reprint, Jackson: University of Mississippi Press, 1994.
19. Margaret I. Jordan, *African American Servitude and Historical Imaginings*, 225.
20. Morrison, "Talk with Toni Morrison," interview with Mel Watkins, in *Conversations with Toni Morrison*, 47.
21. Pitavy, "From Middle Passage to Holocaust," 52.
22. Welty, "A Worn Path," 142.
23. Welty, "A Worn Path," 146.
24. Welty, "A Worn Path," 146.

Bibliography

Harrison, Elizabeth Jane. *Female Pastoral: Women Writers Re-visioning the American South*. Knoxville: University of Tennessee Press, 1991.
Jordan, Margaret I. *African American Servitude and Historical Imaginings: Retrospective Fiction and Representations*. New York: Palgrave Macmillan, 2004.
McWhirter, David. "Secret Agents: Welty's African Americans." In *Eudora Welty, Whiteness, and Race*, ed. Harriet Pollack, 114–30. Athens: University of Georgia Press, 2013.

Morrison, Toni. *Song of Solomon*. New York: Alfred A. Knopf 1977. Reprint, New York: Plume, 1987.

———. "Talk with Toni Morrison." Interview with Mel Watkins. In *Conversations with Toni Morrison*, ed. Danille Taylor-Guthrie, 43–47. Jackson: University of Mississippi Press, 1994.

———. "The Visit of the Writers Toni Morrison and Eudora Welty." Interview with Kathy Neustadt. In *Conversations with Toni Morrison*, ed. Danille Taylor-Guthrie, 43–47. Jackson: University of Mississippi Press, 1994.

Pitavy, François. "From Middle Passage to Holocaust: The Black Body as a Site of Memory." In *Sites of Memory in American Literatures and Cultures*, ed. Udo J. Hebel, 51–64. American Studies Series, vol. 101. Heidelberg: Universitätsverlag, 2001.

Pollack, Harriet. "On Welty's Use of Allusion: Expectations and Their Revision in 'The Wide Net,' *The Robber Bridegroom* and 'At the Landing.'" *Southern Quarterly* 29, no. 1 (1990): 5–31.

Schreiber, Evelyn Jaffe. *Subversive Voices: Eroticizing the Other in William Faulkner and Toni Morrison*. Knoxville: University of Tennessee Press, 2001.

Tolnay, Stewart E., and E. M. Beck. *A History of Violence: An Analysis of Southern Lynchings, 1882–1930*. Urbana: University of Illinois Press, 1995.Wallace, Maurice O. *Constructing the Black Masculine: Identity and Ideality in African American Men's Literature and Culture, 1775–1995*. Durham: Duke University Press, 2002.

Welty, Eudora. *Delta Wedding*. 1946. Reprint, New York: Harcourt Brace, 1991.

———. "Must the Novelist Crusade?" In *The Eye of the Story: Selected Essays and Reviews*. New York: Vintage, 1979. 146–58.

———. *One Writer's Beginnings*. Cambridge: Harvard University Press, 1983.

———. "Place in Fiction." In *The Eye of the Story: Selected Essays and Reviews*. New York: Random House, 1978. 116–33.

———. "A Worn Path." *The Collected Stories of Eudora Welty*. San Diego: Harvest, 1980. 142–49.

PATRICIA YAEGER

"Black Men Dressed in Gold"

Racial Violence in Eudora Welty's "The Burning"

The icon of the white lady on a pedestal, gentle and genteel, has never appealed to me. My mother had the accoutrements of a southern lady (the polish of class, cotillion manners), but at her funeral my brother captured a truth about the steel in her magnolia when he said: "Mickey Mantle and my mother had two things in common. They both loved baseball, and they were both hard-hitters." Since my sisters and I had been struggling to keep straight faces as the preacher spun the dross of the past into fairy tales about my mom's love of cooking and housekeeping, we laughed out loud when my brother spoke the truth, relieved that someone had dared to say how scary my mother was with a switch. The rest of the congregation sat there, frozen. Was this the right thing to say at a Christian funeral?

The white women in Eudora Welty's short story "The Burning" are also hard-hitters. While we never see the actual scoring of flesh, white-on-black violence permeates this story about the Civil War–torn South—a violence that the reader may find hard to assimilate, since Welty writes in a difficult, beautiful style that asks as many questions as it answers, withholds as much as it reveals. "Behind her the one standing wall of the house held notched and listening like the big ear of King Solomon into which poured the repeated asking of birds. The tree stood and flowered. What must she do?" (493).[1] The riddling quality of this passage drenches the reader in metaphor. A wall becomes an ear, the birds its questioners, and the trees must stand before they flower. Welty's gorgeous prose recalibrates the effects of the fires that destroyed Jackson, Mississippi, when Union soldiers burned their way south; Welty explores the blighted white landscapes that give Welty's black protagonist, Delilah, the freedom to roam. Delilah "believed Miss Theo twisted in the grass like a dead snake until the sun went down. She herself held still like a mantis until the grass had folded and spread apart at the falling of dew. This was after the chickens had gone to roost in a strange uneasy tree against the cloud where the guns still boomed and the way from Vicksburg was red. Then Delilah could find her feet" (492). Voudon-like beliefs mingle with surrealism in a landscape scoured with trauma: "She put her arms over her head and waited, for they would all be coming again, gathering under her and above her, bees saddled like horses out of the air, butterflies harnessed to one another, bats with masks on, birds together, all with their weapons bared . . . she dreaded the fury of all the butterflies and dragonflies in the world riding, blades unconcealed and at point" (493). After multiple rapes and an abuse at the hands of her white mistresses, Delilah feels menace everywhere. The miniature world of harlequin bees and writhing insects echoes past furies. Welty asks, "What does a house-slave know about nature? About survival? About her own identity?" Even in her hallucinations, Delilah seems more worldly than the white women who claimed to own her. She makes her way back to the burned-down plantation and transforms trauma into portable property. The expensive, damaged goods she collects from its grounds include a Jubilee cup and a baroque mirror crowned with gilded African men. The extravagance of white people's objects and the violent sources of New World plenitude threaten to overwhelm not only Delilah but Welty herself, even as Welty deploys this overabundance as an imagistic technique for unearthing racial violence. As we will see, "The Burning" offers powerful insights into white women's violence toward blacks in the antebellum South, but through an unexpected symbol system that at first seems minor, even unimportant—whites' and blacks' uneven relationships to everyday things.

In an interview published long after "The Burning," Welty worried that her story was "too involved and curlicued around with things."[2] Despite this worry, I want to commend the finesse of using things to unravel racial asymmetry. The story's thing-obsession unearths a ferocity in the plantation household that transgresses ordinary ideas about white female gentility in the U.S. slave-owning world. Thalvolia Glymph, historian of nineteenth-century plantation America, argues that a house slave's relation to white people's objects—cleaning floors, polishing silver, setting tables, clearing them—"put her in the direct path of her mistress's power" (33). The objects that passed between mistress and slave placed slavewomen in an acute nexus of bodily harm. The remarkable gift of Welty's story—its prescience—is to understand these sadistic asymmetries and to create an intricate analysis of race focused on Delilah's relation to white people's things. Welty's ability to imagine this world from Delilah's perspective may be flawed in its wild poetry and primitivism, but it is also astounding—and critics need to recognize the imaginative risks Welty took in trying to dramatize Delilah's unsung perspective. While André Bleikasten argues that "The Burning" only gradually comes to "concentrate on Delilah," I suggest that Welty uses Delilah as focalizer throughout "The Burning." When he contrasts Welty's story to "the great baroque frescoes of Southern fiction" by calling it "a pocket tragedy, a tempest in a rococo china cup," I disagree. Welty refuses to miniaturize Delilah's psychological maiming, her physical trauma, and the historic consequences of slave-owning women's cruelty; these are world-historic events. But I concur with Bleikasten's assessment that "'The Burning' is a masterpiece—not a *minor* masterpiece" and suggest that it should be taught and read more widely, included among the jewels of the Welty canon.

Although "The Burning" was published in 1951, its insights about white women's abuse of power remain underanalyzed, perhaps because archiving white women's cruelties has only recently become the subject of historical inquiry. As Glymph explains in *Out of the House of Bondage: The Transformation of the Plantation Household* (2008), generalized portraits of the "[c]ollapsed geography of the household" (where women and slaves remained subordinate to men) have allowed scholars to imagine that slave-owning women were less violent and their acts less purposeful than white men's cruelties. In this limited view of southern history, slavewomen were beaten and constrained, but white women also felt the constraints of domestic coercion. Compared to the "more public violence against slaves in the fields . . . white women's violence is rarely analyzed as a central facet of their existence . . . In general, a silence surrounds white women's contributions to the basic nature of slavery, its maintenance, and especially, one of its central tendencies, the maiming and destruction of black life."[3] These multiple cruelties become the mobile, angry center of "The Burning."

Glymph is equally eloquent about the ways in which white men and women shared in the racial atrocities of the antebellum South. Attributing white women's violence to "mere 'petulance' or explaining it as 'spontaneous outbursts' dislodges white women from their place at the slaveholder's table." When scholars focus on victimization, submerging white women's "human and historical agency," they forget that a mistress who struck her slaves in the heat of the moment was "preconditioned to this kind of response. She lived in a world in which actions of this kind were accepted as understandable if not laudatory 'slips.'" She also lived in a world that denied her victims the right to bear witness (30). Miss Theo and her sister, Miss Myra, are preconditioned to treat slaves with nonchalant cruelty; Welty presents their story without sympathy; she steers our perspective on their actions from the vicinity of the house slave Delilah, who, as freedwoman, bears witness to her own silenced history.

Through Delilah's eyes we see heart-wrenching acts of violence. First Miss Theo, attempting to save her own and her sister's bodily integrity, turns Delilah over to Yankee soldiers to be gang-raped. Compounding this trauma, Miss Theo and Miss Myra use Delilah as a launching pad when the white women hang themselves—their response to a post-Confederate world where their plantation has been desecrated and their slaves have fled. The sisters kick Delilah's body as they fly through the air, sharp-shinned even in death. Finally, they leave Delilah's son, Phinny, to die, abandoning him to the plantation house as it burns; Delilah collects his bones at the end of the story.

These events are horrific, but the story exceeds this Grand Guignol legacy by refusing mere melodrama and attending instead to artifacts and slave-owning women's daily, thing-oriented aggression. The plantation home was a workplace where enslaved women killed and dressed chickens; dusted; mopped; wet-nursed; polished floors, silver, and furniture; bathed white owners; "scoured dishes, made biscuits and pies from scratch, churned butter, turned vegetables . . . washed damask tablecloths and every piece of clothing their owners wore . . . They were expected to do these things in silence and reverence, barefooted and ill-clothed. These expectations formed part of the legitimized violence to which they were subjected."[4] To depict this world, Welty contemplates an inequality in objects—the excesses of owning things that promote bodily integrity on one side and a deprivation of ownership and secure embodiment on the other.

Delilah endures this deprivation from the beginning of "The Burning." As Union soldiers maneuver a big white horse through the double doors of Rose Hill, they discover Miss Myra and Miss Theo, relics of the landowning class, stiff-backed among the "precious, breakable things white ladies were never tired of and never broke, unless they were mad at each other" (483). Welty's story is obsessed with genteel excess, with white people's superabundant goods and objects, which depend on a world of slave labor. Breaking into this superabundance, the soldiers rape the white ladies—or at least they try; Welty's prose twists, proliferates, withholds, maddens. Like the ladies' "precious, breakable things," her style cracks and whirrs, refusing to specify the white ladies' trauma. But Welty's writing becomes clear and pointed when Miss Theo offers Delilah as a sexual substitute to the soldiers: "My sister's the more delicate one, as you see. May I offer you this young kitchen Negro, as I've always understood—" (484). The soldiers treat Delilah as a portable object; they carry her into the tall grass where her status as a human commodity breaks away: "she screamed, young and strong, for them all—for everybody that wanted her to scream for them, for everybody that didn't; and sometimes it seemed to her that she was screaming her loudest for Delilah, who was lost now—carried out of the house, not knowing how to get back" (33). Once the house is set ablaze (and no one lifts a finger to help Phinny, Delilah's mixed-race son and the white ladies' nephew, escape the fire), once the white ladies hang themselves by unknotting a left-behind hammock and jumping off Delilah's back, Delilah is released again into designated nothingness.[5] As she looks into a melted mirror from the plantation's parlor and trudges in the direction of the Union troops, Welty surrounds her with a gorgeous, ravishing symphony of sounds and images. Why embroider cruel acts so beautifully? Is this the aestheticization of predation and prejudice? In a thing-encrusted world, the human labor bound up in these objects can become ensnarled or invisible. Welty's prose struggles with this entangling drama.

While "The Burning" is ostensibly about war and its aftermath, I've suggested that it is even more deeply obsessed with things: what it means to have them, to leave them or burn them, to take them from others. Before committing suicide, Miss Myra sits on a hammock picking ants out of a silver cup. Her most natural, most casual assumption is that, as a white woman, she should be surrounded by objects. ("There was some little round silver cup, familiar to the ladies, in the hammock when they came to it down in the grove. Lying on its side with a few drops in it, it made them smile" [490].) Challenging the taken-for-grantedness of ordinary white culture's superabundance, the Caribbean writer Kamau Brathwaite insists on the necessary thinglessness and portability of black culture before and after slavery: "And this total expression comes about because people be in the open air, because people live in conditions of poverty ('unhouselled') because they come from a historical experience where they had to rely on their very breath rather than on paraphernalia like books and museums and machines. They had to depend on immanence, the power within themselves, rather than the technology outside themselves."[6]

When Welty's style brims with this "paraphernalia" and too-muchness, it illuminates the contrast between plantation wealth and the small change allotted to southern blacks. Most stories of the U.S. Civil War invoke past-induced trances of the South's gothic past, with its haunted slave markets, massifications of money, and never-forgotten Lost Cause. But despite "The Burning's" ruined plantations, hysterical sisters, and ferocious injustice, Welty recasts this could-be gothic tale in an excessive and violent lyricism that emanates from Delilah and her forced deprivation. The story's crammed, multimythic style pulses around objects and finally focuses on one luminous object that Delilah knows too well: a Venetian mirror that once hung in the plantation parlor.

When the soldiers erupt into the parlor and force Delilah to hold their horse's reins, she can only see the story unfold at a distance, in the mirror's glaze.[7] "The first soldier shoved the tables and chairs out of the way behind Miss Myra, who flitted when she ran, and pushed her down where she stood and dropped on top of her. There in the mirror the parlor remained, filled up with dusted pictures, and shuttered since six o'clock against the heat and that smell of smoke they were all so tired of, still glimmering with precious, breakable things" (30). "Dusted . . . shuttered": these are Delilah's tasks. She sees this world through its objects, the labor they require, and her own object status. As Carlos Fuentes says of the American baroque, only those who possess nothing include everything, and Welty imagines Delilah's brimming imagination as too image-full, too rich. In fact, when Delilah concentrates on Miss Myra and the soldier who accosts her, Delilah's mind turns to object analogies "the chair in the mirror . . . It was the red, rubbed velvet, pretty chair like Miss Myra's ring box" (483), the mental trick of dissociating from people and attending to things to escape memories of trauma; she imagines the white woman's parallel dissociation as Miss Myra looks up to see "the little plaster flowers going around the ceiling" (483).

While these landowners cling to their propertied sovereignty, Delilah lacks bare ownership. Watching objects in the mirror is one mode of possessing them. Returning to the burned-down plantation after her mistresses' death to collect its charred, empty objects is another. Casting aside "an iron pot and a man's long boot, a doorknob and little book fluttering, its leaves spotted and fluffed like guinea feathers," she spies the melted Venetian mirror "down in the chimney's craw, flat and face-up in the cinders . . . Though the mirror did not know Delilah, Delilah would have known that mirror anywhere, because it was set between black men. Their arms were raised to hold up the mirror's roof, which now the swollen mirror brimmed, among gold leaves and gold heads—black men dressed in gold, looking almost into the glass themselves"

(492). The unknowing, unreflective mirror gives way to a scene of recognition, to an anagnorisis grounded in a lifetime of laboring over white people's objects: "Delilah would have known that mirror anywhere." "The Burning" is "involved and curlicued around with things" because these things open up the labyrinth of southern history. Miss Myra's "bright gold" may adorn these black men, but their raised arms contact cinders; they become archetypes of an abundant penury. In her sudden freedom, Delilah can see and address these brimming images, but burnt into nubbins these men are paralyzed; they can only "almost" look. Charged with supporting the mirror's roof, the mirror's "black men dressed in gold" may seem like idyllic creatures: ornaments sentenced to hard labor. And yet in their weird, melted state they exert a centrifugal energy for Delilah; they project the laboring world's collectivity. Delilah "would have known that mirror anywhere" because she has cleaned it repeatedly, just as her ancestors created the wealth that enabled its purchase. Welty effaces the distance or dissonance between the baroque artificiality of this looking glass and Delilah's workaday world. And Delilah recognizes the mirror as her own object because of its kindredness, because her race is represented there.

The Yankee fire that destroys the plantation's grandiloquence also deepens our sense of these men's ornate pain. The "black men dressed in gold" are "now half-split away, flattened with fire, bearded, noseless as the moss that hung from swamp trees" (44). Delilah's plight as rape victim is amplified in the figures' deformed bodies. But instead of steadying or deepening pain, the mirror slips into another genre; it offers a dream vision: an odd turn, as if it were customary to slide from Faulkner to Chaucer. Again, this object moves the reader deeper into history. The ensuing dream vision features Delilah's encounter with non-synchronous time and space—these men offer her a deep look into ancestral communities: "Where the mirror did not cloud like the horse-trampled spring, gold gathered itself from the winding water, and honey under water started to flow, and then the gold fields were there, hardening gold. Through the water, gold and honey twisted up into houses, trembling. She saw people walking the bridges in early light with hives of houses on their heads" (492–93). Delilah has an Old World vision. She sees the honeyed commodification that flowed from the New World to the Old and back again, the traffic in bodies and goods that turned fields, as well as black and indigenous women and men, into gold.[8] The expenditure and overexpenditure of lives made the money that created the extravagance of beehive hairdos and powdered wigs, a world of slavery-fueled ornament populated by men in long coats looking like "dresses, some with red birds; and monkeys in velvet; and ladies with masks laid over their faces looking from pointed windows. Delilah supposed that was Jackson before Sherman came. Then it was gone. In this noon quiet, here where all had passed by, unless it had gone in, she waited on her knees" (493). What geography greets us here? Is this Venice, Bruges, London, the Caribbean? And what is this carnival of nonsynchronous time doing in Welty's story? Why is it vouchsafed to Delilah?

There may be multiple explanations, but I would argue that Delilah conjures this vision because as Brathwaite suggests, she possesses "a historical experience where [she] had to rely on . . . breath rather than on paraphernalia like books and museums and machines . . . on immanence, the power within [herself], rather than the technology outside."[9] By conveying a sense of Delilah's immanence and power through a mirror that holds multiple pasts, Welty shows that it is possible to colonize these pasts even when they are incomprehensible or out of synch. Even when history maims your people, you can still appropriate (lift/pinch/embezzle/purloin) the past's dead citations and give them outrageous life. That is, Welty recognizes in Delilah much more than the power to care for white people's things. Delilah appropriates and remaps these things' meanings. She possesses a dream vision, a role usually bestowed on poetic white men.

As one vision gives way to another, Delilah gazes into the past-struck mirror and it changes again: "The mirror's cloudy bottom sent up minnows of light to the brim where now a face pure as a water-lily shadow was floating. Almost too small and deep down to see, they were quivering, leaping to life, fighting, aping old things Delilah had seen done in this world already, sometimes what men had done to Miss Theo and Miss Myra and the peacocks and to slaves, and sometimes what a slave had done and what anybody now could do to anybody" (493). The archaic past yields to the near past, to a warring world without order and the memory of Delilah's rape and concubinage—that is, her lack of recourse and inability to bring her tormentors to law. Then, "like an act of mercy gone . . . the mirror felled her flat" (493). The rest could be darkness, but Welty's text keeps going, like Delilah's burned heart. Character and narrator erupt in a surfeit of supernaturalism as Delilah protects herself from an army of dangers, and we enter the insect-driven passage quoted earlier, a universe brimming with marauding insects who "would all be coming again, gathering under her and above her, bees saddled like horses out of the air, butterflies harnessed to one another, bats with masks on, birds together, all with their weapons bared. She listened for the blows, and dreaded that whole army of wings—

of flies, birds, serpents" (45). Again, we greet this story's odd rhythms; Welty's play with exploding forms, with a style that is too hot and perfect, too lyrical to encompass Delilah's terrible history. But even though the supercharged natural world may become a strange outrider for Delilah's fear, in this extraordinary surplus of tiny terrors we stumble across Delilah's mechanism for staying alive. In a South filled with angry white people who've left nowhere to hide, Delilah ratchets up her sensorium. She summons courage, returning to the destroyed plantation to discover the mirror and the bones of her child. Watching the mirror brim with images of conquest and counterconquest, she imagines that the Yankee's threatening horse, wounded, falls away, its "flayed forehead . . . with ears and crest up stiff." Next Delilah imagines a legion of Maroons drumming, "the shield and the drum of big swamp birdskins," and grabs her own piercing weapons: "the horns of deer sharpened to cut and kill with. She showed her teeth." These are figures of enmity that make way for discovery. "Then she looked in the feathery ashes and found Phinny's bones. She ripped a square from her manifold fullness of skirts and tied up the bones in it" (493).

As Delilah gathers this portable property, all the mirror's times remain co-present: the period of decadent white wealth and slave impoverishment stretching from New World colonization to the Civil War; the near past when Delilah was abused by her mistresses and raped by white men; and the present, when Delilah survives and collects the bones of her son as the only item from her private past that can travel. Then she responds to her own "unhouselledness" by assembling more portable property to barter or treasure. "She set foot in the road then, walking stilted in Miss Myra's shoes and carrying Miss Theo's shoes tied together around her neck, her train in the road behind her. She wore Miss Myra's willing rings—had filled up two fingers—but she had had at last to give up the puzzle of Miss Theo's bracelet with the chain. They were two stones now, scalding-white. When the combs were being lifted from her hair, Miss Myra had come down too, beside her sister" (493–94). The text is not judgmental about corpse robbing. The sisters—dehumanized—are reimagined as stones, hot to the touch, punishing, "scalding." Meanwhile, Welty's style continues in its filigree: "In the shade underneath the burned and fallen bridge she sat on a stump and chewed for a while, without dreams, the comb of a dirt-dauber" (494). Palming "her own black locust stick to drive the snakes," her Jubilee cup, her precious rings, "Miss Theo's shoes tied together around her neck," and clutching her bones, Delilah faces a precarious future. Just as the mirror's black men are "dressed in gold," just as, melted, they become fluid, decorative, deconstructive, and subversive, so Welty's scavenging heroine represents the aptitude for bricolage and her need for her own economy. "Submerged to the waist, to the breast, stretching her throat like a sunflower stalk above the river's opaque skin, she kept on, her treasure stacked on the roof of her head, hands laced upon it" (494).[10] Why all these extra words—"like a sunflower stalk"? "opaque skin"? her head like a "roof"? Welty's signs are always exorbitant; here they point to Delilah's willful superabundance, to her wavering life as a black woman dressed in gold.

In following "The Burning's" trajectory from object poverty to object plenty, Welty's story surprises with its historical accuracy. Glymph explains that after emancipation, freedmen's and women's relation to objects shifted. "Many for the first time in their lives came into possession of beds, spoons, forks, crockery, and plates and clothes that did not scratch the skin . . . These transfers of property dramatize 'the meagerness of black people's lives as slaves. Spoons and plates replace communal troughs and tin cups'" (112). What does it mean to live in a world where you own nothing, not even yourself—and then to enter a world where things exist? After the war the newly emancipated Virginia Newman described her idea of freedom as a new dress, "a blue guinea with yaler spots," capturing the pleasure of owning one's first store-bought dress, and with it new control over a whole way of life.[11]

Welty's story limns a path from owning nothing to owning something: self-possession solidified through object possession. Delilah takes a journey from nonentity, from life as an abused possession and caretaker for objects, to seizing rights in the objects she has handled and cared for. "The Burning" may have been a difficult story for a white woman to conjure in the midst of a Jim Crow South that still glorified the beautiful, victimized plantation wife. That is, while praising Welty for her insights, I want to leave room for her authorial confusion, her anxiety about writing a story curlicued with violence-created things. "The Burning" disrupts plantation myths, but it also obscures its subject, makes it opaque or hard to read. Why?

Glymph insists that the plantation world (and its aftermath) was "canted toward falsehood . . . Even though their status had depended upon the work of slave women, former mistresses did not believe their former slaves capable of working" (145). Glymph insists on the dogged presence of historical and ideological screens obscuring the facticity of the plantation household as a place where white women ruled; when we cast these screens away, "the practical world of violence by women and the threat of it comes into view. The point of the screens thus becomes immediately obvious, for the practical reality of routine domination is not easy to look upon" (31). When Miss Theo and Miss Myra emerge from the plantation house and Yankees burn it to the ground, their goods have already been confiscated by "soldiers and Negroes alike" who carry off "beds, tables, candlesticks, washstands, cedar buckets, china pitchers, with their backs bent double" (486). The white ladies emerge with dignity—not as two faces, but "one clarified face" able to "mark every looting slave, also, as all stood momently fixed like serenaders by the light of a moon" (486). Here the white women become the story's focalizers and the slaves, now called "looters," are secondary. They turn into an audience, re-evoking the plantation myths of the lady on a pedestal. But just when these white sisters threaten to derail the story with more myth and magnolias, Miss Myra furrows her "too-white forehead" and the perspective shifts again:

> To Delilah that house they were carrying the torches to was like one just now coming into being—like the showboat that slowly came through the trees just once in her time, at the peak of high water—bursting with the unknown, sparking in ruddy light, with a minute to go before that ear-aching cry of the calliope.
> When it came—but it was a bellowing like a bull, that came from inside—Delilah drew close, with Miss Theo's skirt to peep around, and Miss Theo's face looked down like death itself and said, "Remember this. You black monkeys," as the blaze outdid them all. (486–87)

A tragedy for Miss Theo, a cry for hierarchy, and a return to her old invective represent, for Delilah, a slim chance for theater in a life empty of events. This new ontology of a plantation that can be burned down, this new world "just now coming into being" and "bursting with the unknown" is a too-powerful revelation of the terrors "bellowing like a bull, that came from inside" the plantation house—the possible reversion to a world where, when African Americans become "black monkeys," the plantation mistress remains "like death itself." I suggest that Welty has difficulty portraying the sadistic white mistress and the searching imagination of the about-to-become-free slave together; she gives Delilah priority, but lets her narration veer or become distracted by mythologies of white power as well. Welty's story is, then, flawed and imperfect because, like every work of art, it struggles unevenly with dominant ideologies—but it also struggles intriguingly. Welty inherited a worldview in which "the very idea of a violent white womanhood was antithetical to the reigning ideology and to gender ideals that equated power over slaves with white men. If white women's active participation as members of the master class in the construction and management of slavery is to be minimized or denied, then it becomes necessary to minimize or ignore portraits lodged in the memories of former slaves. Those portraits add violence to the 'lady's' repertoire."[12] Welty adds violence to the lady's repertoire, and she makes Delilah the center of memory. At the same time, "The Burning" keeps leaping from ordinary to extraordinary imagery, as if the scale of the world Welty portrays is too hot to keep in focus. At the end Delilah walks "stilted in Miss Myra's shoes" with a "throat like a sunflower stalk." The charade of incommensurable images suggests a world in which deprivation and plenitude meet, where "entire populations existed as actual or potential commodities and . . . the triangular trade in human flesh, manufactured goods, and raw materials rapidly produced a superabundance unprecedented in both extent and maldistribution. The enduring effects of this superimposition still operate in the fiercely laminating adhesion of bodies and objects, in which the exchange of human flesh signifies the prolific availability of all commodities" (Roach 124–25).[13]

"The Burning" explores the New World's triangular trade in condensed and coded form. Once the commodities of the plantation world have burned to the ground, once the commodification of flesh and bone is no longer legal, what happens? The threat of recurring rape and the maldistribution of goods remain. What fate awaits Delilah when she joins the Union soldiers who have already gang-raped her? Stung by the death of her child, the victim of multiple terrors, Delilah is liberated from slavery but still hungry and shelterless. She still feels the forces of conquest descend: "She listened for the blows, and dreaded that whole army of wings—of flies, birds, serpents, their glowing enemy faces and bright kings' dresses, that banner of colors forked out, all this world that was flying, striking, stricken, falling, gilded or blackened, mortally splitting and falling apart, proud turbans unwinding" (493). The baroque plenitude of Delilah's imagination suggests an impoverished freedwoman's perverse strength in a world flooded with too many pasts. She takes objects that have been emptied of history (that is, deterritorialized or dispossessed) and fills them with expectation. Delilah treats time without ceremony. When treasure is "stacked on the roof of her head," she allows eras of artifice to mingle with the finite everyday: "she did not know what day this was, but she knew—it would not rain, the river would not rise, until Saturday" (494). To own good shoes, good clothes (Miss Theo's train dragged "in the road behind her"), to possess a Jubilee cup to be traded or kept or melted into money—to own anything at all is to come closer to owning one's own "roof," one's own land, one's own being. Welty pulls down as many screens as she can; she suggests the destratification of objects as one route for challenging social stratification. Her story knows, even if she did not, that objects become delicious when they gravitate toward those who cleaned and cared for them: "Light on Delilah's head the Jubilee cup was set. She paused now and then to lick the rim" (494).

Notes

An earlier version of "Black Men Dressed in Gold: Racial Violence in 'The Burning'" appeared in *PMLA* 124, no. 1 (2009), © 2009 by the Modern Language Association of America. It is used here by permission.

1. Subsequent citations of this work appear parenthetically in the text.

2. Gretlund, "An Interview," 246.

3. Glymph, *Out of the House of Bondage*, 25–26.

4. Glymph, *Out of the House of Bondage*, 2.

5. Although the story indicates that Phinny is Delilah's son, at points his status seems ambiguous. Miss Myra claims he is her son and registers surprise when her sister suggests that since Phinny is black, consanguinity would be impossible. Unlike Miss Myra and Miss Theo, Delilah thinks about his fate instead of his color: "'Could be he got out,' called Delilah in a high voice. 'He strong, he.' 'Who?' 'Could be Phinny's out loose. Don't cry'" (489). The sisters remain in a gothic plot of racial torment, but Delilah claims his kinship and carries his bones.

6. Brathwaite, *The History of the Voice*, 19. See my "Ghosts" for an analysis of Brathwaite's relevance to African American literature.

7. Bleikasten aptly describes the mirror as an image of the white ladies' narcissism while I argue that it is Delilah's "speculum mundi."

8. As Galeano comments, "Caribbean island populations finally stopped paying tribute because they had disappeared . . . totally exterminated in the gold mines, in the deadly task of sifting auriferous sands with their bodies half submerged in water, or in breaking up the ground beyond the point of exhaustion, doubled up over the heavy cultivating tools brought from Spain" (15). He adds that the "rape of [Atahualpa's] accumulated treasure was followed by the systematic exploitation of the forced labor of Indians and abducted Africans in the mines" (29).

9. Brathwaite, *The History of the Voice*, 19.

10. Welty carefully balances Miss Myra's combs with the dirt dauber's and the hyperbolic "roof" of the gold mirror with the treasure-laden "roof" of Delilah's head: these parallels contrast white ownership and African American cadences of possession/dispossession. This is an unusual preoccupation for a white woman writing before the civil rights movement, but see the discussion of Welty's WPA photographs of African American women in Westling and in Pollack and Marrs.

11. Glymph, *Out of the House of Bondage*, 10.

12. Glymph, *Out of the House of Bondage*, 25–26.
13. See my "Circum-Atlantic Super-abundance" for an elaboration of Roach's analysis.

Bibliography

Bleikasten, André. "Homespun Horrors: 'The Burning.'" In *Eudora Welty: The Poetics of the Body*, ed. Géraldine Chouard and Danièle Pitavy-Souques, 141–46. Rennes: University of Rennes Press, 2005.

Brathwaite, Edward Kamau. *The History of the Voice: The Development of Nation Language in Anglophone Caribbean Poetry*. London: New Beacon, 1984.

Carpentier, Alejo. "The Baroque and the Marvelous Real." In *Magical Realism: Theory, History, Community*, trans. Tanya Huntington and Lois Parkinson Zamora, 89–108. Durham: Duke University Press, 1995.

Galeano, Eduardo. *Open Veins of Latin America: Five Centuries of the Pillage of a Continent*. New York: Monthly Review Press, 1997.

Glymph, Thavolia. *Out of the House of Bondage: The Transformation of the Plantation Household*. Cambridge: Cambridge University Press, 2008.

Gretlund, J. N. "An Interview with Eudora Welty." In *Conversations with Eudora Welty*, ed. Peggy Whitman Prenshaw, 211–29. New York: Washington Square Press, 1985.

Pollack, Harriet, and Suzanne Marrs. "Seeing Welty's Political Vision in Her Photographs." In *Eudora Welty and Politics: Did the Writer Crusade?*, ed. Pollack and Marrs, 223–51. Baton Rouge: Louisiana State University Press, 2001.

Roach, Joseph. *Cities of the Dead: Circum-Atlantic Performance*. New York: Columbia University Press, 1996.

Welty, Eudora. "The Burning." In *The Collected Stories of Eudora Welty*. New York: Harcourt, 1965. 482–94.

Yaeger, Patricia. "Circum-Atlantic Super-Abundance: Milk as World-Making in Alice Randall and Kara Walker." In "Global Contexts, Local Literature: The New Southern Studies," ed. Annette Trefzer and Kathryn McKee. Special issue, *American Literature* 78, no. 4 (2006): 769–98.

———. "Ghosts and Shattered Bodies, or What Does It Mean to Still Be Haunted by Southern Literature?" *South Central Review* 22, no. 1 (2005): 87–109.

REBECCA MARK

Ice Picks, Guinea Pigs, and Dead Birds

Dramatic Weltian Possibilities in *"The Demonstrators"*

In *The Eye of the Story*, Eudora Welty states: "The mystery lies in the use of language to express human life. In writing . . . we rediscover the mystery."[1] If we
read Eudora Welty's "The Demonstrators" as a detective story, we begin to find
clues that do indeed help us "rediscover the mystery."[2] As in Susan Glaspell's "A
Jury of Her Peers," a detective, blinded by bias, can easily miss the significance
of a dead bird or spilled preserves.[3] Readers of "The Demonstrators" often
overlook the clues and accept the surface reading that the black community
is rife with internalized violence. This reading has led critics to focus more on
Welty's critique of Dr. Strickland's racist projections than on her presentation
of the lives of her African American characters.[4] The intertextual clues suggest that Welty's African American characters do indeed have agency, that their
story is more important than Dr. Strickland's, and that we might be misreading
"The Demonstrators." In particular, these intertextual clues force us to question if Ruby and Dove actually kill each other, and even more startling, whether
they are even dead. The textual evidence suggests that rather than committing
a double murder, Dove and Ruby, with the whole African American community of Holden, Mississippi, behind them, are instead performing an elaborately
choreographed political drama designed to educate the doctor and save their
own people.

Throughout "The Demonstrators," Welty highlights the political power of
performance or "dramaticizing." When Dr. Strickland castigates the young
bearded civil rights worker for writing an article in his paper claiming that
Mississippians made the students go into the fields and pick cotton in hundred-
degree heat, Strickland points out that there is no cotton to pick in June in Mississippi. Dr. Strickland calls the account "lying," but the student responds: "We
are dramatizing your hostility . . . It is a way of reaching people. Don't forget

what they might have done to us is even worse" (*CSEW* 617). By highlighting newspapers, Welty puts all journalists and, for that matter, all writers on the stand, questioning if anyone can actually tell the truth about racial violence (as so many political activists have asked her to do). She reminds us that whatever anyone writes to "dramatize" the situation is in some ways a lie because it always could have been, and already was, so much worse. The bigger lie in this exchange is that neither this young man nor Dr. Strickland mentions that enslaved, sharecropping, and simply underpaid African Americans had been picking cotton in blistering heat in Mississippi for over a hundred years. By not linking his story to the actual lives of the people they are supposedly trying to "heal," the doctor and the activist "play" bridge, or only play at bridging the two communities—a narcissistic altruism.

Throughout "The Demonstrators," Welty warns us that there is a drama going on here and not one that the doctor fully understands. A "negro child" (*CSEW* 608) calls Dr. Strickland out at eleven o'clock on a Saturday night, interrupting his bridge game at the club, drives with him through a labyrinth of back roads, across the railroad tracks, past the cottonseed mill, "into a roomful of women" (*CSEW* 609), where he follows a path of newspapers and sees an injured and, we presume, dying Ruby Gaddy. The account in the *Sentinel*, the white newspaper of Holden, Mississippi, asserts that two common-law African American lovers, Ruby Gaddy and Dove Collins, murdered each other in a Saturday-night brawl. Attributing this incident to black-on-black violence, the unreliable *Sentinel* (the guardian of the white community) defensively quotes Rev. Alonzo Duckett, pastor of the Holden First Baptist Church, who states: "That's one they can't pin the blame on us for. That's how they treat their own kind. Please take note our conscience is clear" (*CSEW* 621). Although Dr. Strickland claims that Dove expired and the *Sentinel* reports that the Gaddy woman died "later this morning" (*CSEW* 621), no African American character acknowledges their deaths.

The *Sentinel*'s account of the "murders" reads like a how-not-to-prove-your-case manual for lawyers: "As Holden Marshal Curtis 'Cowboy' Stubblefield reconstructed the earlier mishap, Ruby Gaddy, 21, *was stabbed* in full view of the departing congregation of the Holy Gospel Tabernacle as she attempted to leave the church" (*CSEW* 619, italics mine). If there is anyone inherently untrustworthy in 1966 Mississippi, Cowboy Stubblefield is your man. Marshals and sheriffs in small towns throughout the South lynched and murdered innocent African Americans. For a writer as technically aware as Eudora Welty, to use a passive voice ("was stabbed") when discussing the murder is a red flag. Welty's *Sentinel* reporter asserts that "witnesses said" but does not name any of these witnesses, nor does he corroborate their stories. Welty is all but shouting, "Do not trust this!" By not questioning the town newspaper and Dr. Strickland's assertion that Ruby and Dove, the two African American lovers, kill each other in a double murder, readers accept the town's claim of innocence. In a town where the white population lives in a stricken, stubblefield wasteland, with dead goldenrod, sick citizens with unmentionable diseases, a fading electrical system, an inadequate water supply, an insatiable cotton mill droning on day and night, looked over by a Dr. Strickland who is himself so sick and tired of life he cannot anesthetize people fast enough, one suspects that Mayor Fairbrothers and these "Fair" (with the double meaning "white" and "evenhanded") brothers have more to account for than they care to admit.

During the years prior to writing "The Demonstrators," Eudora Welty listened to the news reports as FBI agents unearthed James Chaney, Andrew Goodman, and Michael Schwerner's bodies from a clay bank only a few hundred miles from her home, faced Byron De La Beckwith's violent murder of her Mississippi neighbor Medgar Evers, and listened in shocked grief to the report of the death of Addie Mae Collins, Cynthia Wesley, Carole Robertson, and Denise McNair, who were murdered when Chambliss, Cash, Blanton, and Cherry detonated a bomb in the 16th Street Baptist Church in Birmingham. She lived through the assassinations of Martin Luther King Jr. and John F. Kennedy. During this historical moment, the idea that Eudora Welty, a known liberal and self-proclaimed civil rights supporter, a photographer of dignified and respectful images of African American men and women, a person who appreciated African American cultural contributions, would focus only on the *Sentinel*'s preoccupation with black-on-black violence seems unlikely.

Rather then ask why Ruby and Dove kill each other, we need to devil the details and ask: (1) Do Dove and Ruby actually kill each other? and (2) Do we know that they are dead? Welty, who was an avid reader of detective stories, never shows us the most important piece of evidence in any good murder mystery: a dead body. When Dr. Strickland first sees Ruby he observes "a dark quilt was pulled up to the throat of a girl *alive* on the bed" (*CSEW* 609, italics mine). When he observes Dove on the ground, he asks, "So you're *alive* Dove, you're still *alive*" (*CSEW* 619, italics mine). As we open up the multiple interpretations of the text, whether Dove or Ruby is alive or dead at the end of the story— like the often asked question about "A Worn Path," whether Phoenix Jackson's grandson is really dead—is of less importance than what their lives meant to the health of the community.[5]

Repeating the questions—"Who killed Ruby? Who killed Dove?"—Welty develops a resonant space in which we hear echoes (especially since their names are the common bird names dove and ruby red breast) of the familiar 1774 nursery rhyme "Who Killed Cock Robin?" In this childhood verse, each of several animals tells how they are involved in the murder of Cock Robin. The allusion reminds us that in any murder there are multiple players. The ninth stanza reads: "Who'll be chief mourner? / I, said the Dove, / I mourn for my love, / I'll be chief mourner" (*Roud Folk Song Index* 494.17–18).[6] Dove, the man Ruby loved and who loved her, would more likely be Ruby's chief mourner than her murderer. The fact that there is no evidence of marital discord—that especially in the 1960s the dove is the symbol of peace for the antiwar movement and of the Holy Spirit rising in Christian iconography—makes the idea that Dove struck the first blow, or any blow at all, doubtful.

Rather than Strickland's racist stereotypes, the women at Ruby's house are astute observers who know more about life, death, and healing than the good doctor. The old women, young girls, and babies who occupy Ruby's mother's house test, argue with, teach, correct, laugh at, belittle, and generally deride the drama of pompous white male power that the honorable doctor performs. These impatient authors, theater directors, and teachers tell Dr. Strickland when to enter and when to exit. Strickland is in their world, and in the short time that they have with him they try to wake him up to the deadly disease of greed and racism that is destroying their community. While he plies his sedatives, they specialize in stimulants. He remembers that when he was a young man at the train station, "the old tyrant" (Lucille) gave him "boiling hot coffee." They silence his imperious "How?" "What?" "Where?". "When?" journalistic and legalistic questioning, making him stop hiding behind his scientific stethoscope and his dubious newspaper.

When Dr. Strickland asks questions about the murder, both the women inside the house and the men on the porch laugh at him. After guessing and guessing, he finally says in exasperation: "'All right, I heard you. Is Dove who did it? Go on say.' He heard somebody spit on the stove, then: 'It's Dove'" (612). Around the room, the women repeat, echoing the cooing of a dove: "'Dove. Dove. Dove. You got it right that time.' While the name went around, passed from one mouth to the other, the doctor drew a deep breath. But the sigh that filled the room was the girl's, luxuriously uncontained" (612). The cupid valentine on the wall and Ruby's almost postcoital sigh suggest that Dove and Ruby's double piercing might be symbolically sexual, not literally murderous. Dr. Strickland does not ask, "Did Dove kill Ruby?" He asks instead the ambiguous question, "Is Dove who did *it*?" We do not know what the "it" is, and Ruby, in her silence, jealously preserves the indeterminacy of her story.

The *Sentinel*'s detailed description of the "murders" amplifies this multivalent storytelling:

> In the ensuing struggle at the conclusion of the service, the woman, who was a member of the choir, is believed to have received fatal ice-pick injuries to a vital organ, then to have wrested the weapon from her assailant and paid him back in kind. The Gaddy woman then walked to her mother's house but later collapsed . . . Members of the congregation said they chased Collins 13 or 14 yards in the direction of Snake Creek . . . Those present believed him to have succumbed since it was said the pick while in the woman's hand had been seen to drive in and pierce either his ear or his eye, either of which is in close approximation to the brain. (*CSEW* 620)

Our first response to reading this tortured newspaper account might be laughter, but our second response should be horror. The reporter in these few lines has given an exact description of a transorbital lobotomy.[7] In *The House of Cards: Psychology and Psychotherapy Built on Myth*, Robyn M. Dawes writes that this surgery "involves gently lifting the patient's eye ball from its socket, sticking in a thick needle behind it . . . manipulating it to destroy the same brain tissue until the patient becomes incoherent—the ice-pick operation" (49). Harriet A. Washington exposes the fact in *Medical Apartheid: The Dark History of Medical Experimentation on Black Americans from Colonial Times to the Present* that, "Between 1936 and 1960, an estimated fifty thousand lobotomies severed neuronal connections between the frontal lobes and the mid-brain of mental patients, both adults and children" (284). She provides evidence for the fact that in Mississippi, the most likely targets were African American boys.[8]

The powerful eugenics movement, which had taken root during the first half of the century and had spread by the 1930s and 1940s throughout the United States, justified two types of invasive surgery to terrorize, subdue, and exterminate the African American community: sterilization and lobotomies. Although the holocaust sent the American eugenics movement underground, the surgeries, particularly sterilizations, continued unabated until the mid-1970s.[9] In the first half of the century, eugenics proponents, including such prominent spokespeople as Theodore Roosevelt, John D. Rockefeller, Andrew

Carnegie, and Margaret Sanger, believed that by sterilizing the feebleminded, the criminally insane, and the poor, especially the black poor, they would be able to create a healthy, "fitter" (read Anglo-Saxon and wealthy) American society.

When Welty has Dove let those guinea pigs run wild throughout Ruby Gaddy's mother's house,[10] she is not just freeing the symbolic guinea pig of these laboratory experiments but is possibly referring to a particular kind of guinea pig experiment. In the 1920s, proponents of the eugenics movement created what they called Fitter Family Exhibits and took them to state fairs throughout the Midwest,[11] the South, and California. The exhibits usually had one section devoted to "The Six Mendelian Possibilities." The directors of the *Fitter Families* exhibits would kill guinea pigs and pin them to plywood boards, or trap them in small side-by-side cages with labels to "prove" that when you mate black and white guinea pigs, you will eventually end up with mongrelized black guinea pigs and no pure white guinea pigs (fig. 5). They argued that if they did not fight against miscegenation on every front, then racial commingling would end up watering down, dumbing down, and degenerating the genetic pool, gradually taking over the world with hybridized mongrels.

Dove's guinea pigs, like Welty's narrative, cannot be caught, pinned dead to a board, or caged in a little box. When Dr. Strickland imperiously demands that someone "Catch those things!" (611), the healthy African American baby laughs, the rest copy him, and a disembodied voice says, "They lightening" (611)—fast and able to escape and like "lightening" warning of the storm to come. The baby named Roger,[12] born before his mother would have faced the knife of sterilization, is in fact a force of life begging Ruby to live, trying to open her eyes, poking at her, and crying out loud for her. When Dr. Strickland tells them to hush that baby, the women respond that "He going to keep-a-noise till he learn better" (613). The baby will keep making noise until he either learns to keep quiet in white society or until he learns how to speak, to read, and to think. He will keep on making noise until he and all African American children get a better education (i.e., learn better). Ruby's brother, age eight, finds the ice pick in the schoolyard, an ice pick originally belonging to the church. By embedding the ice pick, quite literally in the ground of the schoolyard and in the narrative, Welty foregrounds the political nature of Ruby and Dove's "demonstration." Their ice pick is not a lobotomizing instrument but one that has multiple positive and life-giving associations that can break up the frozen ice of the white world.[13]

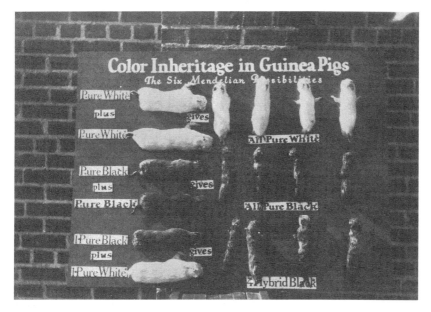

Fig. 5.   Color Inheritance in Guinea Pigs (Mendelian pattern), 1925. American Philosophical Society, Fitter Families Collection, 2000.

Throughout the story, the African Americans are engaged in living—going to church, working as productive members of the community—while the white people are in bad shape. Examples of feeblemindedness, degeneracy, and stupidity are everywhere in this white community and nowhere in the black community. As Marcia Pope knows, Dr. Strickland is not sleeping with his wife and therefore, in any eugenics assessment, would be an anemic specimen, not a Fitter Family contest winner. Not just Ruby and Dove, but poor white trash Billy Lee Warrum, who would have been a primary target of a eugenics campaign, engage in healthy sexual activity. Warrum dies in an accident because he is racing passionately to meet his fiancée. Ruby and Dove have populated the otherwise waning community with a healthy, intelligent child. By contrast, Dr. Strickland's own child is "damaged," unable to walk or talk, almost a vegetable, a "moron" in eugenics language, making both Dr. Strickland and his daughter perfect, though unlikely, candidates for eugenics sterilization. Herman Fairbrothers has a disease (racism?) about which no one wants to talk. Marcia Pope is bedridden with seizures.

Welty opens "The Demonstrators" with Marcia Pope's quote from *The Aeneid*, "Arma virumque cano" (I sing of arms and the man) (*CSEW* 608). In *The Aeneid*, Virgil does not just sing of arms and of the man but of a woman, Dido, the scorned Libyan queen of Carthage. Dido is so angered by her lover Aeneas's departure for Italy that she impales herself on his sword and has her sister burn her body so that Aeneas will see the burning pyre and feel remorse. After consummating their love in a cave during a rainstorm in Carthage, Aeneas, possessed by his desire to follow his destiny (ultimately to found Rome), leaves Dido.[14] Virgil describes her death with these words: "Red were her rolling eyes, and discompos'd her face; Ghastly she gaz'd, with pain she drew her breath" (*Aeneid* 4.649–51).[15] Later in the text he adds, "These boding omens his base flight pursue! She said, and struck; deep enter'd in her side the piercing steel, with reeking purple dyed: Clogg'd in the wound the cruel weapon stands; The spouting blood came streaming on her hands" (*Aeneid* 4.662–69). In "The Demonstrators," Ruby is rolling her eyes. She has trouble drawing breath and blood covers her hands. She and Dove impale each other on the same ice pick (sword). In *The Aeneid*, before Dido kills herself she curses Aeneas and calls out that for generations to come the peoples of Libya and Italy will be at war. It will in fact be Hannibal, an African general, considered the greatest warrior of all time, who fights for Carthage against Rome.

By connecting "The Demonstrators" to *The Aeneid*, and without drawing simple equivalencies like "Ruby is like Dido" or "Dove is like Aeneas," Welty unlocks the textual possibility that Ruby and Dove's love is as epic and powerful, as worthy of inclusion in the canon of Western literature, as Dido's. Referring to the greatest African general and African queen of all time, during a period when white Mississippi isolationism is deadly, Welty transforms the civil rights struggle in Holden, Mississippi, into an epic battle performed on the world stage.[16] It is no coincidence that Welty starts this story with Virgil and a snapshot of Dr. Strickland looking at a newspaper photo of a peace activist. Welty is foregrounding war and reminding us that this moment of racial conflict in Mississippi is a war.

Dove and Ruby would not engage in a life-and-death performance in order to bring about anything but radical change. By the time Welty is writing "The Demonstrators," proponents of the black power movement are moving beyond the nonviolent stance of Martin Luther King Jr. that dominated the civil rights movement in the 1950s and early 1960s. By 1964 groups like the Deacons for Defense start to arm themselves against the KKK and other white supremacist organizations and demand the equality outlined in the 1964 Civil Rights Act.[17] In the summer of 1966, the Deacons accompanied marchers from Memphis to Jackson, where Stokely Carmichael popularized the phrase "black power." The African American liberation movement by 1965 was no longer engaged only in civil disobedience.

If we understand the liminal space that the doctor has been called to occupy—"the other side of the tracks"—as a war zone, then the story takes on a wholly different meaning. If this is a war and a eugenics war at that, then in Holden the African Americans are better organized. The women are holding down the front lines at the train depot, calling out in loud voices, cities along the road to freedom, "Meridian. Birmingham. Chattanooga. Bristol. Lynchburg. Washington. Baltimore. Philadelphia. And New York" (*CSEW* 614)— New York, the ultimate location of great drama. They highlight the fact that profound change requires performative agility. When Dr. Strickland looks at the lights that spell BROADWAY in Holden, the bulbs are all knocked out. Rather than playing bridge, or playing at bridging the two communities, Ruby and Dove are acting their roles. They are not disconnected from history or pain. They are willing to put their bodies on the line. In this case, living on the edge, the railroad station that separates rich whites from poor blacks is so dangerous that Oree, a soldier in this racial war, has lost her legs. In French, *orée* means "boundary, edge." When describing Ruby, Welty writes: "The dome of her forehead looked thick as a battering ram, because of the rolling of her eyes" (609). As a battering ram, the young woman's forehead, her mind, is trying to break through barriers.

In Ruby's bedroom, Lucille tries hard to show the doctor the light, literally sticking "the lamp hot into his own face. 'Remember Lucille? I am Lucille. I was washing for your mother when you was born. Let me see you do something' she says with fury. 'You ain't even tied her up! You sure ain't your daddy!'" (613). Dr. Strickland answers, "Why she's bleeding inside . . . What do you think she's doing?" (613). He condescendingly misses Lucille's declaration of identity, and the point she is trying to make. There is a possibility that while Lucille is angry that the doctor has not stitched up and bandaged Ruby, on another level she is observing that when Dr. Strickland's father came to take care of poor black women, especially women who had already had one baby, he tied them up, the vernacular for tying one's tubes.[18] Lucille does not want Dr. Strickland to tie up Ruby, but she does want him to have enough fight in him to be a worthy opponent, that after they wake him up he will be able to save a life.[19]

After Lucille's outburst, all Dr. Strickland can think about is guinea pigs, another potential connection of the moment to sterilization and the eugenics movement: "For a minute all he heard was the guinea pigs racing. He looked back at the girl; her eyes were fixed with possession" (613). Ruby is still in possession of her own body, her own personhood, and her own fertility. In response to Ruby and to Lucille, Dr. Strickland simply repeats his famous line: "I gave her a shot. She'll just go to sleep" (613). But Ruby does not go to sleep; instead, inverting Dr. Strickland's invasive scientific gaze, she keeps her eyes on the doctor until he leaves: "Then he stepped across the gaze of the girl on the bed as he would have had to step over a crack yawning in the floor" (614). She now has him in her sights, and even refuses to succumb to his drugs. The crack is the space between what she knows and what he is able to see.

If we read the scene at Ruby's house as a birth instead of a death, the reactions of those around seem more appropriate. Everyone appears positive if not cheerful; the men on the porch are laughing, smoking cigarettes, and joking. The doctor even sends a child to boil water. Death in this particular ritual performance is a birth, while birth in the doctor's own child's case is death. Ruby and Dove have given each other the gift of entry into what the "small heel tapping man" calls "the gates of joy" (615). In fact, this slippery line between life and death becomes even more potent as through this multiple and multiplying narrative, Welty appears to give Ruby and Dove the power of resurrection. This is fiction, of course, and in the mythical world of Holden, Mississippi, anything is possible. By including what appear to be references to Fitter Family guinea pigs, a lobotomy, and tube-tying sterilizations, Welty troubles the waters, forcing us to question what constitutes murder, who is really killing whom, and who is dead and who is alive.

Welty interrogates the exact kind of "indirect murder" that Michel Foucault delineates in his lectures at the Collège de France: "When I say killing I obviously do not mean murder as such, but also every form of indirect murder: the fact of exposing someone to death, increasing the risk of death for some people, or quite simply political death, expulsion, rejection, and so on" (*Society Must Be Defended* 256). Welty is "dramaticizing," but in this case she tells a deep truth. A character in a mythical world can die and still be alive; they can mutate, shape-shift, and change forms in any number of ways. The mill is eating Dove alive and indeed Holden alive, and yet the yellow pollen on his body reveals Dove's fertility. The women call him in a triad chant. Dove is at once a bird, a man, and a snake who can climb up from Snake River during the time it takes the seventy-two trains to pass—seventy-two being the number of hours preceding Christ's resurrection. Dr. Strickland finds that Ruby is wearing a "skin tight" white, silky dress with a red banner tied around it. Dr. Strickland does not tie her up but instead unties the knot that reveals her Amazonian warrior breasts and her white tooth necklace. She, like Dove, sheds her white snakeskin, preparing for metamorphosis. By transmogrifying, Ruby and Dove do more then just save themselves, they attempt to save the community not just from racism but from the economic slavery of the mill.

Dr. Strickland asks Ruby if she can breathe a deep breath and if she is coughing up anything. Being unable to breathe deeply and coughing up phlegm are two symptoms of brown lung disease, or byssinosis, a disease caused by breathing in tiny particles of cotton dust. People have known about the disease since the seventeenth century, but not until the late 1960s and early 1970s did the movement successfully force American cottonseed mills to ventilate, provide adequate filtration, etc. Welty in 1965 would already have heard of the disease. The disease only becomes potentially fatal after five years. Dove has worked at the Fairbrothers Cotton Seed Oil Mill since 1959. When Dr. Strickland finds him, he is covered with cottonseed meal. Dr. Strickland describes the mill in a disturbing way: "He passed the throbbing mill, working on its own generator. No lights ever shone through the windowless and now moonlit sheet iron, but the smell came out freely and spread over the town at large—a cooking smell, like a dish ordered by a man with an endless appetite" (615). Dove "dies" hemorrhaging through the mouth, the "death" of a man dying of internal injuries or lung sickness. Dr. Strickland observes that "The telephone wires along the road were hung with shreds of cotton, the sides of the road were strewn with them too, as if the doctor were out on a paper chase" (615). One of the major causes of byssinosis was unventilated workspaces. The cotton gin is windowless—no light shows through.

This complex demonstration involves not just Dove and Ruby but every member of the community. The women in their white dresses and red sashes are also demonstrators. They are following the ritual known in the Mississippi and Louisiana Delta towns as Easter Rock, a ceremony that seamlessly joins West African, Caribbean, and Christian elements and connects directly with the famous Gullah Ring Shout ceremonies in which participants walked in a particular circular pattern thought to be a West African cosmogram. In the Easter Rock ceremony, participants start at nine o'clock on Saturday night (the same time Ruby and her friends leave the church) and engage in a ritual around a table in the church in which twelve women wearing white dresses with red banners follow one male leader and the banner of a paper sun as they dance a rocking song. As documented by Seale and Seale in their 1942 ethnographic work, one of the songs sung in the Easter Rock service is "Meet Me at de Station When Dat Train Come Along." There are hundreds of verses but the ones that apply to this story are:

> (*Three times.*)
> 'Cause Ah may be blin', and Ah ca' not see.
> Meet me at de station when dat train come along,
> (*Three times.*)
> 'Cause Ah may be lame, and Ah ca' not walk.

Oree and the old Tyrant are at the station when the train comes along. Oree is lame. That the "ritual" of the Easter Rock and the "ritual" of the killings occur at the same time reinforce the performative possibilities in the text. The fact that Dove and Ruby pierce each other on Easter adds to their Christ-like martyrdom.[20]

In this mythical multiplicity, Ruby and Dove are representative of every black man and woman who walked over Pettus Bridge. Their bodies are not sacrificial but the body politic of a *Ruby* Bridges, who in 1960 braved federal marshals and tomatoes and racial slurs to walk up the steps to integrate William Franz Elementary School in New Orleans. They are not playing bridge; their bodies are the bridge. Ruby's name means a "precious stone," hard to cut or hurt. Her last name, Gaddy, when shortened to "Gad," means a sharp, metal spearlike object just like an ice pick. If Ruby is a ruby, a hard precious stone and a "gad," a hard, metal spearlike object, then she is not the pierced victim but the weapon itself—the battering ram. Bodies, like those of all civil rights workers, are weapons. During the civil rights movement, at least forty martyrs died putting their bodies on the line. One of the four children killed in the 16th Avenue Baptist Church bombing in Birmingham was eleven-year-old Addie Mae Collins. To name Dove, Dove *Collins* in 1966, just three years after the girls' deaths, seems to make an unmistakable connection to Addie Mae Collins.

In this mysterious dark quilt of a story, life and death have changed places. Ruby and Dove by their performative or real murders save their souls from the terror that is the assault on black bodies, the deadening, cannibalistic nature of the mill, and the horror of eugenics. The lobotomized, sterilizing death machine of white supremacy can drone on, but Ruby and Dove are opting out. In death or the shape-shifting metamorphosis they accomplish, they are more alive then Dr. Strickland is in life. However, Welty does not stop here. When Dr. Strickland sits by the train tracks being *rocked* into momentary awareness, he asks himself if "there was still allowed to everybody on earth a self—savage, death defying, private?" Throughout slavery and into the twentieth century, racist propagandists demeaned African Americans and made them into feared subhumans by calling them "savages." The fact that Welty has Dr. Strickland speak the word to describe the core feeling of being human—"a self, savage, death defying, private"—an individual capable of autonomous action, strips the word, in this context, at least for a moment, of negative and demeaning racist connotations. For this moment, being a self, being savage, is a good thing.

Dr. Strickland's oblique allusion to savage, the presence of Ruby's dog-teeth necklace, the allusion to Amazonian breasts, the Easter Rock ritual, and at least ten other textual traces suggest that Eudora Welty is consciously inviting into her textual universe "Africanisms" or African American cultural practices that can be traced back to specific African communities. These "Africanisms," like the ice pick, function in diametrically opposite ways. They serve simultaneously as signs of Strickland's racist projections and as powerful markers of the cultural continuity in African American communities that anthropologists had documented by the mid-1960s. As she does with all allusions, Welty makes these connections with calculated indirection and some humor. Rather than link Holden, Mississippi, to any particular country or community in Africa, Welty picks up on the guinea pigs again and links Holden and the African American community in Holden to Papua, New Guinea. Any resisting reader would be thinking, as in Momma's phrase from "Why I Live at the P.O.": "Stop right there!" Guinea pigs do not come from New Guinea, and what does New Guinea have to do with African American cultural heritage anyway? Of course guinea pigs do not come from New Guinea, and New Guinea has nothing to do with African American cultural continuity, but this is a detective story full of wit, and Welty has warned us not to be like Dr. Strickland and miss the most important clues.

In 1964 a Harvard professor, Richard Gardner, documented in his famous and highly controversial ethnographic film, *Dead Birds*, what he interpreted to be the ritualized warfare and revenge murders of the community called the Dani in Papua, New Guinea. What tears through the fabric of "The Demonstrators" are what I see as specific allusions to the rituals and rites of the Dani, as mediated and exoticized in both *National Geographic* and the documentary *Dead Birds*—"texts" to which Eudora Welty would have had access. Rather than supporting these texts' "othering" view of New Guinea "savages," she uses the references to the Dani to empower her characters. In a wonderfully imaginative stroke, Welty introduces the cannibal-dark, rain-forest, sharp-teeth-necklace, Amazonian, paternalistic, *National Geographic* view of exotic otherness into the space of white Holden, Mississippi. In her critique of racism Welty reminds us that it certainly does not matter to *National Geographic* if it is Africa or New Guinea. They are all "exotics."

Robert Gardner's film *Dead Birds* supposedly records a ritualistic warfare in which the tribe must revenge the killing of tribal members to appease the ancestral ghosts and regain the health and fertility of the community. According to Gardner, each time a warrior is killed on one side, the other group mourns and gets ready to appease the ghosts by revenging his death with another death. Gardner first showed his film in 1964, right before Welty wrote her story. Even if Welty did not herself view the film, *Dead Birds* garnered massive media attention, because of the shocking nature of the subject, because many believed that Gardner condoned and possibly even started the wars he filmed, and because Michael Rockefeller, Nelson Rockefeller's son, died on a separate expedition after working on the film. As early as 1962 there were *New York Times* articles about the shooting of the film. *National Geographic* had a fascination with New Guinea as early as 1927, when an expedition went up the Strickland River to find disease-resistant strands of sugarcane. From 1927 to 1964 *National Geographic* published at least fifteen articles on peoples in New Guinea, most composed by ornithologists who exoticized the "native" peoples by connecting the beautiful birds of New Guinea to the people decorated with bird feathers.[21]

The intertextual links between "The Demonstrators" and images in *National Geographic* and the documentary film *Dead Birds* are numerous. Many of Gardner's expeditions started on the Strickland River, and the base camp was called Strickland camp.[22] In both the *National Geographic* issues devoted to the Dani and in *Dead Birds*, there are images of young boys tending pigs by holding out greens to feed them. When Welty mentions guinea pigs "running underfoot," she also includes this odd detail: "The little boy with a sanctimonious face had taken the bit of celery and knelt down on the floor; there was scrambling about" ("The Demonstrators" 611). The little boy is kneeling on the floor to feed the scrambling guinea pigs just like the Dani boys feeding their pigs.

Dr. Strickland's description of Dove's death evokes *National Geographic* images of New Guinea women wearing fishing nets that hang from the back of their heads. One of these pictures shows them wearing the nets as they mourn (fig. 6). "The man raised up and looked at him like a seal," Welty writes. "Blood laced his head like a net through which he had broken. His wide tongue hung down out of his mouth" (*CSEW* 619). The Dani live separately by gender, and the women watch over the funeral rites. In the *Demonstrators*, only women and children gather around Ruby as she is dying. The men are on the porch, the women inside the house. Gardner presents evidence in *Dead Birds* that when the Dani women participated in funeral rites, they sometimes engaged in what he calls "cannibalism" by ingesting a small piece of flesh from the dead warrior. *National Geographic* repeatedly calls the New Guinea people headhunters, cannibals, wild men. But in Welty's story the possible cannibals are white. As Dr. Strickland leaned over the bed, "the lamp was brought down closer and closer to the girl, like something that would devour her" (612). Dr. Strickland describes the mill as having "a cooking smell, like a dish ordered by a man with an endless appetite." The cannibalistic mill eats the workers. In his book on *Dead Birds*, Gardner mentions too that after a warrior had been killed, a young girl sometimes had fingers or toes cut off as a way to engage them in the communal moment. Dr. Strickland mentions Ruby's bloody fingers. Oree has stumps for legs.

Fig. 6. Mogei women in mourning darken their faces with soot, Australian New Guinea. John Scofield/National Geographic Stock.

Welty frees the metaphoric "other," the dark savage represented in this text by the New Guinea people from the frame of *National Geographic* and Gardner's documentary. In Native American discussions, the Algonquin people refer to the damaging "othering" implicit in documentaries about Native peoples by calling the films "documentary genocide." In Welty's text the women, like the Dani, are autonomous warriors engaged in their own battle, inscrutable to the Dr. Stricklands, Robert Gardners, and writers for *National Geographic*.[23] Through this subtext Welty exposes not just the deep fear harbored in the southern slaveocracy, that "savage" Africans would rise up and kill those who had treated them as less than human, the psychotic double-edged sword of racism, but the rightful anger of those who have been used. A simplistic rewriting of Welty's subtext would read: you think this African American character is an ignorant maid, but she is a warrior, and for all you have done to her and her people—slavery, lobotomies, sterilizations, lynchings, economic genocide, exposure to environmental hazards—she will not kill you, but she could and perhaps should.

One of the images in *National Geographic* is of brush fires on the hills near where the Dani live. Dr. Strickland observes that "Far down the railroad tracks, beyond the unlighted town, rose the pillow-shaped glow of a grass fire. It was gaseous, unveined, unblotted by smoke, a cloud with the November flush of the sedge grass by day and sparkless and nerveless, not to be confused with a burning church, but like anesthetic made visible" (*CSEW* 616). The fire burns away the anesthesia, the complacency, and revitalizes the fields for planting in the spring.

By 1966 the debate over Africanisms in African American and American culture in general was fully developed. Beginning with Du Bois and continuing through Melville J. Herskovits's famous *The Negro in American Culture*, anthropologists and historians had argued, and were in the process of contextualizing in great detail, ways in which enslaved Africans had preserved and transformed elements of a diverse number of African cultures to develop language, art, music, dance, ritual, intellectual perspectives, educational values, more "African" than European and often a brilliant creolization of the two. Du Bois's and Herskovits's insistence on cultural continuity was a direct reaction to the Eurocentric position that African American peoples had no cultural heritage and thus made no contribution to American culture. The same sort of prejudice plagued Mississippi during the civil rights movement, with even well-meaning liberals assuming a black ignorance, poverty, and desperation that completely ignored the autonomy and continuous intellectual and cultural contribution of the black community. In their eyes, the black community was dying and needed saving by altruistic whites.

As Dr. Strickland is looking around the town, he describes an odd scene that cannot be understood in any purely realistic reading. He wanders through the town and observes "The haze and the moonlight were one over the square, over the row of storefronts opposite with the line of poles thin as matchsticks rising to prop the one long strip of line over the side walk, the dry goods store with its ornamental top that looked like opened paper fans held up by acrobats (*CSEW* 618). The Dani warriors when looking out for their enemies stood on tall poles that looked exactly like "opened fans held up by acrobats" (fig. 7). The acrobat warriors are protecting a town that would otherwise falter.

In an ingenious sleight of hand, Welty rewrites a racism that has situated itself between two stereotypes: aggressive savage and helpless poor folk. But to mention "Africa" would be to open the Pandora's box of the savage stereotype too directly. Instead, Welty critiques the stereotype obliquely by evoking the *National Geographic*'s minimalizing of the Dani culture at a moment in history when these "savages" were most accessible to her readers.[24] Then she asks the question through Dr. Strickland's musing: and what is wrong with being savage? If it means being alive, fierce, connected to the natural world, and ready to die for what you care about, then we should all strive to be savage.

Through allusions accumulating below the obvious surface of the text, Welty takes on the most ridiculous stereotype of black people, the savage cannibalistic beast, to recognize the agency and power that African Americans retained throughout the reign of terror known as slavery and segregation. Evoking the racially charged and traditionally damaging stereotypes of "savage" and "cannibal," Welty imbues the women in Ruby's mother's house with a menacing, mysterious warrior power that diffuses the narrative of victimized Delta sharecropper, raped and beaten African American maid, and jilted common-law wife. Agency replaces subservience. Black power replaces nonviolence.

Ruby and Dove kill off the body that worked for the Man and replace it with the body that they put on the line—the demonstrator, activist, actor—who will pour his and her blood onto the grounds of the new school to make sure that it will prosper and grow. In order to ensure the potency of their magic, they dramatize their case by presenting their bodies to the town doctor. And in the end it is birds, both Dove and Ruby, and the birds he sees in his backyard that ultimately open Dr. Strickland's eyes—a little bit at least.

Fig. 7. Robert Gardener, *Watching for the Enemy*, in *Making Dead Birds: Chronicle of a Film*. Courtesy of the Peabody Museum of Archaeology and Ethnology, Harvard University, ID #2006.12.1.170.27. © President and Fellows of Harvard College, photograph by Michael Rockefeller.

The story concludes with Dr. Strickland's observation that

> a pair of flickers were rifling the grass, the Cock in one part of the garden the hen in
> another, picking at the devastation . . . probing and feeding . . . He was pretty sure
> that Sylvia had known the birds were there. Her eyes would follow birds when they
> flew across the garden.[25] As she watched, the cock spread one wing, showy as a ze-
> bra's hide, and with a turn of his head showed his red seal. Dr. Strickland swallowed
> the coffee and picked up his bag. It was all going to be just about as hard as seeing
> Herman and Eva Fairbrothers through. He thought that in all Holden, as of now,
> only Miss Marcia Pope was still quite able to take care of herself—or such was her
> opinion. (622)

Such was her opinion and if we believe the eugenics subtext, it was not a good
one. The birds, like Dove and Ruby, like the women in the bird pageant that
Eudora Welty photographed, are performing, in this case the showy zebra's
hide, in which white and black merge together in a complex pattern, a zebra-
like creolization not easily discernable, as mysterious as the cock's red seal or a
ruby red breast's markings, a kind of extraliterary text. This ending hints that
Strickland *may* indeed have learned something—if only to drink his coffee,
try to "read" the birds and trees, wake up to his real job of healing the sick-
ened white community, and at the very least do no medical harm to the black
community.

In the Dani culture that Gardner filmed, the objects that the warriors took
from one another during combat were called dead birds. As Ruby is dying, her
sister bids her necklace covered with teeth. Her necklace is a dead bird. Dove
is a dead bird. Ruby is a dead bird. The white dresses and china cups that the
women—who worked as maids in white people's houses—have in their houses
are dead birds, objects taken from the enemy. On his way out Dr. Strickland
bumps into these white starched and boiled dresses from the women in his
life, and they appear as white KKK robes circling the house, as lynched bodies bumping his face, as a reminder of the hours of backbreaking toil that the
women had to endure as maids in white uniforms to feed their children and
stay alive. They stand birdlike as a sign of the ghosts of the ancestors that must
be avenged: "With sleeves, spread wide, trying to scratch his forehead with
the tails of their skirts, they were flying around this house in the moonlight"
(*CSEW* 615). Far from being about black-on-black violence, "The Demonstrators" is instead about African American empowerment, subjectivity, and cultural continuity. It is also about how much a white authority, Welty herself, can

actually know. She asks us, as she asks herself, if she is in danger of telling lies, of hiding murderers, of pretending innocence, always relegated to a *National Geographic*–mediated cultural experience no matter how close she is to her subject?

In death, Ruby and Dove and their whole community literally exit the text, taking with them the right to tell their own story. They are selves, savage, death defying, and private, something Dr. Strickland can only feel as a nauseous moment. Welty leaves open the possibility that what might have happened to Dove and Ruby in this time and place could have been much worse. The marshal whom the doctor sees driving away from the scene of the crime could have killed Dove. Dr. Strickland could have lobotomized him on Sunday morning when he was stitching him up. Dove might have been "tarred and feathered," covered with cottonseed for demonstrating. Welty does not tell us that we should believe one variant over another. "The Demonstrators" should be read as literature, with all the symbolic, metaphoric, allusive, "lying," "dramatizing" qualities that literature brings to politics, not as history, or biography, or political rhetoric. The African American home of Ruby Gaddy's mother is not any "real" or "politically correct" or even "historically accurate" African American home, but the imaginary space created by this one writer who, caught in a particularly violent and fraught moment of cultural dislocation, tries to connect one human being to another, to break down the dividing wall of segregation.

If all we know at the end of the story is that we do not know and should not assume that we do know, then Welty would have successfully broken the narcissistic hallucination that propels racist projection. But we actually know much more than this. Through skillful inclusion of historical references, literary allusions, and cultural markers, Welty forces her readers to question authority, not just social authority but literary authority. Who can be trusted or believed? Whose story should we validate? Who is telling the truth and for what purpose? Who is lying and for what purpose? What can we actually know about one another? Just as Dove and Ruby pierce each other, Welty pierces the textual fabric of segregated society by quilting a text that we can enter through multiple portals of human experience. Welty's contribution to racial understanding is not a didactic blueprint but a human footprint. Her familiarity with the world of 1960s Mississippi makes what she has to say more illuminating and more devastating than what an outsider might have written. She does not have to make up cotton picking in the June heat to dramatize her story. She knows just how much worse, and how much better, it could be.

1. Welty, *The Eye of the Story*, 137.

2. Welty, "The Demonstrators," in *The Collected Stories of Eudora Welty*. All future references will be to this edition.

3. Glaspel, "A Jury of her Peers."

4. In her article "'Racial Content Espied': Modernist Politics, Textuality, and Race in Eudora Welty's 'The Demonstrators,'" Suzan Harrison argues that Dr. Strickland projects onto the black characters a world of "otherness," "illicit sexuality, chaos, madness, impropriety, anarchy, strangeness, and helpless, hapless desire" (94) in the way Toni Morrison outlines in *Playing in the Dark*.

5. Welty, "A Worn Path," in *Collected Stories of Eudora Welty*.

6. *Roud Folk Song Index*.

7. Welty's famous photograph, *Woman with Ice Pick / Hinds County (1930's)*, captures at once the humorous and deadly nature of the symbol and Welty's personal connection to this particular woman's story.

8. Washington relates that "These acts of unbelievable surgical hostility, obliterated a child's very seat of thought, ability and personality—nothing less than a murder of the mind—were forced upon black boys as young as five" (284). She emphasizes the fact that it was a University of Mississippi neurosurgeon named J. Andy, M.D., who performed "many types of lobotomies on African American children as young as six who, he decided, were 'aggressive' and hyperactive" (284).

9. The statistics are staggering: doctors throughout the country performed as many as sixty thousand sterilizations on African American and Native American women in the United States.

10. Suzanne Marrs recounts that Welty actually had an experience being in a house where guinea pigs were running around the floor. Welty's picture 18 in *Eudora Welty Photographs* shows a woman holding a guinea pig. Welty was taking something from her real life and making it into art, giving it metaphoric resonance.

11. From the eugenicsarchives.org website: "The belief in white supremacy was exactly the concept behind *Fitter Families for Future Firesides*—known simply as *Fitter Families Contests*. The contests were founded by Mary T. Watts and Florence Brown Sherbon—two pioneers of the Baby Health Examination movement, which sprang from a 'Better Baby' contest at the 1911 Iowa State Fair and spread to forty states before World War I . . . Each family member was given an overall letter grade of eugenic health, and the family with the highest grade average was awarded a silver trophy."

12. Interestingly enough, Ruby and Dove's baby's name is Roger. There is no reason for Welty to name the baby at all, and Roger is an unusual first name for a southern African American child. Since many of the names are significant and several reference renowned African Americans, I think it is possible that Welty is giving a nod to Jimmy Rogers, who called himself simply Rogers. Rogers was a famous African American blues musician from Mississippi, whose song "Rock This House Tonight" would fit in perfectly with other references to rocking. Dr. Strickland twice feels rocked. Rogers was

famous for his harmonica playing, and Welty mentions harmonicas in the story. He was part of the Chicago blues scene and was known for playing with the Muddy Waters band often referred to as the Headhunters.

13. *The Sentinel* claims that Dove's wounded body rolled down the embankment thirteen to fourteen yards. Specifically in Revelation 13 and 14, God tells his followers to take the scythe and bury it in the earth to enjoy the fruit of the vine. Like the ice pick, the shovel breaking the ground on the new school pierces the earth to enjoy the fruit of the vine, specifically, in this case, educated children.

14. Caves figure prominently in Dr. Strickland's descriptions: "the last electric light of any kind appeared to be the one burning in the vast shrouded cavern of the gin" (609), and "Behind its iron railings, the courthouse-and-jail stood barely emerging from its black cave of trees and only the slicked iron step of the stile caught the moon" (618).

15. Virgil's *Aeneid*, translated by John Dryden, Penguin Classics (all future references to the text will be from this edition).

16. The intertextual parallels to the *Aeneid* allow for the possibility that instead of a double murder, Ruby took her own life after killing Dove, and that she did it not because she was wronged by another woman but for great love, for her people. The *Aeneid*/Dido inversion takes Ruby firmly out of the victim role and makes her the possible agent of her own fate. But it is important not to lean too heavily on the idea that Ruby commits suicide, as it is only one of many narrative options, and one that is as performative as the other possibilities. The point is not to choose one Weltian possibility, but to expand the imaginative field by entertaining all.

17. See Lance Hill, *The Deacons for Defense: Armed Resistance and the Civil Rights Movement*, 2006.

18. In 1964 Fannie Lou Hamer spoke before an "audience in Washington D.C. [and at the Democratic National Convention] telling them that she was one of many black women in her area that had been a victim of a 'Mississippi appendectomy' (an unwanted, unrequested and unwarranted hysterectomy given to poor and unsuspecting Black women). According to her research 60 percent of the black women in Sunflower County, Mississippi, were subjected to post-partum sterilization at Sunflower City Hospital without their permission" (http://mississippiappendectomy.wordpress.com). It would have been impossible for the observant and addicted-to-the-news Eudora Welty to have missed this story. Welty could easily have heard Hamer on the television broadcast but would already have known the story.

19. Even Maria Pope flat on her back in bed is a eugenics soldier. She tells Dr. Strickland: "Richard Strickland? I have it on my report that Irene Roberts is not where she belongs. Now which of you wants the whipping?" (608). According to her, they belong together because they are one of the smartest young men and the "the prettiest girl in the Delta" (61).

20. Two sources: Louisiana Folklife Program/Resources. Documentary: *African-American Easter Rock Religious Service—True Light Baptist Church*, edited from raw field footage by Annie S. Staten (1994) at Original True Light Baptist Church; and Lea

Seale and Marianna Seale, "Easter Rock: A Louisiana Negro Ceremony" (1942), reprinted with permission from the American Folklore Society in *Black American Literature Forum* 25, no. 1 (Spring 1991).

21. The bird/New Guinea connection is a powerful one in "The Demonstrators" and weaves together with Welty's own photographic and written record of the Pageant of Birds in Jackson. The Dani and many other New Guinea people dressed in elaborate bird costumes. One *National Geographic* picture of a Dani warrior has him wearing white wings almost identical to those in the bird pageant in Jackson.

22. "We chartered an auxiliary ketch, the Vanapa of about 100 tons burden, to transport most of our men, our fuel, supplies, and scientific instruments to some yet-to-be found point on the Strickland River, which would later become our first base camp. We decided on the left bank of the Strickland River, above its juncture with the Fly, in a mysterious region regarded by coast folk with superstitious awe" (*National Geographic* 267). The Strickland camp was established early and revisited by many different expeditions. This first description can be found in *National Geographic* 61, no. 3 (September 1929). "Into Primeval Papua By Seaplane: Seeking Disease-resisting Sugar Cane, Scientists Find Neolithic Man in Unmapped Nooks of Sorcery and Cannibalism," by E. W. Brandes, PhD, principal pathologist-in-charge, Sugar Plant Investigations, and leader of the New Guinea Expedition.

23. Tying the body with twine in Dani culture was the first act that the healer would perform to purge a wounded warrior. In *National Geographic,* there are many pictures of warriors being tied with twine after being wounded. This provides us with another reading of Lucille's "Let me see you do something." She said with fury: "You ain't even tied her up! You sure ain't your daddy" (*CSEW* 613)—meaning Ruby is a wounded warrior, and Dr. Strickland has not tied her up.

24. By the 1970s and certainly today we would have no problem recognizing and embracing the cultural continuity of such groups as the Gullah, who are still performing the Ring Shout or the complex "African" roots of the Mardi Gras Indians, the Africanisms embedded in the blues, jazz, and hip-hop.

25. A common image in earlier editions of *National Geographic* is of the ornithologist being carried by Native peoples. Dr. Strickland "felt as though someone had stopped him on the street and offered to carry his load for a while—had insisted on it—some old, trusted, half-forgotten family friend that he had lost sight of since youth" (*CSEW* 618). Dr. Strickland appears to be waxing nostalgic for the old slave or servant who will carry his load. This also makes him part of one of the ornithological expeditions. Since he and his daughter are literally looking at birds throughout the text, this is not such a far-fetched connection.

Bibliography

Brandes, E. W. "Into Primeval Papua by Seaplane: Seeking Disease-resisting Sugar Cane, Scientists Find Neolithic Man in Unmapped Nooks of Sorcery and Cannibalism." *National Geographic* 61, no. 3 (September 1929).

Color Inheritance in Guinea Pigs, ca. 1925. Image #1566 (Mendelian pattern). American Philosophical Society, Fitter Families Collection, in *The Image Archive on the American Eugenics Movement*, 2000. Dolan DNA Learning Center, Cold Spring Harbor Laboratory, Cold Spring Harbor, New York. http://www.eugenicsarchive.org.

Dawes, Robyn M. *The House of Cards: Psychology and Psychotherapy Built on Myth*. New York: The Free Press, 1996.

Glaspell, Susan. *A Jury of Her Peers*. Whitefish: Kessinger, 2010.

Harrison, Suzan. "'Racial Content Espied': Modernist Politics, Textuality, and Race in Eudora Welty's 'The Demonstrators.'" In *Eudora Welty and Politics: Did the Writer Crusade?*, ed. Harriet Pollack and Suzanne Marrs, 89–108. Baton Rouge: Louisiana State University Press, 2001.

Hill, Lance. *The Deacons for Defense: Armed Resistance and the Civil Rights Movement*. Chapel Hill: University of North Carolina Press, 2006.

Louisiana Folklife Program/Resources. *African-American Easter Rock Religious Service—True Light Baptist Church*. Edited from raw field footage by Annie S. Staten (1994) at Original True Light Baptist Church.

Mississippi Appendectomy: A Developing Online Archive of Information about Women of Color and Coercive Sterilization. http://mississippiappendectomy.wordpress.com.

Morrison, Toni. *Playing in the Dark: Whiteness and the Literary Imagination*. New York: Vintage, 1993.

Seale, Lea, and Marianna Seale. "Easter Rock: A Louisiana Negro Ceremony." *Black American Literature Forum* 25, no. 1 (1991): 27–33.

Washington, Harriet A. *Medical Apartheid: The Dark History of Medical Experimentation on Black Americans from Colonial Times to the Present*. Norwell: Anchor Press, 2008.

Welty, Eudora. "The Demonstrators." In *The Collected Stories of Eudora Welty*. New York: Harcourt, Brace, Jovanovich, 1980. 608–22.

———. *Eudora Welty: Photographs*. Jackson: University Press of Mississippi, 1993.

———. *The Eye of the Story: Selected Essays and Reviews*. New York: Vintage Press, 1990.

———. "A Worn Path." In *The Collected Stories of Eudora Welty*. New York: Harcourt, Brace, Jovanovich, 1980.

"Who Killed Cock Robyn?" In *Roud Folk Song Index*, ed. Stephen Roud. London Borough of Croydon.

Virgil. *Aeneid*. Trans. John Dryden. Ed. Frederick M. Keener. London: Penguin Classics, 1997.

JULIA EICHELBERGER

Rethinking the Unthinkable

Tracing Welty's Changing View of the Color Line in Her Letters, Essays, and The Optimist's Daughter

For over sixty years, Welty's portrayals of race and racism in twentieth-century Mississippi have puzzled some readers, many of whom have criticized her for not making it more evident in her fiction that she found Mississippi's racial hierarchy reprehensible. In 1946 Diana Trilling was among the first critics to castigate Welty for her portrayal of privileged white southerners in *Delta Wedding*. Calling the novel a celebration of "the parochialism and snobbery of the Fairchild clan," Trilling announced that she "deeply oppose[d] its values." Welty acknowledged such criticisms in her 1980 introduction to her *Collected Stories*, where she noted, "I have been told, both in approval and in accusation, that I seem to love all my characters." Claudia Roth Pierpont repeated these accusations in her 1998 *New Yorker* essay, asserting that Welty's affectionate portraits of white Mississippians "turned her into Mississippi's favorite daughter—the besieged white public was only too happy to see itself in her adorable eccentrics." Dean Flower, one of the most recent critics to find Welty politically suspect, concludes in his 2007 *Hudson Review* essay that "Welty felt ambivalent about racism" and that scholarly efforts to prove otherwise amount to special pleading.[1]

Welty scholars have offered repeated evidence that Welty's fiction registers the harmful effects of racial, social, and economic hierarchies, and her liberal politics are now well documented. But many readers still see little evidence of Welty's progressive attitudes in her fictional texts, which rarely portray straightforward resistance to racism. Why, if this writer desired a more just, humane, and inclusive society, did she write so few works that directly addressed a problem that was so widespread? Welty set one of her novels, *The Optimist's Daughter*, in 1960s Mississippi, yet the civil rights struggle is only faintly in evidence there. Pierpont, in assessing this seemingly quietist treatment of social upheaval, calls the novel "morally simplified," and Flower faults its focus on "the same non-disruptive familial themes that had generated *Delta Wedding*."[2] Ann Romines notes that in this novel, "the turmoil [of the 1960s] was relegated to the farthest edges of the canvas." Romines's conclusion is not a condemnation; she is contrasting the novel to Welty's 1960s stories "Where Is the Voice Coming From?" and "The Demonstrators," arguing that these stories allow Welty to explore "the possible costs and consequences of filial piety . . . from a stance that was not specifically autobiographical and was specifically political."[3] While I agree that political issues do not take center stage in the novel the way they do in her 1960s stories, I think *The Optimist's Daughter* does situate its protagonist's private family memories within the context of Mississippi's history of white supremacy, as I will demonstrate later in this essay. I also believe that three letters Welty wrote in 1951, describing a hospital similar to the fictional one she would create in *The Optimist's Daughter*, are further evidence that Welty's understanding of race did not remain static throughout her adult life. For many years Welty, like most liberal white southerners, considered the color line to be deplorable but virtually unalterable.[4] Her changing view is reflected, quietly but unmistakably, in her construction of *The Optimist's Daughter*.

The color line in the United States after World War II, a topic that has been widely explored for its own sake, has not foregrounded many discussions of Welty's racial attitudes. Yet it is impossible to assess Welty's presentations of race in her writing without understanding how race was constructed in her time and place. Her pre-1960s writings generally acknowledge the color line without interrogating or explicating it. Reflecting on these omissions in a 1973 interview, Welty said that *Delta Wedding* contained "a lot of things I didn't have the wits to realize would need to be explained."[5] But the characters in that novel, set in the 1920s and written in the 1940s, would have needed no explanations. In the South prior to the civil rights movement, the color line—a web of custom, belief, public discourse, and enforcements both legal and extralegal— was a reality so pervasive that its existence provoked little remark, regardless of one's attitude toward it. Interactions between whites and nonwhites were laden with unspoken imperatives, preexisting classifications that individuals were not at liberty to disregard. Such imperatives are rarely mentioned directly in Welty's fiction or personal letters, but they clearly circumscribed the thoughts and behavior of the people about whom she wrote. It is also clear to me that Welty's attitude toward the color line, which was always progressive compared with most white Mississippians, changed between the 1940s and the 1960s.

Welty's letters help us track her views of the color line, but her private references to race are not exactly transparent to the twenty-first-century reader.[6] Welty's correspondence contains a few—a very few—racially offensive words and phrases; the meanings that Welty may have attached to these words are somewhat cryptic, as Suzanne Marrs has argued. Welty wrote hundreds of letters in the 1940s to John Robinson, a high school classmate with whom she was romantically involved. Four of these letters use the word "nigger" seemingly as a matter of course. Marrs, when commenting on this usage in her biography, notes that these four references constitute a miniscule percentage of the thousands of letters Welty wrote, and that in other letters and conversation in 1949 and 1950, Welty said she considered the term offensive.[7] To this qualification Dean Flower has responded sarcastically, "Why, Eudora is hardly guilty of racism at all."[8] For my part, instead of excusing or implicitly damning Welty for such language, I wish to keep it—its presence and its rarity—in mind as I analyze other references to race in her private letters and public statements.

Another 1948 letter to Robinson is also potentially problematic: Welty praised Mississippi journalist Hodding Carter for defending the South's record on race relations. This discussion, too, is impossible to parse without its rather intricate context. Carter, whom Welty and Robinson knew socially, had appeared on a 1948 radio program opposite Fred Sprigle, a white northern journalist who had just published a series of articles entitled "I Was a Negro in the South for 30 Days." Welty said of the radio program, "It was gratifying," adding that Carter had "done a good piece of journalistic research in getting a quote from a Negro newspaper . . . saying the Negro does better down South, in opportunities for small business etc."[9] What did she mean by this? If we read the transcript of the radio program, Welty's support for Carter's performance sounds troubling; Carter blamed southern blacks' disenfranchisement on outside interference—people during the Reconstruction era "who came down to the South in the guise of reformers and tried to handle that vote on their behalf. That's when the Negro lost the vote."[10] Here Carter sounds like a reactionary white conservative. Yet his Pulitzer Prize–winning editorials were regarded as liberal in the 1940s, both inside and outside the Deep South.[11] Moreover, in the same letter that praised Carter's radio appearance, Welty wrote that she "was surprised [Carter] came out for Dewey," the Republican who opposed Truman in the 1948 presidential election. "How could any soul?" she wondered to Robinson. This was a rhetorical question; Welty would have been well aware of how many Mississippi voters hated Truman. His Democratic Party platform had been much discussed in Mississippi; it contained a few sentences about civil rights—sentences that sound innocuous and even timid to most twenty-first-century readers—that had enraged and frightened many white Mississippians.[12] Welty clearly had a different view of Truman's politics; in this letter to Robinson, she said of Truman's recent victory, "I suppose Mr. Truman was the nearest to liberal choice—and that far it's good."

Similarly inscrutable attitudes appear in letters Welty wrote in 1951, describing a New Orleans hospital where her brother was being treated. These letters are worth more detailed scrutiny, because I believe they functioned as precursors to the fictional New Orleans hospital Welty created in *The Optimist's Daughter*, and they help us trace Welty's changing view of the color line and race. By the late 1960s, when Welty wrote *The Optimist's Daughter*, the color line had not disappeared, but it was fundamentally altered. Welty's 1951 letters both accommodate and contradict the color line's raison d'être, a belief in white supremacy.[13] Her later fiction, however, bears witness to her support for changes that had once seemed all but impossible.

First let us examine these New Orleans letters, written in 1951 to John Robinson and to Diarmuid Russell, Welty's literary agent and close friend. Welty described her experiences at the Ochsner Foundation Hospital, a research clinic in New Orleans filled with a diverse array of patients and staff.[14] Welty and her sister-in-law stayed at Ochsner for several days while doctors tried to diagnose her brother Walter's illness. After exploratory surgery suggested Walter did not have lung cancer, Welty reported the good news to Robinson. Writing in longhand, she crossed out some phrases and interpolated others in her attempt to describe her impressions of the clinic: "Now that a part of the worry has almost safely gone I can really note all with some (I don't know what) (strange kind of fascination) (in the café is a *place*) all sorts of course—Spanish I hear spoken every day (to the best of my belief)—also of course French, Cajun, & New Orleans-talk." Some of the people amused her, such as Rita, one of Walter's nurses, who "arrives at 6:00 AM & he thinks straight from a Rodeo, she has the armband on & shouts out how many bulls she got last night—Is getting divorce—'When I get on dat witness stand he's going to be sorry he ever born.'" Welty cataloged others who interested her:

A Bombay, India lone soul is in a bed nearby—No one seems to know how or why he has ended up there—A very young, bearded, dignified, wonderful face—Just rests on bended elbows, hands behind head, gazes out over at nothing—and so far from home—3 French people, darling, family—3 Cajuns, 2 daughters and Mama, at eternal dominos in lounge—Daughters with structural hair-dos, Mama's hair is coming out but still has 2 colors, black & yellow—She is fat & walks like a bear— The waitresses are like nurses, & the nurses are like waitresses—[15]

In her next letter to Robinson, Welty provided more entertaining details: "Such a place! Rita the nurse (while out) was riding a 2-legged horse the other night— the other man in him fell down.* [In margin:] *She calls her hair moss—Gave herself a Toni last night. Has a daughter who is a majorette at St. Francis of Assisi. She takes lessons in twirlin'."[16] In this letter, Welty expressed concern over the fate of the Indian patient:

The Bombay man gets out today, rejoins his ship he was taken off of & is going straight back to India, never expects to leave again. His final humiliation: the negro girl (who came to work today in blue uniform over long sleeved plaid wool lumber-jack & nun-like cowl which she wore all morning) who brings you water & things like that fixed him up to go & said to a friend "I combed his hair, scraped out de dandruff, greased him, shave off dat beard, & got him dressed up." She fixed him to look just like a Negro, of course. I guess I could have learned what ailed him—oh so easily, a talkative crowd.

The "crowd" included Smitty, a man who was "either (a) a gambler or (b) night spot owner or (c) sheriff," who "carries his arm in a brace—so—[here Welty drew a stick figure]. Has a wife with diamonds & also a television set with him at hospital." Welty reported that Smitty and "another patient on the hall (curtains for walls, it's really only a ward in effect)" tried to learn Walter Welty's story: "The other night Smitty* suddenly lowered his voice & said 'Say, quiet. Do you know what he does.' (Walter.) 'He ain't never said.' W. gave them a quiet Jack Holt look—never said."[17]

A few days later Welty wrote to Diarmuid Russell about the clinic, again speaking sympathetically of the Indian man—"young, dignified, bearded, with his hands clasped behind his head staring out into a point in space, unvisited and so black." Welty's account of how the man's beard was shaved is almost identical to what she sent Robinson. "The colored help were fascinated by him," she told Russell, then described how she had overheard one of the staff describing how she had combed and dressed the patient's hair and shaved his beard. "She made him look, of course, colored. The poor man was probably feeling some final humiliation—he was going to New York straight and catch his boat back to India—went out into the ice and snow. I hope he gets there, and his religion takes him back—what about that lost beard? He just has long, zoot-looking sideburns now."[18] Here, again, is another story to puzzle the contemporary reader. Readers who already suspect Welty of being a closet racist may see these letters as further evidence that she regarded African Americans as inferior. But in the Deep South of the 1950s, what did this patient's experience, and Welty's response, signify?

Mississippi custom and law had long distinguished "white" from "colored" or nonwhite.[19] The patient from Bombay, despite being, in Welty's words, "so black," was in the same ward as white patients, hence not classified as "colored"—a circumstance that would have seemed strange to most southerners of this era, on both sides of the color line. Hospital facilities were segregated in many regions of the country, and most in the South remained strictly segregated until the mid-1960s, when the 1964 Civil Rights Act required hospitals to desegregate in order to receive federal funding.[20] The Ochsner Hospital served patients from throughout the Deep South and from Latin America, but the reaction of the hospital staff suggests that a man from Bombay was out of the ordinary, and that staffers rarely, if ever, saw a man with skin this dark who was not African American.[21] Welty's comment to Russell, that "the colored help were fascinated by" this dark-skinned patient, further indicates that within the hospital, he was not perceived or classified as "colored." However, as Suzanne Marrs suggests earlier in this volume, in her analysis of this incident, the woman who prepared this man for discharge may also have assumed that once he left the hospital, he would need to comport himself differently—to "look like a Negro." This staff member, whom Welty identified as "the colored maid" and as "the negro girl . . . who brings you water and things like that," was performing the kind of personal service that whites in 1951 might expect to receive from African Americans. A dark-skinned man receiving such care next to white patients would have displeased many white southerners.[22]

Yet Welty's letters, though they are full of detail about the hospital's poor heating and the nosiness and hairstyles of other patients, record no objection or discomfiture by herself or her family over the Bombay man's presence in a hospital bed near Walter Welty. Instead, they suggest that she felt a similar empathy for both men. The Indian man seemed to bear his illness patiently, like Welty's brother, of whom she wrote, "Walter is just so *good*—all those bad sounding bronchoscope & oil examinations." The Bombay man and Walter were unlike the "talkative crowd" of other patients, and both had mysterious ailments that might not be curable. "That shadow in [Walter's] lung just can't be accounted for so far," Welty had written Robinson.[23] Amid Welty's sympathy for this stranger, two of her letters also contain a suggestion of racism in the way they conflate the man's loss of his beard—a clear violation of "his religion"—with his partial transformation into an African American: in her account, the staff member "made him look, of course, colored," like someone on the wrong side of the color line, someone who has no right to occupy a bed in this part of the hospital. If Welty believed that "look[ing] just like a Negro" was *not* inherently humiliating, she did not bother to clarify her attitude in these private letters.

Did these 1951 experiences—the hospital visit and the letters describing it— affect a work of fiction Welty began writing sixteen years later? She did not have the letters in her possession when writing the novel in the late 1960s, and she may not have been conscious of using this particular experience when she created the fictional hospital where the protagonist's father seeks treatment.[24] But this 1951 hospital scene, surely made more memorable because she had written letters about it, could certainly have returned to the artist's imagination many years later. Welty often acknowledged that she drew on her memory for many details, gestures, scenes, and sensory experiences in her fiction.[25] Of this novel in particular, she told one interviewer that "anyone who's ever had anyone in the hospital will recognize the people who sit in the waiting rooms and eat and drink and talk. I wouldn't want anyone to think I was using their *sick* in the novel, but these things come back to me, like air, and I use them."[26] The writer's imagination selects and rearranges details from the past in a process that is not always conscious. Welty discussed this in her 1984 memoir: "Attached to [my fictional characters] are what I've borrowed, perhaps unconsciously, bit by bit, of persons I have seen or noticed or remembered in the flesh—a cast of countenance here, a manner of walking there—that jump to the visualizing mind when a story is underway."[27] As she explained in a mid-1970s interview, a writer creates fictional dialogue from "a fund in your head, having heard people talk and noted in your mind all your life the way people say things. And it will come back to you at the right time."[28]

It's reasonable, then, to posit that these 1951 New Orleans experiences were part of the "fund in her head" from which Welty drew in creating the New Orleans section of The Optimist's Daughter. Both the novel and the 1951 experience feature a woman at a relative's bedside in a New Orleans hospital during carnival season. In the novel, Laurel's father is as helpless as Walter Welty and the patient from Bombay were. Clinton McKelva is bound tightly to his hospital bed, following his doctor's instructions, "holding himself motionless" with his one unbandaged eye often closed.[29] This resembles Welty's account of the Indian man who "rest[ed] on bended elbows, hands behind head, gaz[ing] out over at nothing—and so far from home."[30] The staff in Welty's fictional hospital obey the doctors' orders, rather than improvising like the woman who shaved the Indian patient in the Ochsner clinic. In the novel, it is Laurel's stepmother, Fay, rather than a hospital orderly, who improvises a method of caretaking, shaking her husband and shouting, "Enough is enough!" (901). The 1969 version of Welty's novel features more verbal abuse than the 1972 version,[31] but even in the final version, Laurel feels that Fay has "assail[ed] a helpless man" (962), much as Welty's letters suggest that the 1951 hospital worker assailed the Bombay patient. Fay, like the 1951 worker who expressed apparent satisfaction in having shaved the Indian patient, is proud of the way she has treated Clinton. "I tried to make him quit his old-man foolishness. I was going to make him live if I had to drag him!" she tells Laurel. "And I take good credit for what I did! . . . I was being a wife to him!" (989). Like the Ochsner staff member, Fay tries to fit her patient into a role she deems more appropriate for him; unlike the Indian patient, Clinton does not survive his treatment.

In creating the fictional hospital where Laurel loses her father, Welty seems to have drawn on the carnival atmosphere of the 1951 clinic, where the uniformed staffer was dressed in motley semicostume, "a plaid wool lumberjack shirt on under her uniform and a nun-like cowl around her head."[32] In The Optimist's Daughter, narrated from Laurel's point of view, Fay and the carnival seem to be collaborators in Clinton's decline. When she enters his hospital room after hearing Fay shouting, Laurel sees grotesque suggestions of carnival costuming. "Her father's right arm was free of the cover and lay out on the bed. It was bare to the shoulder, its skin soft and gathered, like a woman's sleeve. It showed her that he was no longer concentrating" (902). This patient has not been made to "look colored," like the patient from Bombay, but part of his identity seems to have been stripped from him, for he no longer looks like a man. When Doctor Courtland listens for a heartbeat, Laurel sees that her father's "upper lip had lifted, short and soft as a child's, showing ghostly-pale teeth which no one ever saw when he spoke or laughed. It gave him the smile of a child who is hiding in the dark while the others hunt him, waiting to be found" (902). While the doctor tries to revive her father, Laurel observes other families in the waiting room "raggedly laughing." Telling tales about other patients who refused to follow doctor's orders, they vow to give water to their own dying relative. Welty's narration of this scene stresses an upending of protocol, a melting of boundaries: "'We'll pour it down him!' cried the mother. 'He ain't going to stand a chance against us!' The family laughed louder . . . other families joined in. It seemed to Laurel that in another moment the whole waiting room would dissolve itself in waiting-room laughter" (906). The laughter and the dissolution Laurel perceives in this waiting room are, to her, a kind of soundtrack for the mistreatment of her father. She looks on helplessly, the medical staff labor uselessly, her father dies, all while carnivalesque laughter seems to "dissolve" the waiting room.[33]

Laurel's anguish over her father's condition clearly resembles Welty's 1951 concern for her brother and the patient from Bombay. However, in scenes from *The Optimist's Daughter* where a patient is misunderstood, ill-treated, or violated, there are no references to race or the color line; nothing that threatens Clinton's health or dignity is associated with racial boundaries. No "humiliation" of being made to "look colored" occurs, and indeed, there is not a single African American in evidence within this hospital. I believe that these peculiar omissions, along with Welty's references to race in the rest of the novel, reflect her changing attitude toward the color line. By the 1960s, as the color line was being defended more stridently in her home state, it was also beginning to look more malleable than Mississippians would have ever thought possible.

Why might Welty, an unconventional and imaginative artist, have believed that the color line was unlikely to be changed in her lifetime? To answer this question, I will briefly revisit a few instances of struggles over civil rights in Mississippi, a story whose broad outlines are familiar but whose details still have the power to shock. White Mississippian resistance to Truman's 1948 Democratic platform, with its modest claims for civil rights, was mild compared with the backlash that was to come. From the late 1940s to the late 1960s, challenges to the color line in Welty's home state met with escalating violence, disinformation by the Mississippi press, and intimidation by state and community officials. Such challenges undoubtedly made things worse in Mississippi in the 1950s. After the Supreme Court's 1954 *Brown* decision outlawed segregated schools, the state of Mississippi established an agency whose stated aim was "to protect the sovereignty of the State . . . from encroachment thereon by the Federal Government."[34] The Sovereignty Commission, in Taylor Branch's words, "worked an intermediate ground between press conferences and cross burnings."[35] It publicly promoted the virtues of segregation and privately did extensive surveillance on anyone suspected of opposing it. At the commission's request, Jackson newspapers omitted news stories that might seem to favor desegregation, and Jackson television station WLBT refused to broadcast content that could be favorable to African Americans.[36]

White-owned newspapers in the South had a long-standing practice of omitting African Americans in photographs or news stories unless they were portrayed in a subservient or unfavorable light.[37] This practice continued in their 1955 coverage of the murder of fourteen-year-old Emmett Till. Although Mississippi editorials initially expressed regret that a child had been brutally murdered, the tone of the coverage altered once the NAACP had denounced the crime. From then on, most news coverage was sympathetic to the defendants, portraying them as protectors of the young white woman that Till had supposedly endangered.[38] For most Mississippi papers, coverage of the murder trial became an occasion to revile the NAACP, to vow to maintain segregation, and to reassert the wisdom of white supremacy. As one Jackson paper put it, the NAACP was to blame for any racial disharmony that existed in the state: "Mississippians have long understood the inability of the Negro to live with comprehension in a white man's complicated society without minor rebellions and backsliding into his ungoverned heritage."[39] Till's killers were acquitted after the defense attorney presented contradictory explanations for the evidence against them and said in closing arguments, "Every last Anglo-Saxon one of you has the courage to free these men."[40] Even editorials expressing surprise at the acquittal restated the importance of maintaining the color line: "A mistake in the Till decision is infinitessimal [sic] in comparison with what the Supreme Court did in the segregation cases," wrote a Natchez editor.[41]

Violence in defense of the color line became more public as civil rights advocates challenged Mississippi's "way of life" in the 1960s.[42] In 1962, when the Supreme Court ordered Ole Miss to admit James Meredith, Governor Ross Barnett announced his secession-like plan of "interposition" against federal authority, and was praised by the Jackson newspaper.[43] Two weeks after Meredith began taking classes at Ole Miss under the guard of federal marshals, a riot broke out in Oxford, killing two foreign journalists and injuring many others. In 1963 NAACP's Mississippi field secretary Medgar Evers was murdered, a few weeks after he was finally allowed to appear on WLBT,[44] and on the same night that President Kennedy had endorsed civil rights legislation in a television address.[45]

Worse still was the campaign of terror waged against challenges to the color line in 1964. Activism in the state increased when COFO (the Council of Federated Organizations, a coalition of CORE, SNCC, and NAACP) organized

Mississippi Freedom Summer, bringing hundreds of out-of-state volunteers to help local organizations run Freedom Schools, desegregate public places, register voters, and monitor elections. During this period, when the murder of three young civil rights workers put Mississippi in the national news, countless other acts of harassment, bombings, wrongful arrests, and murders were committed by, or with the full cooperation of, local police. Mississippi's newspapers often omitted or distorted reports of these events.[46] For example, a COFO attorney "was arrested on charges of reckless driving after a local white, Travis Hamilton, slammed his truck into Connelly's car, smashing it and injuring a passenger," but the incident went unreported by the local newspaper, as historian Susan Weill writes.[47] Earlier in the summer, this newspaper did report that a group of African Americans said they had been beaten by police, but the article's headline discredited their account: "Negroes Claim Beat By Police, Commie Type Propaganda Found in Car Says Sheriff."[48] The conflation of Communism with resistance to racism would have been familiar to Welty, who had been called a Communist when she criticized Bilbo in a 1945 letter to the *Jackson Clarion-Ledger*.[49]

It seems patently unfair to characterize Welty as "ambivalent about racism" during this turbulent period, but she does appear to have felt ambivalent about what to *do* about the racism on display in her home state. In 1962 Welty declined the *New Republic*'s request for a public statement about the Ole Miss riots, telling her high school friend Frank Lyell that she had declined "because (a) I'm a coward [. . .] (b) it wouldn't help."[50] Yet in 1963, in the tense aftermath of the Oxford riots and of an African American boycott of Jackson stores, Welty chose to read "Powerhouse" to an integrated audience at Millsaps College. As Marrs notes, as a white writer reading her portrait of a black artist, Welty risked offending the few African Americans present, and at the same time, her gesture would certainly have offended many white Jacksonians.[51] When Evers was murdered in June of that year, two months after the reading, Welty did not hesitate to publish "Where Is the Voice Coming From?" as her attempt to anatomize the mind of a murderous racist. But in July her concern for her mother's safety caused her to cancel a television interview with Ralph Ellison scheduled for later that summer.[52]

From a comfortable distance of fifty years, Welty's choices may strike some readers as less than heroic. But many liberal white southerners were reluctant to make public statements on racial injustice; Hodding Carter wrote in 1963 that "One can count on two hands those Jacksonians who are willing to speak out against any status quo."[53] Preoccupied with caring for her mother, often traveling to give lectures as her primary source of income, Welty declined most requests (some in the form of late-night phone calls from strangers) that she speak out on Mississippi's social upheaval.[54] Her most famous demurral, "Must the Novelist Crusade?," began as a 1964 lecture entitled "The Southern Writer: An Interior Affair." Welty's essay, arguing that it is not in the nature of fiction to deliver any particular message, is eloquent and insightful, but its accompanying admonitions can be read in ways she surely did not intend.[55]

Like Bible verses, many of Welty's sentences are subject to multiple interpretations, especially if quoted in isolation. "The novelist works neither to correct nor to condone, not at all to comfort, but to make what's told alive," she wrote.[56] This statement expresses a writer's understanding of the special characteristics of literary art, but it could also be interpreted as a dismissal of all social activism, as a suggestion that critics of the South's social order should mind their own business. "The crusaders' voice is the voice of the crowd and must rise louder all the time . . . the voice that seeks to do other than communicate when it makes a noise has something brutal about it; it is no longer using words as words but as something to brandish, with which to threaten, brag, or condemn . . . Nothing was ever learned in a crowd, from a crowd, or by addressing or trying to please a crowd" (809). Here Welty is not so much deriding political activism as she is honoring the way fiction can act in a different sphere. As "an interior affair," fiction's calling is to awaken the inner life of the reader.[57] Welty's essay makes clear her solidarity with the civil rights movement; in the next sentence, she continues, "To deplore a thing as hideous as the murder of the three civil rights workers demands the quiet in which to absorb it. Enormities can be lessened, cheapened, just as good and delicate things can be. We can and will cheapen all feeling by letting it go savage or parading in it" (809). Here and in her later praise for E. M. Forster's treatment of "race prejudice" (810), Welty speaks explicitly against racism and says nothing that condones Mississippi's status quo, yet in suggesting that some expressions of social protest can be so shrill or "savage" that they do harm, Welty uses phrasing that would have appealed to someone eager to classify all threats to Mississippi's status quo as uncivilized.

A short time after delivering her December 1964 lecture, Welty and other Jackson residents had the opportunity to hear more accounts of white supremacist violence against COFO workers and others involved in civil rights efforts.

In early 1965 the Federal Civil Rights Commission conducted hearings in Jackson that were broadcast on local television stations (their licensure was then under review by the FCC). Both black and white victims testified, and the commission subpoenaed several law enforcement officers, asking them to explain why civil rights activists were regularly jailed on any possible pretext, while perpetrators of violence went unpunished and suspects were rarely even questioned.[58] As one commissioner told a police chief, in a supremely understated summary of that morning's testimony, "Some of the colored people believe that your force is not protecting them as well as white people . . . [I]t looks very bad on paper."[59] A Jackson citizen and civil rights activist said later of these broadcasts, "Many people realized that the stories they had been hearing were not just fabrications of the imaginations of a deprived people . . . people for the first time realized, well now, maybe there is something to it. Maybe there are things going on in my state that I didn't know about."[60] Welty was already aware that organized criminal activity in the service of racism was occurring in her state, and we have no record of her reaction to these hearings, but by November 1965 she had completed "The Demonstrators," a work that documented some of these conditions. Set in Mississippi a year after Freedom Summer, the story includes white supremacist terrorism, complicity by white newspapers, and a white protagonist who fails to see the reality of his neighbors' lives. This story and "Where Is the Voice Coming From?" were Welty's only two published works of fiction from the early 1960s. A few months after writing "The Demonstrators," in 1966, Welty's work as family caregiver was ended by the deaths of her mother and surviving brother, Edward (Walter had died in 1959). The following year, in the wake of these profound losses, Welty began writing the story that became *The Optimist's Daughter*.

By 1967, Welty had been exposed to thousands of instances of whites making distorted or slanted references to African Americans in order to reinforce their own prejudices and justify a white supremacist status quo. Her awareness of whites' distorted perception of blacks had always been keen, but I believe it was significantly heightened by the events of the 1960s. This context may explain the way Welty presented the color line in *The Optimist's Daughter*. First, she seems to have written African Americans out of her fictional New Orleans hospital. Her omission of nonwhite characters from the hospital section of the novel may or may not have been a conscious choice, but it functions as an interesting reversal of southern newspapers' omissions of African Americans from coverage that did not present their supposed criminality or inferiority. Welty's omission, by contrast, makes it impossible for a reader to associate Clint McKelva's death with any care provided by African Americans. Nor does Welty's narrative associate African Americans with the Greek chorus of hospital patients who side with Fay and whom Laurel considers to be part of the heedless confusion accompanying her father's death. On the other hand, when the protagonist returns to her hometown to bury her father, the novel explicitly acknowledges Mississippi's tradition of white supremacy.

Evidence of this tradition surfaces in conversations Laurel overhears on the day of her father's funeral, when mourners recall how her father once "stood up and faced the White Caps" (930) and apparently prevented a lynching. (The White Caps were a Mississippi organization very similar to the Ku Klux Klan.) Laurel focuses not on the story itself but on the inaccuracies she thinks are in it; she believes that her father would not have taken the sort of risk this story-teller claims to remember. "They're misrepresenting him," she says. "The least anybody can do for him is *remember* right" (933). With the novel's protagonist focused on the funeral and private family memories, some readers might not linger over the particulars of a story another mourner tells. Yet the story would have been familiar to Welty and many of her readers as a miniature version of white supremacist violence in twentieth-century Mississippi.

Major Bullock tells the story, saying that "Mount Salus volunteers" had expected to arrive at the town jail in time to help Clinton prevent the band from breaking in. Since "the White Caps . . . came a little bit earlier than they promised," Clinton faced them down alone, demanding that they remove their hoods (930). In the Major's account of this scene, Clinton was heroic. "He says, 'Back to your holes, rats!' And they were armed!" His bravery sent the White Caps "back into the woods they came from. Cooked their goose for a while!" (931). The Major's story contains several details that conveniently distance him from racist violence. The lawless band is not from Mount Salus but from some indefinite elsewhere—"the woods where they came from." Mount Salus residents, by contrast, are eager to defend the rule of law. This story corroborates a view of lynching and other racial violence that many southern apologists held—that such acts were perpetrated by underclass "rats" who did not share the ideals and gentility of true southern gentlemen.[61] Yet even if McKelva did stand up to a band of would-be lynchers, Major Bullock's story leaves doubts about the motives of the rest of Mount Salus—he says that the White Caps had announced their arrival time beforehand (which was true of some lynchings) but "came a little bit earlier than they promised, little bit earlier than the rest of us got on hand" (930). The late arrival of the opposition may indicate that no one else in Mount Salus was sufficiently concerned to show up in time to prevent the planned lynching, and that the storyteller is now revising history to place himself on the side of justice, law, and order. After all, the parlor is filled with people telling stories that are obviously incomplete if not false—think of Mrs. Chisom's story of her son committing suicide, for reasons she seems determined not to acknowledge, "her face arranging itself all at once into an expression of innocence" (928). No one in the room is allowed to rebut the Major's account; when Laurel tries to dispute it, he replies, "Honey, you were away. You were up yonder in Chicago, drawing pictures. I saw him!" (931).

A few minutes later, Laurel overhears another anecdote about her father that also connects violence with race:[62]

> "Clint's hunting a witness, some of the usual trouble, and this Negro girl says, 'It's him and me that saw it. He's a witness, and I's a got-shot witness.'"
> They laughed.
> "'There's two kinds, all right,' says Clint. 'And I know which to take. She's the got-shot witness: I'll take her.' He could see the funny side to everything."
> "He brought her here afterwards and kept her safe under his own roof," Laurel said under her breath to Miss Adele . . . "I don't know what the funny side was."
> "It was Missouri, wasn't it?" said Miss Adele.
> "And listening," said Laurel, for Missouri herself was just then lit up by a shower of sparks; down on her knees before the fire, she was poking the big log. (931–32)

The storyteller does not notice Missouri, the black housekeeper who is stoking the fire Major Bullock asked for. Nor do any listeners ask what "some of the usual trouble" was, although it seems to have been racially charged. Clinton apparently protected Missouri from this "trouble" by inviting an African American to stay "under his own roof." Before the 1960s, such individual acts of kindness were the closest many liberal Mississippians had come to crossing the color line. Many other whites looking across this divide, like the heedless storytellers at the McKelva home, and like Richard Strickland in "The Demonstrators," could "see" only anonymous servants or laborers rather than valued members of their community. Laurel, however, notices Missouri when others overlook her, and values her human presence. When Missouri arrives at their home on the morning of the funeral, her affection and Laurel's gratitude are evident.

"Am I supposed to believe what I hear?" asked Missouri.

Laurel went to her and took her in her arms.

[. . .] "Well, *I'm* here and *you're* here," said Missouri. It was the bargain to give and take comfort. After a moment's hesitation, Missouri went on, "He always want Miss Fay to have her breakfast in bed."

"Then you'll know how to wake her," said Laurel. ". . . Do you mind?"

"Do it for him," said Missouri. Her face softened. "He mightily enjoyed having him somebody to spoil." (917)

Here Missouri is acting as a housekeeper and servant to Fay, but also as a friend to Laurel. Sympathetic to Laurel's dislike for Fay, Missouri reminds Laurel that Fay did make her father happy. As Welty said in a 1978 interview, "Missouri is her maid in the household, but they were also big friends and both of them knew it."[63]

By the time Welty wrote this novel, she had experienced relationships with black Jacksonians that were deeper than this fictional one, including sustained contact with one woman who worked in the Welty home in her youth and then "went on to better things," and with another woman, "a schoolteacher who helped me on weekends to nurse my mother," who "was beyond a nurse, she was a friend and still is, we keep in regular touch." Welty discussed these relationships in a 1973 interview with Alice Walker, who asked if Welty had "known any black women? Really known them."[64] In her answer, Welty was careful not to overstate the connections she had made: "Of course I've met black people professionally. Lecturing introduced us. The first college anywhere, by the way, that ever invited me to speak was Jackson State—years ago . . . Now I don't count meeting people at cocktail parties in New York—black or any other kind—to answer the rest of your question. But I do know at least a few black people that mean a good deal to me, and I think they like me too."[65] In later interviews, Welty also acknowledged how much she did *not* know about black Jacksonians when she was younger. Asked in 1978 about her childhood years, she said that she "never saw black people except in a white household as a servant or something, and . . . I never heard black people talking among themselves."[66] In 1979 she told Louis Rubin, "It's awful people my age didn't even really know the conditions of the black schools."[67] And in 1981 an interviewer asked Welty about a sentence in "Must the Novelist Crusade?" stating that understanding between the races "is no harder now than it ever was, I suppose." Welty told the interviewer that when she made that statement, "I was sincere as far as I knew, but I didn't know enough. It was harder."[68] These comments show that Welty came to believe that her own knowledge had been incomplete, and that she consciously revised some of her earlier impressions of black experiences.

In a study of Jackson broadcasting during the civil rights era, one historian has correctly observed that "segregation and racism are poorly explained if they are simply attributed to a few individualized subjects."[69] By placing Welty's private and public references to the color line within the tangled web of her time and place, I do not seek to prove she was an unerring saint who never made statements or harbored thoughts that we would now consider racist. What I hope I have demonstrated is how much more and how differently the color line signified in Welty's time than it does in the twenty-first century, now that its legal status has been substantially undermined and enforced racial segregation is no longer openly championed. In 1951 even a partial dismantling of the color line could have seemed as distant as a trip to the moon, or the election of a nonwhite president. Hodding Carter said as much in a 1952 review of *South of Freedom*, a book that was for him "a vivid reminder that changes which a white Southerner thinks are swift seem snail-like and indecisive to a Southerner who is not white." Carter called the book's African American author "a loyal and perhaps unquietly desperate American, who will not find in his lifetime full acceptance as a first-class citizen everywhere in his country."[70] Within twelve years of Carter's review, however, the book's author, Carl Rowan, was appointed to high-ranking government posts: delegate to the United Nations, U.S. ambassador to Finland, and a member of the National Security Council.[71]

Before the 1960s, Welty, like Carter, seems to have believed that the injustice of the color line would remain for a very long time. In 1949 she reviewed Faulkner's *Intruder in the Dust*, in which two white characters exhume a corpse in search of evidence that could free Lucas Beauchamp, accused of murdering a white man and now in jail, awaiting a trial that may soon be preempted by a lynching. Welty wrote, "Out of the diggings comes a solution and an indictment, defining a hope, prayer, that we should one day reach the point where . . . Lucas Beauchamp's life will be secure not despite that fact that he is Lucas Beauchamp but because he is."[72] Welty's "hope, prayer" was for "one day" in the distant future. In 1949 even progressive southerners like Welty believed that the color line was as solid, as dangerous to cross, and as permanent as the Berlin Wall.

And of course the color line did not disappear, as Welty acknowledged in a 1993 interview with Jan Nordby Gretlund. She told Gretlund that, although race relations in Jackson had come a long way by the 1990s, such progress was "slow, too slow, too late, but . . . not too late, can't be too late."[73] Yet in the words of historians Davis Houck and Matthew Grindy, "The changes [in Mississippi] more than fifty years later are breathtaking."[74] Their assertion comes at the end of a book-length analysis of the 1955 Mississippi press coverage that, in effect, justified Till's murder and the state's failure to convict his killers. In 2005 the Mississippi State Senate renamed a highway as a memorial to Till. Houck and Grindy argue that the Till Memorial Highway sign, despite being only a symbol, is powerful: it "functions as visual and state-sanctioned confirmation of the formerly displaced memories born in 1955."[75]

Welty also believed in the power of symbolic gestures. While she was writing *The Optimist's Daughter*, she saw a hopeful emblem in the form of a 1967 recital that Leontyne Price sang in Jackson. Welty had heard the African American singer, a Mississippian, years before. As she wrote her friend William Maxwell, "The only other time she'd appeared in Jackson was when she was a young girl . . . and it was private and invitational because it was in a downtown hotel and at that time you could only integrate privately." This time, the performance was public, and Price "was all radiance and glory."[76] In 1980 Welty expressed similar delight at having participated, along with Price, in a symposium celebrating the inauguration of governor William Winter. "It was all so joyous," she said. "Everybody just thought, the top rail is on top instead of on the bottom, where it had been for so long."[77]

There are no public symbols of a changed Mississippi in *The Optimist's Daughter*. Laurel's family are gone; all their shared experiences, both joyous and painful, are now in the unchangeable past. But Laurel's dream at the end of the novel reveals to her that memory, unlike the past, is alive, and "will come back in its wounds from across the world . . . calling us by our names and demanding its rightful tears" (992). Through memory and the powerful emotions it awakens in her, Laurel restores her connection to those she has lost. As she takes leave of her family home, Laurel performs several gestures that seem designed as private symbols, outward signs of her inner transformation. She gives Adele Courtland the small carved boat her father once gave her mother, acknowledging Adele's unspoken love for Clinton; she cleans the breadboard Phil made, then leaves it behind, announcing that she does not need the object when she has her more precious recollections. And in another gesture,

Laurel collaborates with Missouri, the character with the most direct experience of Mississippi's troubled racial history. In order for Laurel to free the bird trapped in her family home—a particularly potent symbol of the imprisoned grief that Laurel must release—Missouri must help her. As in other Welty texts, this novel shows the reader that the subjective experience of one individual resonates with many others, whether or not they realize it. Private as Laurel's transformation may seem to her, Welty links it to the possibility of a transformed society.

Consistent with Welty's inclusion of Missouri in Laurel's story is her "omission," probably an unconscious one, of African Americans from the New Orleans hospital in her novel, where their race could be mistakenly associated with Laurel's devastating personal loss. In the New Orleans clinic in 1951, Welty had watched as a stranger, "unvisited and so black," suffered with a disease no one seemed able to cure.[78] Her empathy for this patient reappeared years later, in the form of Laurel's pained compassion for her dying father. Welty's experiences at the Ochsner clinic had remained in the artist's "fund in her head," the storehouse of memories and observations that she drew upon for her fiction. By 1967, that "fund" also included a more acute awareness of many whites' racial hatred and of their reflexive tendency to perceive African Americans as inferior. The New Orleans hospital of Welty's novel, unlike her 1951 letters, no longer provided any fulcrum for white supremacist self-justification, for a derogatory interpretation of people living on the "other" side of the color line.

Notes

I wish to thank Harriet Pollack, Scott Peeples, and Mike Duvall for their helpful comments on earlier versions of this essay. I'm also grateful to Suzanne Marrs and Peter Schmidt for their comments on the conference paper that led to this essay, and to Rachel Reinke for her research assistance and insights while I was writing that paper.

Letters quoted in this essay that are not otherwise identified are from the Eudora Welty Collection in the Mississippi Department of Archives and History, and are reprinted by the permission of Eudora Welty, LLC, copyright © Eudora Welty.

1. Trilling, "Fiction in Review," 104; Welty, *Collected Stories*, xi; Pierpont, "A Perfect Lady," 101; Flower, "Eudora Welty and Racism," 331.

2. Pierpont, "A Perfect Lady," 103; Flower, "Eudora Welty and Racism," 327.

3. Romines, "A Voice from a Jackson Interior," 121.

4. For another pre-1960s assessment of the color line as unjust but unchangeable, see "How the South Feels," a 1944 *Atlantic* essay by Mississippi native David L. Cohn.

Southern society, he wrote, "was kept going more by unwritten and unwritable laws than by the written law affecting the races; by an immense and elaborate code of etiquette that governs their daily relations . . . by adherence to a labyrinthine code of manners, taboos, and conventions" (48). Cohn, who was clearly sympathetic to the suffering of black southerners, argued that white southerners "will not at any foreseeable time relax the taboos and conventions which keep the races separate, from the cradle to the grave . . . No notable improvement of race relations can be achieved, in my opinion, unless the ground is cleared by a recognition that (a) the problem is incapable of solution, and (b) the issue of segregation must not be called into question" (50). Welty told John Robinson that she had read this essay and thought Cohn's account a reasonable one (Welty to John Robinson, July 13, 1944).

5. Gretlund, "Seeing Real Things," 255.

6. Welty was definitely ambivalent about the study of an author's personal letters. In a 1977 review of William Faulkner's letters, she wrote, "It would deny the author's whole intent, in a lifetime of work and passion and stubborn, hellbent persistence, to look in his letters for the deepest revelations he made" (*Eye of the Story* 219). I believe, however, that Welty's letters can offer "deeper revelations" about her fiction, particularly on this topic that seems to vex so many readers.

7. Marrs, *Eudora Welty*, 94. During the 1940s Welty wrote well over 350 letters to Robinson alone, and about the same number to Diarmuid Russell.

8. Flower, "Eudora Welty and Racism," 330.

9. Eudora Welty to John Robinson, November 1948. This letter, dated only as "Friday," was written shortly after Carter's November 9 radio appearance; the Friday following November 9 was November 12.

10. Carter, "What Should We Do About Race Segregation?" 15.

11. Carter's profile of Theodore Bilbo, a senator whose racism was noteworthy even for the Deep South, ran in the *New York Times* in 1946. Bilbo had attracted national attention for urging whites to prevent blacks from voting. Carter reported that in his speeches, Bilbo stated that Mississippi would not convict any registrar for "refusing to register a nigger," but that "You know and I know what's the best way [to intimidate black voters] . . . You do it the night before the election." Carter also noted in this article that Bilbo denounced Carter, along with other whites who did not support Bilbo, as "a nigger-loving communist" (Carter, "The Man," 12).

12. The 1948 platform read, "The Democratic Party commits itself to continuing its efforts to eradicate all racial, religious and economic discrimination. Basic rights are (1) the right of full and equal political participation, (2) the right to equal opportunity employment, (3) the right of security of person, and (4) the right of equal treatment in the service and defense of our nation" (Weill, *In a Madhouse's Din*, 23).

In February 1948 the Mississippi Legislature convened a special meeting to denounce Truman and the Democratic Party's platform and to recommend a separate convention of, in their words, "true white Jeffersonian Democrats" (Winter 142). In mid-February 1948 Welty wrote John Robinson, "I feel like burning the *Clarion-Ledger* every morning. Well, I just won't go into it. And the Legislature a disgrace every day, and altogether

Mississippi seems to get more hopeless all the time . . . The other day a bill was proposed wherebody (whereby anybody) who didn't like Mississippi could get a free ticket out of it, the state to provide the RR fare and a ten dollar bill to spend when you've got out. Hooray! I'll be the first one—I'll go somewhere nice and be a twenty-minute queen" (Marrs, *Eudora Welty*, 162). At the 1948 Democratic National Convention, all of Mississippi's delegates walked out and joined like-minded southerners in Alabama, where they formed the States' Rights (Dixiecrat) Party and nominated Strom Thurmond for president (Weill 29–30).

13. To many Mississippi editorial writers in this period, the term "white supremacy" was an uncontroversial, self-evidently necessary condition of civilization. A 1947 article in the *Jackson Daily News*, reporting on rising numbers of African Americans registering to vote, asked readers "whether you want a white man's government, or will you take the risk of being governed by Negroes?" This article was entitled "White Supremacy Is in Peril" (Dittmer, *Local People*, 26). In 1948, when the civil rights plank of the Democratic platform infuriated many whites in Mississippi, a Natchez editorial stated, "Anti-lynch, anti-poll tax, and anti-segregation are all aimed at negro votes and the death of white supremacy. These measures do not better the condition of the negro" (Weill, *In a Madhouse's Din*, 24).

14. See Wilds and Harkey for a discussion of the early years of the Ochsner clinic.

15. Eudora Welty to John Robinson, January 28, 1951.

16. Eudora Welty to John Robinson, February 1, 1951.

17. Eudora Welty to John Robinson, February 1, 1951.

18. Eudora Welty to Diarmuid Russell, n.d., February 1951.

19. For a history of the legal definition of whiteness in the United States, see Haney-Lopez, *White by Law*. Whiteness, a prerequisite for U.S. naturalization from the eighteenth century through 1952 (Haney-Lopez 28), had varying legal definitions during this long period. In 1923 the Supreme Court wrote that "the knowledge of the common man" should be used in deciding who was not white, and ruled that this knowledge clearly classified Bhagat Singh Thind, an Indian-born U.S. Army veteran, as ineligible for naturalization. Between 1923 and 1927, the *Thind* decision caused the citizenship of at least sixty-five previously naturalized Asian immigrants to be revoked (Haney-Lopez 61–64). In the twentieth century many states' laws defined a person with any "Negro" ancestry as nonwhite (Haney-Lopez 83). An article in 1973 in the reference work *A History of Mississippi* provides population statistics only for "White" and "Negro" while also noting that the 1960 census recorded almost five thousand "nonwhite" and non-Negro Mississippians out of more than two million (Burrus, "Urbanization in Mississippi," 368–69).

The U.S. Census made distinctions more elaborate than the "white" and "colored" of Jim Crow segregation. In 1930 and 1940 U.S. census workers were instructed that "a person of mixed White and Negro blood was to be returned as Negro, no matter how small the percentage of Negro blood," but the forms listed several other racial classifications (Bohme, *200 Years of U.S. Census Taking*, 60). In 1960 census instructions said that Asian Indians "were to be classified as 'Other,' and 'Hindu' written in" (Bohme 78).

20. Ray Sprigle, the journalist who debated with Hodding Carter on the radio program Welty heard in 1948, wrote a series of articles about blacks in the South; one article was about people whose relatives had died while trying to reach a hospital that would admit blacks (Sprigle, "Marble Monument"). For a discussion of desegregation of health care in the U.S. South, see Beardsley, "Good-bye to Jim Crow." The Hill-Burton Act, passed in 1946, appropriated $75 million over a five-year period for states to "create a system of hospitals and public health centers that would enable all Americans to receive healthcare at modern institutions" (Beardsley 369). The act still permitted segregated wards; hospitals feared offending white patients who might object to being treated alongside blacks (368–70). Very few white hospitals in the South were desegregated or open to black patients before the 1960s (371–72). A U.S. Circuit Court of Appeals overturned the "separate but equal" aspect of the Hill-Burton Act in 1963, ruling that all hospitals that had accepted Hill-Burton funds were required to admit black patients as well as doctors (379).

21. Wilds and Harkey, *Alton Ochsner*, 141.

22. Hodding Carter, in a *New York Times* article on white southerners' response to the Democratic Party's 1948 civil rights proposals, included among his examples "the churchgoing young woman . . . who refused to help make hospital bed-jackets from old shirts because their recipients would be Negro patients" (Carter, "Civil Rights Issue," 54).

23. Welty to John Robinson, January 28, 1951.

24. In 1967 a more recent real-life hospital incident would have been much fresher in Welty's mind. During the final hospitalization of Welty's brother Edward, a nurse had told Welty that Edward's "frantic wife came to the hospital where he was stretched in a harness with a broken neck and hit him." In a letter to William Maxwell, Welty described this incident when discussing the *New Yorker* version of *The Optimist's Daughter* (Welty, *What There Is to Say*, 225).

25. In her memoir, explaining how she came by her fiction writer's interest in chronology, Welty wrote that in her home "we grew up to the striking of clocks . . . It was one of a good many things I learned almost without knowing it; it would be there when I needed it" (*Stories, Essays, and Memoir* 839). In an interview, Welty noted, "while you don't use exact things people say in a situation, you can often use an exact thing someone has said—adapt it to your situation . . . it's not taking it out of one box and putting it in another, you know. It's a transformation, a magician's act—if it's good, I'm talking about" (Ferris, "A Visit with Eudora Welty," 162). When asked about movies that may have influenced her, Welty told Ferris, "I must have absorbed things . . . these things come into your mind, and you learn from them without really knowing" (169). To another interviewer she explained, "The act of imagining has its own velocity, its own power . . . it calls up what it needs as it goes on. I know I'm sounding too fancy. But you can't unthink something, and you can't disremember something" (Powell, "Eudora Welty," 178).

26. Woolf, "Some Talk About Autobiography," 162–63.

27. Welty, *Stories, Essays, and Memoir*, 944.

28. Ferris, "A Visit with Eudora Welty," 162.

29. Welty, *The Optimist's Daughter*, 894, in *Complete Novels*. Subsequent parenthetical page references come from this edition of the 1972 novel.

30. Welty to Diarmuid Russell, n.d., February 1951.

31. Welty, "The Optimist's Daughter," 44. This early version of the novel was published in the March 15, 1969, issue of the *New Yorker*.

32. Welty to John Robinson, January 28, 1951.

33. For two discussions of the role of the carnival in this novel, see Brinkmeyer and Trouard.

34. Quoted in Classen, *Watching Jim Crow*, 38.

35. Branch, *Pillar of Fire*, 240.

36. Classen, *Watching Jim Crow*, 38–40. The NAACP protested the station's slanted or nonexistent coverage in a series of lawsuits. They pointed out that, for example, a national program with a black actor in a lead role was not aired on WLBT, and that an interview with Thurgood Marshall was preempted by a sign falsely claiming technical difficulties (Dittmer, *Local People*, 65). In 1957, after Eisenhower had voiced support for integration of Little Rock's schools, WLBT omitted its customary playing of the national anthem and ran ads recruiting members for the Citizens' Council (Classen, *Watching Jim Crow*, 43). Medgar Evers repeatedly asked the station and other reporters to cover crimes committed against civil rights workers, and to allow black Mississippians to express their own views on civil rights (Classen 43–46). In 1962 the station allowed a black candidate to buy airtime only after extensive pressure from the FCC, President Kennedy, and others (Classen 66).

37. Mississippi journalist Ira Harkey writes that through the 1960s, African Americans only appeared in white newspapers when the story was negative. Black residents' marriages, births, and school honors were never published, but "a Negro in trouble got space. A captured black fugitive even got his picture in the paper" (Harkey xi). Harkey's autobiography reports that when he worked for the *New Orleans Times-Picayune*, the paper's policy was to remove images of black people from street scenes. "Photos of street scenes were scrupulously scanned . . . and every perceivably black face . . . incised by scissors or erased by air brush" (Weill 90).

38. For a detailed analysis of numerous Mississippi newspapers' coverage of the murder, the trial, and ensuing discussion of the Till case, see Houck and Grindy. Christopher Metress's *The Lynching of Emmett Till* gathers both state and national coverage as well as numerous memoirs, poems, and other interpretations of Till's murder and its aftermath.

39. Houck and Grindy, *Emmett Till and the Mississippi Press*, 75.

40. Houck and Grindy, *Emmett Till and the Mississippi Press*, 104.

41. Houck and Grindy, *Emmett Till and the Mississippi Press*, 110.

42. The state of Mississippi was notorious, but certainly not unique, in its incidents of white supremacist rhetoric and violence in this period. For a summary of relevant events in this decade, see the database *The African American Experience* ("Timeline"). For detailed accounts of the period from 1954 to 1968, see the trilogy by Taylor Branch, one of many historians who documents how many people outside the South also opposed civil rights activism.

43. Weill, *In a Madhouse's Din*, 76.

44. Classen, *Watching Jim Crow*, 46.

45. Dittmer, *Local People*, 165–66.

46. "We killed off CORE purposively," a Meridian editor acknowledged later. "There would be an attempted sit-in or something and those folks would be hauled off to the police station immediately. We didn't give it any publicity and if you don't get publicity for something like that, you can't get far" (Weill, *In a Madhouse's Din*, 145).

47. Weill, *In a Madhouse's Din*, 130.

48. Weill, *In a Madhouse's Din*, 130.

49. Marrs, *Eudora Welty*, 141; Eudora Welty to Diarmuid Russell, December 30, 1945.

50. Marrs, *Eudora Welty*, 293.

51. Marrs, *Eudora Welty*, 299–301.

52. Marrs, *Eudora Welty*, 304–5.

53. Carter, "Mississippi Now—Hate and Fear."

54. Welty described these phone calls in "Must the Novelist Crusade?" and numerous interviews.

55. In her introduction to *Eudora Welty and Politics: Did the Writer Crusade?* Harriet Pollack observes that Welty's 1960s text "is not an essay that communicates effortlessly today" (1).

56. Welty, *Stories, Essays, and Memoir*, 808. Parenthetical page references to "Must the Novelist Crusade?" come from this volume.

57. Barbara Ladd's essay "Writing Against Death" argues that in Welty's 1950s essays, her assertion of the importance of the inner life of the individual was itself a political statement, opposing what Welty called "the complicated, almost oriental threats that are constantly being made against our living at all" (qtd. in Ladd 175).

58. Law enforcement officers' testimony during these hearings rarely made sense. The sheriff of Madison County, who had arrested a poll watcher because her presence could "cause a breach of the peace," did not answer repeated questions about why he arrested the woman rather than attempting to protect her (U.S. Commission on Civil Rights, *Justice in Jackson*, 246–53). The sheriff finally said, "I have tried my best to answer [those questions] for you, sir. I can't seem to get an understanding between us" (253). The Laurel chief of police testified that while local youths were attempting to desegregate a lunch counter, he saw a man hitting one of the diners, an eleven-year-old, with a baseball bat; in his testimony the chief noted that it was "one of these small child's" bats (174) and the child "was a pretty good-sized boy" (184). The perpetrator was arrested and paid a $25 bond, but was never convicted; the chief explained that the defendant failed to appear for his trial and "no one appeared against him"—despite the fact that he, the arresting officer and a witness, was present when the case came before the court (175). Later that year, people sitting in at a Laurel coffee shop were arrested for disturbing the peace and required to post $100 bonds (174–85).

59. U.S. Commission on Civil Rights, *Justice in Jackson*, 270.

60. Classen, *Watching Jim Crow*, 48.

61. Historian Joel Williamson calls the blaming of racist violence on poor whites "the grit thesis" (*Crucible of Race* 292–95).

62. Marrs notes that this incident was not in the first version of the novel but was included in the 1972 version (Marrs, *One Writer's Imagination*, 251).

63. Gretlund, "An Interview with Eudora Welty," 225.

64. Walker, "Eudora Welty: An Interview," 136.

65. Walker, "Eudora Welty: An Interview," 137.

66. Nostrandt, "Fiction as Event," 14.

67. Rubin, "Growing Up in the Deep South," 42.

68. Jones, "Eudora Welty," 337.

69. Classen, *Watching Jim Crow*, 13.

70. Carter, "Bitter Search."

71. Fuller, "Carl T. Rowan."

72. Welty, *The Eye of the Story*, 208.

73. Gretlund, "Seeing Real Things," 256.

74. Houck and Grindy, *Emmett Till and the Mississippi Press*, 164.

75. Houck and Grindy, *Emmett Till and the Mississippi Press*, 162.

76. Marrs, *Eudora Welty*, 330; Welty, *What There Is to Say*, 217.

77. Ruas, "Eudora Welty," 68.

78. Welty to Diarmuid Russell, n.d., February 1951.

Bibliography

Beardsley, E. H. "Good-bye to Jim Crow: The Desegregation of Southern Hospitals, 1945–70." *Bulletin of the History of Medicine* 60, no. 3 (1986): 367–86.

Bohme, Frederick G. *200 Years of U.S. Census Taking: Population and Housing Questions, 1790–1990*. Washington, D.C.: U.S. Department of Commerce, Bureau of the Census, 1989.

Branch, Taylor. *At Canaan's Edge: America in the King Years, 1965–1968*. New York: Simon & Schuster, 2006.

———. *Parting the Waters: America in the King Years, 1954–1963*. New York: Simon & Schuster, 1988.

———. *Pillar of Fire: America in the King Years, 1963–1965*. New York: Simon & Schuster, 1998.

Brinkmeyer, Robert. "New Orleans, Mardi Gras, and Eudora Welty's *The Optimist's Daughter*." *Mississippi Quarterly* 44, no. 4 (1991): 429–41.

Burrus, John N. "Urbanization in Mississippi, 1890–1970." In *A History of Mississippi*, ed. Richard Aubrey McLemore, 2: 346–74. Hattiesburg: University & College Press of Mississippi, 1973.

Carter, Hodding. "The Bitter Search for First-Class Citizenship." *New York Times*, August 3, 1952. Accessed July 7, 2010. http://search.proquest.com/docview/112464108.

———. "The Civil Rights Issue as Seen in the South." *New York Times*, March 21, 1948. Accessed July 7, 2010. http://search.proquest.com/docview/108230020.

———. "'The Man' from Mississippi—Bilbo." *New York Times*, June 30, 1946. Accessed July 23, 2010. http://search.proquest.com/docview/107512966.

———. "Mississippi Now—Hate and Fear." *New York Times*, June 23, 1963. Accessed July 7, 2010. http://search.proquest.com/docview/116454124.

Classen, Steven D. *Watching Jim Crow: The Struggles over Mississippi TV, 1955–1969.* Durham: Duke University Press, 2004.

Cohn, David L. "How the South Feels." *The Atlantic* 87, no. 1 (January 1944): 47–51.

Dittmer, John. *Local People: The Struggle for Civil Rights in Mississippi.* Urbana: University of Illinois Press, 1994.

Ferris, Bill. "A Visit with Eudora Welty." In Prenshaw, *Conversations with Eudora Welty*, 154–71.

Ferrone, John. "Collecting the Stories of Eudora Welty." *Eudora Welty Newsletter* 25, no. 2 (2001): 19–22.

Flower, Dean. "Eudora Welty and Racism." *Hudson Review* 60, no. 2 (2007): 325–32.

Fuller, Lorraine. "Carl T. Rowan." In *American National Biography Online.* Accessed August 29, 2011. http://www.anb.org/articles/16/16-03489.html.

Gretlund, Jan Nordby. "An Interview with Eudora Welty." 1978. In Prenshaw, *Conversations with Eudora Welty*, 211–29.

———. "Seeing Real Things: An Interview with Eudora Welty." 1993. In Prenshaw, *More Conversations with Eudora Welty*, 248–61.

Haney-Lopez, Ian. *White by Law: The Legal Construction of Race.* New York: New York University Press, 1996.

Harkey, Ira. Foreword to *In a Madhouse's Din: Civil Rights Coverage by Mississippi's Daily Press, 1948–1968*, by Susan Weill, ix–xii. Westport, Conn.: Praeger, 2002.

Houck, Davis W., and Matthew Grindy. *Emmett Till and the Mississippi Press.* Jackson: University Press of Mississippi, 2008.

Jones, John Griffin. "Eudora Welty." 1981. In Prenshaw, *Conversations with Eudora Welty*, 316–41.

Ladd, Barbara. "Writing Against Death." In Pollack and Marrs, *Eudora Welty and Politics*, 155–77.

Marrs, Suzanne. *Eudora Welty: A Biography.* New York: Harcourt, 2005.

———. *One Writer's Imagination: The Fiction of Eudora Welty.* Baton Rouge: Louisiana State University Press, 2002.

Metress, Christopher, ed. *The Lynching of Emmett Till: A Documentary Narrative.* Charlottesville: University of Virginia Press, 2002.

Nostrandt, Jeanne Rolfe. "Fiction as Event: An Interview With Eudora Welty." 1978. In Prenshaw, *More Conversations with Eudora Welty*, 14–30.

Pierpont, Claudia Roth. "A Perfect Lady." *New Yorker*, October 5, 1998, 94–104.

Pollack, Harriet. "Eudora Welty and Politics: Did the Writer Crusade?" In Pollack and Marrs, *Eudora Welty and Politics*, 1–18.

Pollack, Harriet, and Suzanne Marrs, eds. *Eudora Welty and Politics: Did the Writer Crusade?* Baton Rouge: LSU Press, 2001.

Powell, Danny Romine. "Eudora Welty." 1988. In Prenshaw, *More Conversations with Eudora Welty*, 167–182.

Prenshaw, Peggy Whitman, ed. *Conversations with Eudora Welty.* Jackson: University Press of Mississippi, 1984.

———. *More Conversations with Eudora Welty.* Jackson: University Press of Mississippi, 1996.

Romines, Ann. "A Voice from a Jackson Interior." In Pollack and Marrs, *Eudora Welty and Politics*, 109–22.

Ruas, Charles. "Eudora Welty." 1980. In Prenshaw, *More Conversations with Eudora Welty*, 58–68.

Rubin, Louis D., Jr. "Growing Up in the Deep South: A Conversation with Eudora Welty, Shelby Foote, and Louis D. Rubin, Jr." 1979. In Prenshaw, *More Conversations with Eudora Welty*, 31–53.

Sprigle, Ray. "A Marble Monument to Cruelty." *Pittsburgh Post-Gazette*, August 1948. Rpt. in Post-Gazette.com. Accessed August 29, 2011. http://www.post-gazette.com /sprigle/199808SprigleChap15.asp.

"Timeline of American Race Riots and Racial Violence." In *The American Mosaic: The African American Experience.* ABC-CLIO, accessed May 5, 2011. http://african american2.abc-clio.com.

Trilling, Diana. "Fiction in Review." *The Nation*, May 11, 1946, 578. Rpt. in *The Critical Response to Eudora Welty's Fiction*, ed. Laurie Champion, 103–5. Westport, Conn.: Greenwood Press, 1994.

Trouard, Dawn. "Burying Below Sea Level: The Erotics of Sex and Death in *The Optimist's Daughter.*" *Mississippi Quarterly* 56, no. 2 (2003): 231–50.

U.S. Commission on Civil Rights. *Justice in Jackson, Mississippi: Hearings Held in Jackson, Miss., February 16–20, 1965.* New York: Arno Press, 1971.

Walker, Alice. "Eudora Welty: An Interview." 1973. In Prenshaw, *Conversations with Eudora Welty*, 131–40.

Weill, Susan. *In a Madhouse's Din: Civil Rights Coverage by Mississippi's Daily Press, 1948–1968.* Westport, Conn.: Praeger, 2002.

Welty, Eudora. *Collected Stories.* London: Harcourt Brace Jovanovich, 1980.

———. *The Complete Novels.* New York: Library of America, 1998.

———. *The Eye of the Story: Selected Essays and Reviews.* New York: Vintage Books, 1979.

———. "The Optimist's Daughter." *The New Yorker.* March 15, 1969, 37–128.

———. *Stories, Essays, and Memoir.* New York: Library of America, 1998.

Welty, Eudora, and William Maxwell. *What There Is to Say We Have Said: The Collected Correspondence of Eudora Welty and William Maxwell*, ed. Suzanne Marrs. New York: Houghton Mifflin Harcourt, 2011.

Welty, Eudora, Collection. Series 29b: Select Correspondence. Mississippi Department of Archives and History, Jackson, Miss.

"What Should We Do About Race Segregation?" *Bulletin of America's Town Meeting of the Air* 14, no. 28 (November 9, 1948). ABC Radio's Town Meeting of the Air. Columbus, Ohio: Town Hall, Inc.

Wilds, John, and Ira Harkey. *Alton Ochsner, Surgeon of the South.* Baton Rouge: LSU Press, 1990.

Williamson, Joel. *The Crucible of Race: Black/White Relations in the American South Since Emancipation.* New York: Oxford University Press, 1984.

Winter, William. "New Directions in Politics, 1948–1956." In *A History of Mississippi,* ed. Richard Aubrey McLemore, 2: 140–53. Hattiesburg: University & College Press of Mississippi, 1973.

Woolf, Sally. "Some Talk About Autobiography: An Interview with Eudora Welty." 1988. In Prenshaw, *More Conversations with Eudora Welty,* 158–66.

Contributors

MAE MILLER CLAXTON is Associate Professor of English at Western Carolina University. She is the editor of *Conversations with Dorothy Allison* (University Press of Mississippi, 2012). She also worked as a contributing editor for the sixth edition of *The Heath Anthology of American Literature*. Her articles on Welty have appeared in *Mississippi Quarterly*, *Southern Quarterly*, and the *South Atlantic Review*, among others.

SUSAN V. DONALDSON is National Endowment Professor of English and American Studies at the College of William and Mary. She is the author of *Competing Voices: The American Novel, 1865–1914* (1998) and some fifty journal essays and book chapters, as well as co-editor, with Anne Goodwyn Jones, of *Haunted Bodies: Gender and Southern Texts* (1997), and guest editor of three special issues of *The Faulkner Journal*. Most recently, she co-edited with Amy Louise Wood a special issue of *Mississippi Quarterly* on lynching and American culture. Currently, she is chair of the Department of English at the College of William and Mary.

JULIA EICHELBERGER is Professor of English at the College of Charleston. Previous publications include *Prophets of Recognition: Ideology and the Individual in Novels by Ellison, Morrison, Bellow, and Welty* (1999) and essay reviews and articles in *The Eudora Welty Review*, *Studies in American Jewish Literature*, *Mississippi Quarterly*, and *The Southern Quarterly*. *Tell About Night Flowers: Eudora Welty's Gardening Letters, 1940–1949* will be published by the University Press of Mississippi.

SARAH FORD is Associate Professor of English at Baylor University, where she teaches colonial and southern literature. She has published essays on Eudora Welty, William Faulkner, Ebenezer Cook, and Sarah Pogson.

JEAN C. GRIFFITH is Associate Professor of English at Wichita State University. Her articles on white racial identity have appeared in journals such as *Studies in the Novel* and *Western American Literature* and her book, *The Color of Democracy in Women's*

Regional Writing (2009). She is currently at work on two projects: one that examines the ways differing theories of time have structured the depiction of American Indians, and another that examines the influence of the orphan figure in twentieth-century constructions of race.

REBECCA MARK teaches American literature at Tulane University. She is the author of *Dragon's Blood: Feminist Intertextuality in Eudora Welty* and is presently finishing a book entitled *Ersatz America: Hidden Traces, Graphic Texts, and the Mending of Democracy.*

SUZANNE MARRS is the author of *One Writer's Imagination: The Fiction of Eudora Welty* and of *Eudora Welty: A Biography.* Marrs received the Phoenix Award for Distinguished Welty Scholarship from the Eudora Welty Society and the Distinguished Professor Award from Millsaps College, where she is Professor of English and Welty Foundation Scholar-in-Residence. She is the editor of *What There Is to Say We Have Said: The Correspondence of Eudora Welty and William Maxwell* and a co-editor, with Harriet Pollack, of *Eudora Welty and Politics: Did the Writer Crusade?*

DONNIE MCMAHAND teaches at the University of West Georgia. His research investigates shifting representations of contemporary southern black subjectivity, ranging from incidents of black rage and self-destruction to an ongoing struggle to affirm black identity against a precedence of internalized hatred.

DAVID MCWHIRTER is Associate Professor of English at Texas A&M University. He is the author of *Desire and Love in Henry James* (1989) and editor, most recently, of *Henry James in Context* (2010). He is currently completing a monograph on James's late 1890s fiction and editing *Roderick Hudson* for the forthcoming Cambridge University Press Complete Fiction of Henry James series. McWhirter is 2012–13 President of the Eudora Welty Society; his articles on Welty have appeared in *Mississippi Quarterly* and *Modern Fiction Studies.*

HARRIET POLLACK, Professor of English at Bucknell University, received the 2008 Phoenix Award for exceptional contributions to Welty scholarship and studies. She is the co-editor with Suzanne Marrs of *Eudora Welty and Politics: Did the Writer Crusade?* (2001) and with Christopher Metress of *Emmett Till in Literary Memory and Imagination* (2008), as well as editor of *Having Our Way: Women Rewriting Tradition in Twentieth-Century America* (1995). She served as the director and program chair of the 2009 Eudora Welty Centennial Academic Conference and Celebration, "Welty at 100" (Jackson, Miss.), and *Eudora Welty, Whiteness, and Race* has developed from that event. She is now completing a monograph entitled *The Body of the Other Woman in the Fiction and Photography of Eudora Welty.*

KERI WATSON is Assistant Professor of Art History at Auburn University Montgomery. She specializes in modern and contemporary visual culture and the history of photography. She has published articles on Patricia Cronin's sculpture, Judy Chicago's feminist pedagogy, and 1930s popular culture. Currently, she is researching the Peppler Collection of Civil Rights photography at the Alabama Department of Archives and History.

PATRICIA YAEGER is the Henry Simmons Frieze Collegiate Chair at the University of Michigan and is the author of *Honey-Mad Women: Emancipatory Strategies in Women's Writing* (1988) and *Dirt and Desire: Reconstructing Southern Women's Writing* (2000). She has published recent essays on Charlotte Delbo, Flannery O'Connor, Eudora Welty, Kara Walker, and Alice Randall. She is working on a book called "Luminous Trash" and was editor of PMLA from 2006 to 2011.

Index

Mark, Rebecca, "Ice Picks, Guinea Pigs, and Dead Birds" 18, 199–223

Marrs, Suzanne: *Eudora Welty* by, 3, 44, 90n6; factual basis for "Keela," 53; "The Metaphor of Race in Eudora Welty's Fiction" by, 2; *One Writer's Imagination* by, 23; "Welty, Race, and the Patterns of a Life" by, 12–13, 23–47; on Welty's interest in photography, 52, 75; on Welty's use of the word "nigger" in her letters, 4, 12, 24–25, 43, 226

material possession/dispossession: "The Burning" on inequality in objects and, 12, 17–18, 186, 188–91, 193–95; "The Little Store" (Welty) images on racial differences in, 4, 12, 14, 99–101; "Livvie" (Welty) description of, 12, 14, 103–5; *Making a Date* and *Window-Shopping* on racially divided, 12; postemancipation shift in freedmen's relation to objects and, 194, 196–97; Welty on whiteness implications for, 11–12. *See also* poverty

Max ("Keela" character), 41

McCarthyism, 31

McGill, Ralph, 36

McHale, Brian, 135, 136

McHaney, Pearl, 75

McMahand, Donnie, "Bodies on the Brink" by, 10, 17, 165–84

McWhirter, David, "Secret Agents," 14–15, 114–30

Medical Apartheid (Washington), 203

"Meet Me at de Station When Dat Train Come Along" (Seale and Seale song), 210

Memphis Commercial Appeal, 82

"Metaphor of Race in Eudora Welty's Fiction, The" (Marrs), 2

Mezei, Kathy, 136, 144

Millsaps College (Mississippi): desegregation (1965) of, 41; interracial events at, 43; "The Southern Writer Today" lecture by Welty at, 40; student response to Welty's lecture at, 38; Welty reading of "Powerhouse" at, 42, 234; "Words into Fiction" lecture by Welty at, 36–37

Mississippi: historic "River of Death" in, 176–77; NAACP boycott of Jackson stores (1962) in, 108; Sovereignty Commission of, 39, 232–33; Welty on public assumptions regarding whites from, 28–29; Welty's opposition to Senator Bilbo's reelection in, 29–30, 234; Welty's photographs of African American life in, 26

"Mississippi appendectomy," 221n18

Mississippi Art Association exhibit, 80–82

Mississippi Delta culture: *Delta Wedding*'s description of the, 1–2, 151–52, 155–62; ideal of white womanhood in, 185, 195–96; racial epithet use as part of, 25; racial identities in, 177–78; *spectragraphia* phenomenon as element in mindset of, 169–70; Welty on public assumptions regarding racism of, 28–29; white supremacy belief of the, 244n11. *See also* color line

Mississippi Freedom Summer, 234, 236

Mississippi State College for Women, 116

Mogei women in mourning (New Guinea), *214*

"Monkeying Around" (Bearden), 7

Moody, Anne: on attending Welty's reading, 38; *Coming of Age in Mississippi* by, 109

Morrison, Toni: black subjectivity probed by, 167–68; commendation of Welty's black characters by, 177–78; her template applied to Welty's *Delta Wedding*, 116; *Playing in the Dark* by, 115; *Song of Solomon* by, 17, 167–68, 179–82; on "white man's symptom," 118

Mulkay, Michael, 137

Museum of Modern Art photography shows, 85–86, 88, 92n49

"Must the Novelist Crusade?" (Welty), 7–8, 40, 42, 52, 165, 235

NAACP, 233, 246n36; boycott of Jackson stores (1962), 108

interview with William Buckley on, 41–42; white gaze and meaning of black body in, 10, 166–83; "Words into Fiction" lecture by Welty on her, 36–37. *See also* Welty's readership; Welty's titles

Welty's lectures: "The Southern Writer Today," 40, 235; "Words into Fiction," 36–37

Welty's photographs: African American life presented in, 26, 78–79; "Black Saturday" (unpublished), 52, 76, 77–80, 82, 88; *Courthouse town/ Grenada/1935*, 101; discrimination in consumer culture represented by, 12, 95, *96, 97, 98*, 101; Lugene Photographic Galleries exhibition of, 85–86; *Madonna with Coca Cola*, 85; *Making a Date*, 12, *13–14*, 73, *74–75*, 77, 80–89; *One Time, One Place*, 2, 8–9, 52, 76–77, 87–89; unique images of African Americans by, 76; Welty on what she learned from photography, 48; *Window Shopping/Grenada/1930*, 12, 97, *98*, 111; *Woman of the 1930's*, *64, 65*. *See also* African American life; African Americans

Welty's readership: *Delta Wedding* humor used to inform, 15–16, 132–35, 137–45; Eichelberger's examination of shifting cultural awareness of, 2, 18–19, 224–42; "schooling" in *Delta Wedding*, 136–37. *See also* Welty's fiction

Welty's titles: "At the Landing," 57; "Black Saturday" (Welty, unpublished), 52, 76; "The Burning," 11, 12, 17–18, 185–97; "Clytie," 60–61; *The Collected Stories*, 2, 148, 160–61, 224; "A Curtain of Green," 12, 13, 58; *A Curtain of Green*, 49, 50, 53, 57–58; "The Demonstrators," 8, 12, 18, 41–43, 116–17, 148, 236; *The Eye of the Story*, 199; "Flowers for Marjorie," 57; *The Golden Apples*, 2, 12, 25, 121–22; "Keela, the Outcast Indian Maiden," 4, 12, 40–41, 42, 53–54; "Lily Daw and the Three Ladies," 59–60; "The

Little Store," 4, 12, 14, 99–101, 103–5, 109–10; "Livvie," 4, 12, 14, 103–5; *Losing Battles*, 132; "Must the Novelist Crusade?," 7–8, 40, 42, 52, 165; *One Time, One Place*, 2, 8, 52; "One Time, One Place" preface, 48, 64; *One Writer's Beginnings*, 12, 116, 117, 119–20, 122, 127, 166–67, 169–71; *The Optimist's Daughter*, 12, 19, 33–34, 42–43, 224–42; "Petrified Man," 60; *Photographs*, 8–9; "Place in Fiction," 166–67; "Powerhouse," 4–7, 10, 12, 37, 42, 66–67, 114–15, 168; "Where Is the Voice Coming From?," 3, 4, 5, 8, 12, 14, 16, 38, 66–67, 109, 148, 156–62, 234, 236; "Why I Live at the P.O.," 60; *The Wide Net*, 57; "A Worn Path," 4, 12, 14, 102–3, 109, 168, 182–83. *See also Delta Wedding* (Welty); Welty's fiction

"What Did I Do to Be So Black and Blue?" (Armstrong song), 11

"Where Is the Voice Coming From?" (Welty): *Collected Stories* preface explanation about, 160–61; comparing *Delta Wedding* to, 149–62; as economic story of threat to racial status quo, 14; examined in context of Welty's biography, 12; examining Welty's message on "whiteness" in, 5, 8; Flower's commentary on, 3–4; Harrison's "'It's Still a Free Country'" on, 3; historic and social setting of, 156–57; killer's references to degrading images of African Americans in, 158–60; reflecting changes in consumer culture, 109; as response to assassination of Medgar Evers, 38, 108, 131, 148–49, 160–62, 234; violence perpetrated against an African American in, 150–51; Welty on "the changing sixties" represented in, 148, 156, 236; whiteness and material possession central to, 12; whiteness asserted by murderer in, 16. *See also* civil rights movement

White Caps (*The Optimist's Daughter*), 237–38

whiteface performance: *Delta Wedding*
depiction of racial identity in, 11; Ford
on black recognition of, 11

white gaze: *Delta Wedding* (Welty)
use of, 168–83; white myopia and
spectragraphia representation, 169–70

white men: Cohn's essay (1944) on
mindset of southern, 28; comparison
of *Delta Wedding* and "Where Is
the Voice Coming From?" black
characters and, 149–62; *Delta
Wedding* depiction of racial identity
performance by, 11, 149–62; examining
Welty's fiction featuring violence
between black and, 16; interference
in *Delta Wedding* violence between
two black characters, 149–50, 153–55;
"Where Is the Voice Coming From?"
construction of racial identity of,
159–60. *See also* black men; racial
identities

whiteness: *Delta Wedding* depicting
Troy's probationary whiteness form
of, 151–53; "The Demonstrators"
understanding of meaning and
offensiveness of, 8; Faulkner's naming
of, 10; legal definition in the U.S. of,
244n19; Welty on material possession/
dispossession and, 11–12; Welty on
Mississippi State College for Women's,
116; Welty's understanding of material
implications of, 11–12; "Where Is the
Voice Coming From?" examining
meaning of, 5, 8. *See also* awareness of
whiteness

white privilege: allowing a white man
to interfere in violence between
black characters of *Delta Wedding*,
149–50, 153–55; *A Curtain of Green*
(Welty) on female, 58–60; "Where
Is the Voice Coming From?" murder
in order to preserve, 157–58. *See also*
power

whites: black performance of white
Deltan masculinity in *Delta Wedding*,
11; character-corrupting influence
of Jim Crow on, 27; *Delta Wedding*

humor about, 143–44; white Citizens'
Council's intimidation of "moderate,"
40, 246n36

white social structure: *Delta Wedding*
examined in context of, 16, 155–56,
159–60; destratification of objects
as route for challenging, 196–97;
Mississippi Delta cultural ideal of
white womanhood in, 185, 195–96;
racial codes of behavior in consumer
culture and, 106; scholarship tracing
Welty's opposition to unjust, 18–19;
Welty's "The Burning" on slave labor
for upkeep of, 3, 12, 17–18, 194–95;
Welty's understanding of hierarchy
of, 11–12; "Where Is the Voice Coming
From?" (Welty) in context of, 156–57

white supremacy: eugenics "science" on,
151, 203–9, 220n11, 221n18; Mississippi
Delta culture on, 244n11

white womanhood: "The Burning"
depiction of, 185–86, 187–97; "Clytie"
(Welty) on white blindness of, 60–61;
comparing *Delta Wedding* and "Where
Is the Voice Coming From?," 159–62;
A Curtain of Green (Welty) on power
to destroy black males by, 58–60; "A
Curtain of Green" (Welty) examining
racial interactions by, 13, 57; greater
awareness of racial patriarchy by,
155; humor missed by *Delta Wedding*
white female characters, 134–35;
"Livvie" on differences between black
and, 104–5; Mississippi Delta cultural
ideal of, 185, 195–96; "Petrified Man"
(Welty) on, 60; racial patriarchy
in context of gender and female
role, 107–8, 111, 149–62; response
to male *Delta Wedding* violence by,
153–55; segregated society mandate
to "protect," 57–58; strict codes
of behavior in consumer racial
interactions, 106; Till's murder due
to violating racial code of behavior
toward, 107–8, 111, 233; Welty's "The
Burning" slave-owning world of, 3, 12,
17–18; "A Worn Path" (Welty) images

of shopping experience of, 102–3; Wright on vulnerability of blacks in presence of, 56–57. *See also* gender

"Why I Live at the P.O." (Welty), 60

Why We Can't Wait (King), 148

Wide Net, The (Welty), 57

Wide Sargasso Sea (Rhys), 119

Wiegman, Robyn, 60

Window Shopping/Grenada/1930 (Welty photograph), 12, 97, *98*, 111

Winogrand, Garry, 88

Woman of the 1930's (Welty photograph), 64, *65*

Woodburn, John, 33

"Words into Fiction" lecture (Welty), 36–37

Works Progress Administration, 53

World War II, 29, 31

"Worn Path, A" (Welty): awareness of black southern life revealed in, 168; on consumer culture, 102–3; courageous journey of Phoenix Jackson, 102–3, 110, 131, 182–83; deeply segregated society examined in, 109; as economic story, 14

Wright, Richard: *American Hunger* by, 50–51; "Big Boy Leaves Home" by, 56–57; *Black Boy* by, 50, 56–57; comparing Jim Crow impact on fiction of Welty and, 13; differences in childhood experience of Welty versus, 100; "Down by the Riverside" by, 62; "The Ethic of Living Jim Crow" by, 55–56; "Fire and Cloud" by, 62; on his own encounter with the color line, 55–57; "Long Black Song" by, 62; *Native Son* by, 54, 57; racial experiences in America, 64, 66; *12 Million Black Voices* by, 50, 61, 63, 64, 66; *Uncle Tom's Children* by, 13, 50, 61–62, 63; writing on emotional damage of Jim Crow, 49, 52

Writing Diaspora (Chow), 118

Writing History, Writing Trauma (LaCapra), 54

Yaeger, Patricia: "'Black Men Dressed in Gold'" by, 17–18, 185–98; *Delta Wedding* response by, 131; *Dirt and Desire* by, 3; on history of material possession framed by "The Burning," 12

Yardley, Jonathan, 52

You Have Seen Their Faces (Bourke-White and Caldwell), 78, 80